'Does readers the important service of placing the debates about Indigenous policy—and Indigenous futures in remote Australia—into a theoretically coherent framework.'

From the foreword by Professor Fred Myers, New York University

'In an original and highly provocative critique, Diane Austin-Broos asks whether anthropologists' commitment to cultural difference, and failure to treat the residents of remote Aboriginal communities as historical subjects, blinded them to inequality created by the legal system and the state. This lucid and accessible genealogy of the divergent streams of recent anthropological thinking and debate is a must read for anybody with a serious interest in understanding the current conflicted views about remote Aboriginal futures.'

Nicolas Peterson, Professor of Anthropology, Australian National University

'Once more there is an Aboriginal "crisis", this time in Alice Springs as more members of remote communities move to overcrowded town camps. Where do we turn to understand better why this is happening and what should be done? Austin-Broos discusses why these questions have not been answered well by anthropologists, economists and opinion writers. She analyses the unsettled debate and polarization about policies for remote communities. This book is an important contribution. Ideas generate policy and we all have an interest in the way in which ideas are developed in our universities and think tanks. In this insightful and different book Austin-Broos challenges us all.'

Bob Gregory, Professor of Economics, Australian National University

Other titles by Diane Austin-Broos

Arrernte Present, Arrernte Past: Invasion, violence and imagination in Indigenous Central Australia
Jamaica Genesis
Urban Life in Kingston, Jamaica
Australian Sociologies

A DIFFERENT INEQUALITY

THE POLITICS OF DEBATE ABOUT
REMOTE ABORIGINAL AUSTRALIA

DIANE AUSTIN-BROOS

First published in 2011

Copyright © Diane Austin-Broos 2011

All rights reserved. No part of this book may be reproduced or transmitted in any form or by any means, electronic or mechanical, including photocopying, recording or by any information storage and retrieval system, without prior permission in writing from the publisher. The Australian *Copyright Act 1968* (the Act) allows a maximum of one chapter or 10 per cent of this book, whichever is the greater, to be photocopied by any educational institution for its educational purposes provided that the educational institution (or body that administers it) has given a remuneration notice to Copyright Agency Limited (CAL) under the Act.

Allen & Unwin
83 Alexander Street
Crows Nest NSW 2065
Australia
Phone: (61 2) 8425 0100
Fax: (61 2) 9906 2218
Email: info@allenandunwin.com
Web: www.allenandunwin.com

Cataloguing-in-Publication details are available
from the National Library of Australia
www.trove.nla.gov.au

ISBN 978 1 74237 049 1

Index by Frances Paterson/Olive Grove Indexing Services
Set in 11/13.5 pt Bembo by Bookhouse, Sydney

10 9 8 7 6 5 4 3 2 1

The Indigenous Australian population has altered fundamentally from one typical of the former hunter-gatherer way of life to one that is very poor, marginalised, powerless and sedentarised.
>
> Marcia Langton, The Shock of the New: A postcolonial dilemma for Australianist anthropology

Poverty is not a certain small amount of goods, nor is it just a relation between means and ends; above all it is a relation between people. Poverty is a social status. As such it is the invention of civilization. It has grown with civilization [and] invidious distinction.
>
> Marshall Sahlins, *Stone Age Economics*

Contents

Foreword		ix
Preface		xix
Abbreviations		xxiii
1	Two debates	1
2	Culture and ethnography	25
3	A postcolonial critique	51
4	Opposing separate development	79
5	Defending the homelands	106
6	The politics of difference and equality	135
Notes		169
References		178
Index		194

Foreword

It should be no secret to any reader that there is a crisis in Australia's remote Indigenous communities, a crisis of social suffering and failed expectations, and there is a crisis in thinking about these communities and their futures. When Diane Austin-Broos asked me to write a foreword for this book, I was hesitant—as an American living in the US—to step into the breach of the swirling controversies, unsure of my own position. I wish it were otherwise. In 1973, when I began my research in remote Australia, the great work of W.E.H. Stanner (1968) and C.D. Rowley (1972) seemed to promise a path to an exciting future for Indigenous communities.

The suffering in remote Australia is now, again, a national scandal. It is not new. What is newer is the fading of possibilities, the decline of expectations for the 'not-yet'. This flows from an exhaustion of paradigms of hope. When I began professional life as an anthropologist, in the early 1970s, the paradigm of 'assimilation' as a solution for what was called then 'the Aboriginal problem' had faded. Charles Rowley's famous study, *The Destruction of Aboriginal Society* (1972), had definitively illuminated the failure of 'assimilation' and the suffering of Aboriginal people on remote government settlements. He likened their depression and loss of hope—their 'pathology'—to the experience of inmates of 'total institutions'. Under the direction of the new Labor Government and Gough Whitlam, federal policy shifted to a focus on 'self-determination'. This was not, as some have tried to argue, driven by anthropological desires to sustain cultural ghettos, but followed a trend internationally for 'self-determination'. It was imagined that allowing people to develop and plan their own futures, and respecting their political autonomy, would provide them with the confidence and energy to make their own way in the world.

For whatever reasons, and there is profound disagreement about these, after nearly four decades the social situation in remote communities has not followed anyone's hopes. With the collapse of a dominant paradigm, ideological warfare has broken out in the ranks of analysts, critics and casual observers. Old allies have fallen out, and—especially among anthropologists—the moral anguish of political commitments is palpable. What answer do we have for the old Aboriginal Lutheran evangelist who observed to Basil Schild, a young Lutheran pastor and activist, that 'God like whitefella more better I reckon'? (Schild 2008)

Diane Austin-Broos's book attempts to square the circle, to find a space of discussion and debate in a field of great national importance and passionate ideological disagreement. In an era when it is widely recognised that social analysis cannot escape ideological frameworks, this is a daunting task. Austin-Broos does readers the important service of placing the debates about Indigenous policy—and Indigenous futures in remote Australia—into a theoretically coherent framework. In her analysis, the debates revolve around two paradigms of value that rehearse a well-known theoretical and political divide. The two paradigms are those of cultural difference and of economic inequality. As she writes:

> For some, remote Aboriginal life is a site of enduring and remarkable difference while for others, the hallmark of that same site is poverty and deep distress. Consequently, this book is not simply about inequality and difference but also the politics and policies that these issues have produced.

Austin-Broos is herself an Australian but unlike many who have specialised in the anthropology of Aboriginal people, she studied anthropology outside of the Anglo-Australian nexus (in the US) and she developed her distinguished reputation as a scholar of Caribbean life in societies dramatically reorganised by colonisation. For her, from this context, culture difference and political economy cannot be disentangled. What might this mean in an Australia milieu? Let me write from a personal perspective.

In 1981, the World Council of Churches visited Australia. As it happened, they visited the remote community of Papunya, in the Northern Territory, where I was living temporarily as an anthropologist in an Aboriginal camp, awaiting the return of an initiatory party. The initiation camp was in an area isolated from the main camp—next to the dump and its collection of old, rusting Holdens and Fords. I never met the Church visitors, but soon after, an article appeared in a national newspaper (as I remember), expressing their horror at the living conditions of Indigenous people at Papunya. For me, accustomed after many field trips to living in Aboriginal communities, the location in the dump as very different. The site had been chosen both for its isolation and because it had been cleared by bulldozers, leaving the wide and open space necessary for an initiation ceremony. In the dry desert sun, there was no smell of rotting garbage. The Yirkapiri (mourners) kin of the initiates were comfortable and life was proceeding quite amiably without intrusions.

In 1981, we were not yet met with the soaring rates of disease, mortality, violence, and—by reports—sexual abuse, but alcohol abuse was already common. Indeed, in 1981, because of the perception that living in large communities, in proximity to towns, made alcohol too accessible and brought people of different communities into violent conflict, the Pintupi residents of Papunya and its close outstations made the most of their opportunities to return to their traditional country, at Warlungurru in the Kintore Ranges. In contrast to the current criticisms of 'homeland communities', discussed by Austin-Broos, the Pintupi move was, in the eyes of most people, a triumph—reversing the historical processes that had removed Pintupi people from their Western Desert homelands and brought them to more easily resourced but foreign traditional country. The move was documented not only in Pam Nathan and Dick Leichleitner Japanangka's *Settle Down Country* (1983) but also in the beautiful

CAAMA documentary *Benny and the Dreamers* (1993). As I can testify as witness to these historical events, the Pintupi who struggled to regain their homelands with government support did so in order to gain greater autonomy politically and also to create space between themselves and the sources of alcohol that had been devastating their small population. 'Too many people have died,' they said.

Warlungurru was supported and legitimated by the desires of the elder members of the group to teach their young about their country and to hand on this knowledge of custodianship, to protect it from intrusion, and also to care better for the younger people. It was imagined that this remote community would be healthier, stronger, a basis for moving forth into the world. The wanted schools; they wanted medical help; they wanted food. This was not simply a 'traditional community'. But, support for medical help was not forthcoming—as it conflicted with programs of the Northern Territory Health Service—and education depended on sympathetic local schoolteachers. In this crucible of self-determination, a particular vision developed at Warlungurru, articulated in 1988 in a series of teacher-education training programs as the necessity of the people '*lingkitu kanyintjaka ngurra*'—strongly holding their country. One hears it still.

Self-determination was supposed to be the basis of Aboriginal futures in remote Central Australia. Yet, a visit to Warlungurru in the present—as to many other Central Australian remote communities today—confronts those of us who return with the untimely death of many of our friends, at ages significantly different from the white population of Australia. Many others, not necessarily obese or alcoholic, are 'on the machine'—regular attendees at the dialysis clinic. Too numerous to tell are the names of those who have died in car crashes and rollovers, in violent drunken encounters or in other manner of misfortune. School attendance has declined dramatically. Many of the houses are in shocking states of disrepair, so much that one longs for the time when we all lived in tents. Obesity is more common than wellbeing. You hear that there aren't really many older people left to teach the younger. And there are now so many young people that the population is skewed. These are current realities.

Friends are happy to see a once familiar face; the styles of engagement are not radically different from the past. These are still the people I knew. Acrylic painting has been a sensational economic and cultural success, providing recognition, respect and resources for many in the community. It is a flowering of culture in a difficult environment, one of the good things that have happened. Some people still look to the future with hope; some have been ordained as pastors, a few others advanced in teacher training, but the fundamental administration is in the hands of White outsiders and the community is in some disarray. From one day to the next, you never know where to find people—so pronounced is the mobility that takes people hundreds of kilometres to town and back, to visit relatives elsewhere, to attend funerals. To follow the position of Indigenous intellectual and activist Marcia Langton (2010), the conditions of classical Indigenous life are no longer present—especially in the face of a demographic transformation that has so challenged the possibilities of cultural transmission.[1]

People are making do, and some might say that what I describe is the effect—or largely the effect—of cultural difference, the choice. Others look at the situation and see the necessity for a change, for drastic measures to improve the health and wellbeing, and opportunities, for people born into such a community. To those of us who began our engagement with a profound suspicion of paternalism and of assimilation policy failures, such interventions seem impossible to think.

Where, then, do we stand? How are we to understand what we see—and what, indeed, do we see? Austin-Broos lays out the range of positions that have been taken up in the wake of a radical collapse of the conventional paradigms. She is particularly concerned to outline the frameworks of anthropologists, the discipline perhaps most identified with remote communities and which has come under attack for failing to articulate the devastations in them.

On the whole, Austin-Broos writes, anthropologists have been more inclined to see the situation in remote Australia as a consequence of cultural differences and to portray the lack of material accumulation as a consequence of distinctive cultural values (on sharing, on obligations to kinship, commitment to living on the land, and so on). In this view, the observable lack of material wealth, jobs and work, then, is not necessarily itself a problem but is a bearable consequence of the significance of other values. For the most part, anthropologists have—or perhaps had not—seen the circumstances in remote communities as 'pathological'. The circumstances in the remote areas are to be seen as legitimate artifacts of 'self-determination'. Anthropologists who find the current conditions to be 'pathological', such as Peter Sutton (2001, 2009a), are inclined to locate this pathology in the unsuitability of traditional culture in the contemporary context, and they have found 'self-determination' to be a failure. Those critics focused on economic inequality—mainly non-anthropologists—see violence, illness and sexual abuse as a salient condition in remote Australia and attribute this to economic inequality. They aim to rectify this by a program of 'marketising' Indigenous society—in developing ways for Indigenous people to enter the workforce and to participate in or be integrated into mainstream society. The proposals have included repealing land rights, sequestering welfare payments and so on.

In reading this book, one will certainly have a better understanding of the positions taken up by various analysts, their strengths and weaknesses, and—to some extent—of their predilections for them. I would like to add a few of my own thoughts on anthropological—especially ethnographic—attentions to the local desires and intentions, and our implication in the paradigm of 'self-determination'.

Anthropologists working in the context of self-determination studied or analysed the ways in which Aboriginal people in remote communities defined or knew their world; the concepts of person, power and place through which they distributed value. In this vein, for example, I studied the politics of the Pintupi people's engagement, trying to interpret and represent what people in these communities 'understood' of their situation and how they acted from that. I saw this as having consequences—the conflicts of their model of politics in enacting new rules for collective life.

Of course this was, and is, one source of disarray in contemporary communities, and many analysts have recognised the problems of such 'cultural' misarticulations. But when Austin-Broos examines the entanglement of difference and inequality she specifies something *else*, something that perhaps escapes the lens of local understanding. Crudely put, and in repeatedly criticising treatments of Indigenous social formations in remote communities as 'bounded' societies or cultures, Austin-Broos reinvigorates an approach that looks for broader, underlying—even global—forces that organise and reorganise societies themselves.[2] 'In reality,' she writes, 'there are no bounded cultures involved . . . the maintenance of customary ways as they exist today relies on remote Aboriginal people grasping a secure position for themselves within the state and its economy. This is a process that creates conflict within individuals and their communities—not simply between separate cultures.' Thus, the relevant parties to social interaction are not 'communities' but rather people, young and old, male and female, variously engaged and interested within community life and outside it. And as this approach implies, further along she insists that 'The connections between Fitzroy Crossing, Maningrida, Ntaria and Bourke need to be underlined, as well as the differences.' The significance of economy for remote communities, she maintains, has been insufficiently regarded in the struggles over 'cultural rights' and 'self-determination'.

This is not an accident. Yes, we can see, as one might say, that 'men'—and most particularly men—do not live by culture alone. There is—and has been—no work, no meaningful work in remote Australia since the advent of the self-determination policies, and foraging in the settled circumstances of Indigenous desert communities is not very productive. Is it surprising that alcohol-inspired intensifications of sociality are so attractive to people who find themselves with little in the way of making themselves relevant? In this, Marx may have astutely understood the importance of human beings defining themselves as *homo faber*, through practical labor. But as much as there is not work, so also are young Indigenous people unprepared for work in the market economy. Literacy, for example, has declined significantly in these communities. Here, Austin-Broos suggests, is room for a productive intervention.

In the light of much contentious debate about the Federal Government's Northern Territory Intervention, and also about the policy of self determination, Austin-Broos should be commended for drawing attention to a central issue—of wellbeing perhaps—of work. For much of the self-determination period, remote communities did not have many opportunities for wage labor, economic work. Their locational disadvantage ensured there would not be many opportunities, and it combined with Indigenous desires to remain on their land, near their kin, and to be involved with their cultural obligations. Initially, straight welfare payments provided the (insufficient) cash income that people needed for food and clothing. Somewhat later, this was replaced with Community Development Employment Projects (CDEP). Yet, it is probably fair to say there has not been much enthusiasm for work in these later generations. We understood it was not really meaningful culturally. Nor did young people approach education with the idea of working later.

One thing is clear, and painfully so. Our paradigms are collapsing. The once widely shared commitment to 'self-determination' or an emphasis on protecting indigenous rights as *the* solution to inequality and disempowerment has withered (but not necessarily endorsement of these rights as an inalienable human right). Anthropologists are now deeply divided among themselves about policy options, often along regional lines—northern Australia as a region that seems able to support a hybrid economy solution vs. Central Australia as a region without economic options; remote Australia vs. settled Australia on the importance of cultural difference vs. the hegemony of the State; neoliberal pro-integrationist policy writers who pathologise cultural difference vs. anthropologists who see room for particular Indigenous solutions.

Anthropologists have had long associations with the remote communities of Australia and deep knowledge of what life is like in those communities. I think few of us were under any illusions about the difficulties of life in these communities; the ravages of alcohol, the debilitating violence, the difficulties of leadership. We have been accused, collectively in recent years, of ignoring or whitewashing these difficulties, of neglecting the real lives of people in pursuit of a reified and romantic 'culture'. We have been accused of defending a 'traditional culture' that increasingly came to be pathologised in what has seemed to be unending articles in the popular press. If culture was not to be the 'solution', and the right to culture no longer the fundamental axis of Indigenous politics, the discourse of policy-makers turned back to models that resonated significantly with a worldwide turn to neoliberal economic principles. This is not what Austin-Broos's analysis recommends, not a wholesale abandonment of cultural difference and cultural value, but a reinscription—as it were—of culture and economy. Literate education and employment are the prescription, but she maintains that:

> Routes to literate education and employment need to address and not dismiss the cultural difference in communities, including an inclination not to migrate away from country on a permanent basis. This circumstance also reflects the need for a mix of policy, and not the polarisation that took place in the remote communities debate. If elements of tradition tie remote Aboriginal people to the local, their status as Australian citizens and market participants requires that some among them move beyond the local to negotiate a larger world and its economy as well as regional and national politics.

Diane Austin-Broos's book has the merit of focusing on the human capacities as well as the suffering of people in remote communities. Proposing that disadvantage be addressed through practical literacy education and opportunities to enter into the wage economy, 'to negotiate a larger world and its economy', without insisting on radical assimilation, recognises the historical agency of people in remote communities and the complex nature of contemporary identities, not singular but, as she says, 'multifaceted'.

Fred Myers
New York University

Preface

Remote Aboriginal Australia is one place where great beauty can be juxtaposed with seemingly endless grief. Such a situation allows ample scope for silences of one type or another about remote Aboriginal life as it is described in Australia's urban centres. This is a book about such silences and arguments not carried forward. Its focus is cultural difference and inequality as each bears on those who live remote—especially in the tropical north and in Central Australia. I treat cultural difference and inequality as facts that are given more or less weight according to the form and politics of the analysis involved. For some, remote Aboriginal life is a site of enduring and remarkable difference while for others, the hallmark of that same site is poverty and deep distress. Consequently, this book is not simply about inequality and difference but also the politics and policies that these issues have produced. *A Different Inequality* describes some forms of recent and continuing disagreement. The touchstone for the book is the debate about remote communities that both preceded and followed the Northern Territory Intervention of 2007—a debate that began in earnest in the 1990s and continues to this day. I lead into this dispute with an account of another one within the universities. This was a postcolonial critique of anthropology that foreshadowed issues raised in the remote communities debate. My discussion thereby ranges across both an academic and a public policy domain. It concludes with the proposal that we need to reconcile two forms of politics—those of culture difference (or identity) and those aimed at pursuing equality for remote Aboriginal Australians. Cultural difference does not override socioeconomic disadvantage, but neither can that difference be ignored if the object is to lessen disadvantage in remote communities. Land rights, education and employment need to be addressed in concert—a proposal that is easy to write but not so easy to formulate in policy terms.

Disappointment with public debate created the impetus for this book. At the time of the Intervention, I had just completed another work based on many years of engagement with Western Arrernte (Aranda) people in Central Australia. My disquiet came from the Arrernte's circumstances and from the tenor of debate about their lives and other comparable lives in remote Australia. Uncharacteristic at the time, my unease was with both sides: with my colleagues in the universities and with the opinion writers and private think tanks that provided a competing view of remote communities. The polarisation of opinion was marked. Each side accused the other of ulterior motives. As the words flew thick and fast, in my view they reflected real dilemmas in the analysis of a confronting human situation. I was led to think more broadly about universities and their approaches to research among Indigenous Australians. I realised that if anthropology must change so too must some of the other disciplines involved. Yet in recent times, if the universities have not always served remote communities well, this is also true of an Australian polity that allows a crucial debate to be mired in prejudicial accounts of Aboriginal people. In the end, the loser is policy for remote communities, deprived of the scrutiny it deserves in the public domain.

While this book is a critical reflection on anthropology, my own discipline, it also discusses the work of other academics and policy consultants who have written about inequality, poverty and cultural difference in remote Aboriginal Australia. As a result, the book is directed to an audience beyond anthropology and the universities. The range of material covered demonstrates the need to build a forum for discussion that can dissolve some current and quite unhelpful boundaries. I have tried to keep the language plain and as direct as possible although the discussion ranges from traditional Aboriginal culture through 19th century debates about 'the Aborigines' to pressing issues of illness and unemployment today. This is a discussion of the contemporary circumstance of those who live remote. It also provides some perspective on the past in order to suggest how the present and its politics have been produced. Terminologically, I employ 'Indigenous' and 'Aboriginal' to refer to group identities in the present. The terms are more and less inclusive. With regard to Aboriginal customary ways—specific elements of culture that are not shared with Torres Strait Islanders—I use the term 'Aboriginal'. This designation is especially pertinent when the discussion turns to the *Aboriginal Land Rights (Northern Territory) Act 1976* and its social corollary in a homelands movement that fostered outstation life. At other times, and especially in the course of my discussion of the postcolonial critique of anthropology, I use the term 'Indigenous Australians' to refer to both Aboriginal people and Torres Strait Islanders. Finally, when I am referring to original peoples of the continent, rather than to an objectified identity, I use the term 'indigenous'. I have tried to keep my usage consistent.

In this work, my first debt always is to my friends at Ntaria. One family in particular has been my mainstay over many years and I am now growing old with them. My thanks go out to some very special women for keeping me abreast of family matters over many years. I also wish to thank Jeremy Beckett of the University of Sydney and Nicolas Peterson of the Australian National University who read a part or the whole of the book in earlier drafts. The responsibility for the final version is my own but their early input helped me greatly. There are three other colleagues I wish to thank. One is my departmental associate Gaynor Macdonald. Over many years, we have discussed the types of issue raised in this book. Through our teaching, public debate and publishing we have sought to encourage broader conversations, especially within anthropology. Another is Marie de Lepervanche with whom I worked at Sydney University prior to her retirement. Marie has shared my vision for a critical anthropology in Australia and I have valued her companionship. In different ways, each of us has raised issues that concern the intersection of economy and law as they shape particular lives within the state. The other colleague I wish to thank is my friend Geoffrey Hogbin, a neoclassical economist. Geoff and I met at the University of Chicago when we were both doctoral students, he in economics and I in anthropology. We have never agreed about much. Yet without our conversations, also over many years, this book would not have been written.

Finally, I wish to thank my own small family. Close at hand, and at a slightly greater distance, my husband Frank and our son Harry have lived with me through almost every paragraph. Their own engagement with the Western Arrernte, anthropology and the remote communities debate helped me to complete this project.

Diane Austin-Broos

Abbreviations

AA	Alcoholics Anonymous
AAS	Australian Anthropologial Society
AAAS	Australasian Association for the Advancement of Science
ABR	Aboriginal Benefits Reserve
ABT	Aboriginal Benefits Trust
ADC	Aboriginal Development Commission
AEDP	Aboriginal Employment Development Project
AFL	Australian Football League
ANU	Australian National University
ASSA	Academy of the Social Sciences in Australia
ATSIC	Aboriginal and Torres Strait Islander Commission
CAEPR	Centre for Aboriginal Economic Policy Research
CAAMA	Central Australian Aboriginal Media Association
CDEP	Community Development Employment Projects
CIS	Centre for Independent Studies
CLC	Central Land Council
COAG	Council of Australian Governments
CRC	COAG Reform Council
CYI	Cape York Institute
DAA	Department of Aboriginal Affairs
DATSIPD	Department of Aboriginal and Torres Strait Islander Policy and Development

DSS	Department of Social Security
FACS	Family and Community Support (NT government)
HREOC	Human Rights and Equal Opportunities Commission
MP	Member of Parliament
MRE	Mining Royalty Equivalents
NAC	National Aboriginal Conference
NACC	National Aboriginal Consultative Council
NLC	Northern Land Council
NIRA	National Indigenous Reform Agreement
NSW	New South Wales
NT	Northern Territory
NTAC	Northern Territory Aboriginal Council
OSICP	Office of Social Innovation and Civic Participation (US)
SA	South Australia
SCRGSP	Steering Committee for the Review of Government Service Provision
SIHIP	Strategic Indigenous Housing and Infrastructure Program
TGT	Territory Growth Towns
WA	Western Australia

1
Two debates

Mathew's story

I met Mathew on my first trip to Ntaria, the site of the famous Hermannsburg Mission to Western Arrernte people in Central Australia. The town is located on Aboriginal land about 120 kilometres due west of Alice Springs. I had been in Ntaria for just a few months, starting fieldwork among Western Arrernte people. Normally I camped or lived in a caravan but at the time I had managed to borrow a house for a while (my young son had a broken arm). I was learning Western Arrernte using a small grammar compiled by the Lutheran mission and spending as much time as I could with an Arrernte woman who had become my teacher and guide. We travelled to her son's outstation and camped for days with just a mob of grandchildren and her late husband's aging next elder brother and his wife. All the other brothers were dead. These two old people told me stories about the mission and also, in the wife's case, what it was like to see the last senior and ritually active man in her father's line pass away. 'He just finished,' she said.

Mathew was related to these people although that hardly distinguished him given the very large network of relatives that each Arrernte person has. He was about twenty when we met, smart and lively and, I imagine, normally not inclined to speak to strange middle-aged women including white ones from the coast. I had seen him around Ntaria occasionally, mostly in the camp called 'middle east' with some of his brothers (his male siblings and the sons of his *father's brothers). For a few days in each week, he worked across the Finke River at Tjuwanpa helping to construct the new outstation resource centre. One of his tasks was to drive the earthmover. I used to wave to him as we drove by on our way to country. Mathew came to see me to deliver a message from a relative. I drove a Toyota Hilux truck with a large tray and people used to line me up for lifts into Alice Springs. He wanted to confirm a trip for his relative and to ask if he could come along. As a young initiated man, he knew he would probably sit in front. I had bent to this delicacy among the Western Arrernte. Unless elderly women were coming, men sat in the front with me. In those days—things have changed so rapidly, really—hardly any Arrernte women around Ntaria drove a car. It was a male thing. When the cabin was full of men, I became almost a part of the truck I drove.*

On that day, Mathew walked in and looked at my books. Previously I had worked for twenty years in the Caribbean and, in particular, on ghetto life in Kingston, Jamaica. I had always been interested in people in transition: from country to town, from high life to low life, seeking new religions, cultures and class milieus, across established boundaries and borderlands. Hailing from a suburban family with a modest rural background, I was myself an in-betweener. I had brought the books with me in order to finish an article on Jamaica, maybe my last for a while. Mathew delivered his message in Arrernte, saw me struggle, translated into English, and then allowed me to respond in my own stumbling version of his language. He decided that English was the best way to go, and began to pick up various books and ask me what they were. He read out the titles of some. I explained my past research projects and remarked that I had lived 'in America' for a while. He rummaged through more books, read a sentence here and there, mouthed more titles and then, not looking up, suddenly said in English, 'Maybe you know Martin Luther King. Arrernte mob, that's what we need. Some fella like Martin Luther King.' I told Mathew that I had never known Martin Luther King—killed before my time in the USA. However, I knew about him and I knew a bit about the mob from Africa who were taken to that part of the world as slaves. Mathew asked me if they still spoke 'language'. I said that they didn't, not the ones that I knew, although they did speak Kriol 'little bit same' as mobs up north and in the Kimberley. He nodded and a long silence followed. I think we exchanged remarks about Tjuwanpa and then he left.

The next time I had occasion to speak to Mathew at any length—and those 'lengths' with Arrernte men were always pretty short—I was driving him back from the Alice Springs jail after a three-month stint. It was about two years later. I knew his relatives a great deal better and I had been recruited to collect him because his family wanted Mathew taken directly to an outstation—away from Alice Springs, straight through Ntaria and out the other side, further west. He was slim and looking good: healthy. It had been his first time in the Big House and he was predictably sober; chastened as well as engaging in sobriety. Mathew told his mother and me that he would become a Lutheran pastor. He had even brought a Bible from the jail and was flicking through it. He said he wouldn't drink anymore and would live on the outstation with his brothers. We laughed a lot and talked about names from the Bible for his recently born third child. I remember I put a Western Arrernte country-and-western tape in the cassette deck. We sang 'Hermannsburg Mountain' together. Then we all sang a hymn as well.

Things didn't last on the outstation, though, and Mathew had disengaged from Tjuwanpa. He pulled his CDEP pay and often went directly into Alice Springs. His wife began to follow him, leaving the children with relatives. Soon they were both drinkers, and fighting too. Jail visits became a regular feature of my trips. Sometimes I went inside, both to the security part, and also to the low-security shelters that look out over the Aussie rules football ground. The place where the prisoners meet their visitors could as well be a footy club barbecue area. Other times, depending on how many relatives I had brought, I stayed outside and chatted with an attendant. Mathew was only one of many young men that people I knew visited, and there were always kids to see their fathers and brothers, and sometimes the person who called the jail prior to the visit forgot to give my name. Without advance notice, visitors were not allowed inside.

Time passed and it became clear that Mathew's life was on that track. Mostly he went down for driving under the influence and without a licence. Sometimes he was disorderly but as the years passed he became so thin that he didn't have much strength to hit, except his wife, who left pretty quickly and went back to country. Of course there was much I didn't see and would not have been told about. The only incident I did see concerned an argument linked to a payback. Mathew had taken off from Ntaria in a car—drunk and careering into Alice Springs with his eldest brother's unlicenced rifle. He was angry and ready to kill. An auntie who was about at the time went to the Ntaria constables and told them to call Alice Springs. They should set up a roadblock on Namatjira Drive and stop him going into town. Mathew went down again, for a longer time.

Nonetheless, his family agrees that only relatives and the jail have kept Mathew alive. Relatives look after him and so does the jail, where the regular food and respites from alcohol put fat back on his bones. And it has been a life worth living. I have seen two of his sons with their brothers returning to Ntaria after their initiation ceremonies. I have seen more children born and noticed that, looking good or bad, Mathew generally is present at family events—not just funerals but baptisms and confirmations and barbecues at the outstation. If someone dies, he does 'sorry' too, at least for a while. The naming of his children, and projected marriages, maintain generational and regional ties. The latter involve people whose first language is an Arrernte dialect or a Luritja one, spoken by people to the immediate west and south of the Western Arrernte. It seems likely that Mathew's grandchildren will continue in this path. Moreover, this enduring form of sociality extends into the urban milieu. We meet up in the Alice Springs mall, in his town camp, at the football and the hospital, or on someone's veranda in Ntaria.

About nine years after I first met Mathew we visited in the security section of the jail. Mathew had been in a bit of trouble and there was also family consternation about a young relative who was in jail for the first time. The young man was very depressed, in part caused by the sudden cessation of constant cannabis use. A lot of discussion took place about who to put him with and how to look after him and what to say to the jail staff. I was sitting half turned away from the animated crowd, looking at a wall. Suddenly, Mathew said to me above the hubbub, 'Diane, I'm doing adult literacy. Maybe I can read.' I told him that was great, and I nearly cried in frustration.[1]

•

This book stems from my experience in Ntaria, and debates over many years concerning remote communities, especially in the Northern Territory (NT). It is not a book about Ntaria or about remote Indigenous life as such. It is not about the NT Intervention (2007), although that event bears on this discussion. The focus of the book—debates about remote Aboriginal Australia—draws on my knowledge of Ntaria and on my engagement with various proposals for people like Mathew: who he is, what he wants and chooses, and how his community should be run. These debates concern a population of possibly 80,000 people living in the remote parts of the NT and some states.[2] Writers also offer a figure of 120,000 Indigenous people, mainly Aboriginal people, living in remote and very remote Australia. In other words, the lives to which this book responds are led by quite a small proportion even of Indigenous Australians. Not many live remote and the Western Arrernte, who count as remote, are not nearly as remote as some. The numbers then are very small but, in policy terms, the issue is a big one.

For readers who follow public affairs, Mathew's story should bring few surprises. To put it bluntly, in the time I knew Mathew he became a remote Indigenous alcoholic. Everyone has read about a Mathew juxtaposed with a story on Aboriginal art (just to place the focus on hope and not despondency). But how many of us have thought about a life like his and how it bears on his relatives, especially his wife and children, and his brothers and sisters. His mother died some years ago and his father when he was just a boy. How much do we know about such families, and how much do we really care? Let me make four observations. Mathew is culturally different from non-Indigenous Australians, and even pretty different from many other Indigenous Australians. Some are more traditional than Mathew. Many are much less traditional. Mathew's life has been one of unspectacular cultural difference. Yet for a range of reasons that I have signalled in my short description, Mathew would have found it difficult to leave his milieu at Ntaria. I think he was probably curious to leave when I first met him. From time to time, he had seen others leave because both women and men travelled out on church excursions, to land rights conventions, to DAA (Department of Aboriginal Affairs) or ATSIC (Aboriginal and Torres Strait Islander Commission) meetings, to commercial consultations and the like. For a while, Mathew's father drove a car and the family travelled north. Nonetheless, for Mathew and many others, a foreign land began right outside Central Australia, and still does. He was curious about life elsewhere, but the how and why of getting there was difficult to negotiate due to limited education and cultural difference. Like the figures in *Samson and Delilah,* a feature film about Central Australia, the route from outstation to a fulfilling life seemed illusive for Mathew, if not closed.[3]

My second observation is that Mathew's life has been marred by alcohol. His passage into alcohol dependence was chillingly swift. Between one year and a couple more Mathew seemed entirely gone, although he had relatives who seldom drank and others who had successfully availed themselves of AA (Alcoholics Anonymous). Moreover, it seems very clear that his passage into alcohol dependence was closely connected to things culturally Aboriginal. Even with post-Intervention income management, the consumption patterns of remote Aboriginal Australians and a gender order that subordinates women mean too much money is still left for grog. Again, it does seem that for young men drinking becomes an assertion of autonomy and even a competitive assertion. Freedom is performed among one's siblings and cousins and everyone can harass a mother or a wife. The intensity of kin relations seems to exacerbate the binge drinking, both Indigenous and non-Indigenous, that is common throughout Australia. Furthermore, the dense network of relatives from Ntaria into Alice Springs that has kept Mathew alive has also kept him drinking. Conviviality among male kin seems to demand it, even of men who have led lives shaped by careers and achieved considerable distinction. No one is immune. The social–cultural and historical context and the emotional temper of Mathew and his consocaites seem over-determining where grog is concerned.

Mathew should stop drinking and so should his hard-drinking relatives, and all the other hard-drinking people in the Western Arrernte mob. Yet that seems unlikely without some concomitant change in the form of life that the Western Arrernte lead—and this is my third point. Mathew is culturally different and his life has been marred by alcohol abuse. In addition, Mathew has also been disadvantaged with a dearth of options in education, in employment, and in the ability to travel for pleasure and curiosity's sake beyond his immediate domain. Owing to his cultural difference, and his country and kin commitments, Mathew has lived in a local context of second-rate services and very high unemployment. There are few commercial ventures in Ntaria and limited employment options in Alice Springs for Aboriginal people with poor education. Moreover, apart from the clinic, the Alice Springs hospital and an improving Ntaria School, services are at their best in the Alice Springs jail. In fact, it is a life-cycle stop for many young Western Arrernte men and an increasing number of women. Central Australia begins to look a little like a version of ghetto life in the United States, where burgeoning poverty and distress also bring criminalisation of the population—often described as the US 'ghetto–jail' complex. Where other late teen and post-teen Australian youth are in tertiary institutions, Western Arrernte are often in jail.[4] In sum, cultural difference is important in itself and also important because it has become a site of marked inequality.

Owing to distinctive patterns of sociality and consumption, remote Aboriginal people are often less tightly tied to continuing paid work than many other Australians. In conjunction with poor education and meagre employment opportunities, this difference brings a disengagement from lifestyle aspirations common elsewhere in both Aboriginal and non-Aboriginal Australia. By virtue of the range of values in play, an experience similar to discouraged worker syndrome becomes more complex and widespread in communities. This situation would be unproblematic if cultural difference were in fact the sole cause. Aboriginal people including Mathew would go their own way and the incidence of substance abuse would be significantly less. But the issues are not so simple. In fact, remote Aboriginal people have a foot in two worlds, Aboriginal and European, that inform their local life. Along with poor services, this conflict undermines aspiration, personal health and many local forms of authority. Governments, be they federal or state/territory ones, have responded poorly to this situation. A century of policy and practice has held remote Aboriginal people on the very margin of society in mission stations and the like. These have been attractive policies because they played to cultural difference in a way that masked the inequality of services. In the eyes of many Australians, these were indigenous people who required very little from mainstream society. More recently, the 1967 referendum enabled federal government to include Aboriginal people in the census and also legislate on their behalf. Yet people who live remote have little federal electoral significance, notwithstanding NT land rights. As a result, the inequality that cultural difference masks has endured and divided people like the Western Arrernte from other Australians, including other Aboriginal people who do not live remote. Mathew's life is as it is because of inequality and the cultural difference that makes that inequality natural in the eyes of many citizens. How many readers of this book have thought that employment is irrelevant to remote areas because 'they're traditional'; or perhaps that if those who live remote really want equality 'they should change'? But is it so easy for the Mathews of Australia either to live apart from the mainstream, or drop all their customary ways? The 'space' of difference, as Marshall Sahlins calls it, must be redefined to address this different inequality (see Sahlins 2000:494).

My final point is that Mathew, like other Arrernte, has experienced *all* these factors: the comfort and constraint of minority culture, the highs and lows of substance abuse, the boredom of disengagement from a working life, and the intermittent, often flailing attempts to change things. Not surprisingly, this book is about cultural difference and inequality but also about the fact that neither critical nor policy debate has addressed the full range of issues involved. My proposal is that this failure can be traced in part to a failure in critical thought among anthropologists. But cognate disciplines are also involved, including history and Indigenous studies. I call them the 'humanistic social sciences'.[5] The silence of these disciplines concerning remote community distress left a space that was filled by opinion writers whose pronouncements were not always well informed. Their accounts underlined inequality in remote Aboriginal Australia but took little or no account of the cultural difference that makes that inequality hard to address. Concurrently, influential Aboriginal leaders, including Noel Pearson, turned their backs on academics, or at least on anthropologists. Consequently, there has been no searching critical debate, just policy camps doggedly defended. The outcome for the universities has been mentioned in a recent publication: Hinkson notes a new indifference to anthropology in policy circles that count (Hinkson 2010:12). How did it come to this?

Difference and inequality

Before I proceed, let me define two terms that are crucial to this book. The terms are ubiquitous in social science but in this context have a particular import.

As understood in anthropology, I take the concept of cultural difference to apply to a way of life, society or other bounded social milieu which can be modelled as a distinctive whole. Aboriginal culture, especially in its traditional form, has been modelled in this way and, as discussed in Chapter 2, numerous university texts and other tracts have been written about this 'other' or 'different' culture. Crucial to the understanding of this difference is a range of institutional forms including a hunter-gatherer economy, a specific cosmology and ritual forms (the Dreaming), and an elaborate kinship system, one role of which has been to facilitate the organisation of a regional life in the absence of centralised governance. This distinctive set of institutions was aided in its reproduction by a range of Aboriginal languages, only a small minority of which are still spoken today.

When one writes of Aboriginal cultural difference the reference is generally to elements of practice and belief, some of them implicit and some explicit, that can be linked more or less closely with this 'traditional' way of life. Importantly, these current elements of practice and thought have also been attenuated, changed and repositioned in the course of histories that have involved encapsulation in the Australian state and marginalisation in its capitalist economy. Moreover, in this process quite new forms of specific practice and belief have been generated in accord with transformed elements of the past—for instance, new ways of understanding the 'spiritual' presence of antecedents in the land and of classifying relatives in response to contemporary life. New, specifically Aboriginal iconographies have been created, including both genres of fine Aboriginal art and the types of graffiti found in remote communities today. Nonetheless, all these forms have some link with a historical experience grounded in that initial cultural difference and the impact on it of the state, modern capitalism and their associated institutions. Albeit in more diffuse and elusive ways, this cultural difference is patterned today just as it was in the past. In some degree, the difference in remote Aboriginal life therefore stands in contrast both to non-Indigenous life and the distant past of remote Aboriginal people. Still, that past is a touchstone for discerning the present.

The inequality in remote Aboriginal life with which this book is most concerned is a legacy of invasion and the history of European settlement. This is not to say that traditional indigenous societies had no inequalities. Clearly they did. By and large, women were unequal to men and younger generations were unequal to their elders. In terms of knowledge accumulation some men and women were ritually unequal to others of their gender. Some were clearly unequal in terms of strength, beauty, dexterity and motor skills, including those involved in dance, hunting and the like. Nonetheless, the specific inequality that bears on this discussion is that which began to unfold once Aboriginal Australians were encapsulated in a European-derived state and became increasingly positioned by a capitalist economy. By virtue of laws concerning citizenship, property and association—not to mention crimes and misdemeanours—Aboriginal people became encapsulated by the state. These laws were applied to them and enforced. Where economy is concerned, the expansion of capitalism meant the obliteration of hunter-gathering, or its attenuation and repositioning in almost all parts of the continent.

In short, the inequalities created by these factors of law and economy are the ones of interest here. Aboriginal people in particular lacked many citizen rights and still lack equality in terms of service deliveries deemed the right of all citizens. The unequal delivery of services, including education, housing and health, ramify in the domain of economy. Many remote Aboriginal youth are poorly equipped in terms of their capacity to find jobs of any sort in remote Australia today. Uneducated and often suffering the effects of poor health or substance abuse, their chances of economic success in rural and remote Australia are quite slim. A legal status that in the past facilitated policies that held remote Aboriginal people on the margins of capitalism has promoted poverty today. Moreover, held in this position as much by law as by cultural inclination, remote Aboriginal people have responded by building forms of practice and belief that make them feel at home in this world of state encapsulation and economic marginalisation. It is at this point that inequality and cultural difference intersect, each now intensely reactive to the other.

The change that has been the result of encapsulation has not been simply loss. New institutional forms responsive to Aboriginal experience have been created. Moreover, Aboriginal people have taken on new capabilities as they have lost old ones—in language, technology, practical knowledge, ritual, and ways of organising social, political and economic life. Many would argue that in a literate, global world these new capabilities are more valuable than those that have been lost. Be this as it may, the question remains whether or not remote Aboriginal people have had an opportunity equal to that of other citizens to own these new capacities and employ them fruitfully. If the answer to this question is 'no', this may be because remote Aboriginal people are culturally disengaged from market society, or it may be that marginalisation has reduced their opportunities to engage. Alternatively, both these and other reasons may explain the structural inequality of most Aboriginal people in Australian society today—unable to realise and explore all the forms of human capital that the state purports to offer them.[6]

In sum, to grasp the circumstance of remote Aboriginal people requires an understanding of both cultural difference and inequality. Mathew's life underlines this fact, which I pursue throughout this book. Two further points follow: first, with the advent of an Australian state, Aboriginal culture has always been something positioned within the state and in relation to a capitalist economy. This history of inequality—for that is what it is—has always been a factor bearing on the shape and extent of cultural difference. Aboriginal cultural difference—as it is known now, and in the past—has always been a difference interpreted through inequality. Second, the forms that this inequality take, including issues of service delivery and market capacities, are often exacerbated by neglect of relevant, mundane cultural difference; for example, how to get children to school when obligations to relatives call, and how to promote employment as an integral part of life even in remote locales. In short, Australian society and the state have been perennially disinclined to address Aboriginal inequality in the context of continuing cultural difference—a difficult and also an expensive enterprise. Rather, the proposal has been that if inequality is to be addressed, it can only be addressed by obliterating difference. Alternatively, some have suggested that so different are remote Aboriginal people that inequality as I have described it does not really amount to an experience of poverty as such.

This book has been shaped by just these issues and their impact on Mathew over time. My contention is that cultural difference does not override inequality or redefine it as experience. The prevalence of lifestyle disease, substance abuse and violence in communities attests to this. At the same time, inequality cannot be addressed except through the cultural difference of those who live remote. Routes to a good literate education and market capacities that facilitate employment, even from a remote base, should address and grapple with the cultural difference in communities. There is no simple route around the conflicts involved between institutions that derive from very different cultures (see Myers 1986:258–285). This is not to deny that Aboriginal people have hard choices to make. History is never fair. Nonetheless, the Australian electorate and the state have their own commitments to make on remote communities before Australia can describe itself as a fair and just society.

Two debates

The failure of anthropology and its cognate disciplines to address these issues convincingly created a space that was filled by others, some of whom were antagonistic to cultural difference. This process found its culmination in 2007 with the NT Intervention that brought a range of policy change to remote Aboriginal communities. Rather than extol or deplore the Intervention, the focus here is on the fact that academics were unable to divert it and were virtually silenced by it. Theirs was not the policy voice heard in spheres of government. Two debates, one within the universities and one in the public domain, throw some light on why this was so.

In the 1980s and 90s, some historians and some anthropologists launched a postcolonial critique of Australian anthropology. In essence, the proposal was that this anthropology did not attend to Indigenous people as historical agents; that is, as people who change, and who negotiate the orders of power with which they are confronted, especially as these are manifest in the state and its legal system. Australian anthropology lacked an analysis of the dynamics of British settlement and of Indigenous people's fight against becoming subjects merely fashioned by the state. A variety of concerns informed this debate: the initial *fin de siècle* construction of the 'savage' in natural science; racism in Australian society; the authenticity that land rights conferred on only some Aboriginal people; and anthropology's preference for an abstracted social analysis that masked the 'blood and sweat and tears' of Aboriginal life. All the niceness in this normal science misrepresented both traditional society and the limits placed by the state on an Indigenous response to the exigencies that people faced. The debate about the Stolen Generations and those excluded from land rights—did they count as Aboriginal people?—gave a practical edge to this postcolonial critique. It was used to question the ahistorical portrait of hunter-gatherer Aboriginal people that still resided within anthropology.[7]

Though less remarked upon, the postcolonial critique also rested on the fact that, once encapsulated, Aboriginal people were subject to the dynamics of a capitalist economy, its market institutions and, by and large, its variable interest in regions where they remained the majority. The intersection of economy and law not only secured land for the Crown, but also at a later date determined the forms of marginalisation that various Aboriginal people would experience—as itinerant or seasonal workers, wards of state or welfare recipients. The dynamics of change that produced Indigenous political advance cannot be separated from this positioning that capitalism brought. Nor were these advances left uncontextualised when presented in histories of pastoralism, pearling and itinerant labour in the eastern and southern states. Yet for remote Aboriginal communities, the record is a patchy one.[8]

An early collection on the impact of mining, for instance, did not foster a genre of critical research either ethnographic or historical (see Berndt 1982). Most historians stayed away from cultural difference and the domain of the Land Rights Act. Most practitioners in the field of Indigenous studies were inclined to do the same, although the field has produced its own notable literature.[9] Notwithstanding important examples of genres mixed and boundaries crossed, the 'homeland' communities that grew in the wake of NT land rights have remained the bailiwick of anthropologists, their particular focus of research.[10] For this reason, it is significant that most anthropologists did not come to grips with two major postwar changes in remote Aboriginal conditions. These were the incorporation of Aboriginal people in an Australian welfare state *and* the rapid escalation of unemployment in rural and remote Australia.[11] Soaring unemployment came to remote Aboriginal communities in the context of bounded and highly local lives subsidised by the state. In these milieus, consumption has been organised through kinship networks which are resilient but also vulnerable now to manipulation by bullies who transgress old ways. At the same time, and with welfare ensconced, it is ties to country or locality rather than a working life that have sustained both status and identity. Importantly, this situation signals something in addition to a simple continuity of culture and location. The status confirmed through land rights and its valorisation of tradition also filled the gap that unemployment left (see Beckett 1988:9–15). Traditional ownership became the route along which most resources travelled, many in the form of government grants. As a result, some in communities became involved in a torrid resource politics to secure goods for their relatives (Austin-Broos 2003). Others unable to enter this contest have been involved in substance abuse and personal violence. Health has been a casualty as the epidemiology of remote communities came to resemble that of other indigenous peoples who have been marginalised (see Trovato 2001).

The tendency of anthropologists has been not to look too closely at these forms of change and distress. Consultancy reports commissioned on the homelands seldom brought critical reflection on the frameworks prescribed for that research. In the 1970s and 80s this was also true of the ethnographers. They produced a portrait of continuity and cultural difference that responded to a land claim context with its particular evidentiary requirements.[12] Professionally, history and Indigenous studies dismissed this ethnography as lacking interest for those who worked in south-east 'settled' Australia. Yet this meant that in the everyday of public discourse, the image of remote Australia as a bounded traditional milieu lived on. It lingered not only in the other disciplines but also among those anthropologists who were not ethnographers as such. Consultant anthropologists advised on services delivered to traditional people as portrayed by ethnography. A sense of remote Aboriginal people as historical subjects marked by inequality as much as cultural difference remained elusive. Furthermore, the *range* of remote historical experience and the range of communities produced were barely canvassed. As a result, a romantic and reified image of remote Aboriginal life survived the postcolonial critique. This would influence anthropology's response to another debate.

From the late 1990s, a vigorous campaign began to emerge concerning violence and poor health in remote communities. Before long, there was steadily mounting critique from opinion writers and private think tanks. Noel Pearson published his *Our Right to Take Responsibility* in the year 2000. In that same year, conservative critics came together in a *Quadrant*-sponsored conference, followed by formation of the Bennelong Society in 2001. The latter was headed by Peter Howson and Gary Johns, ex-politicians drawn from the two major parties, Liberal and Labor respectively.[13] In 2001, Peter Sutton published his paper on the 'politics of suffering' that critiqued the violence in remote Aboriginal communities. In his discussion, Sutton held a misguided service bureaucracy and its cultural relativism to account. Yet, by and large, he let anthropologists off the hook and took care to cite colleagues working in Cape York where he had done his doctoral research.[14] Around this time, *The Australian* newspaper began to run an editorial campaign. Its impact was augmented by various writers who included Noel Pearson, Peter Howson, Gary Johns, Nicolas Rothwell and economist Helen Hughes.[15] A disregard for difference was common, though not uniform, among these writers. Some of them opposed land rights and all placed an emphasis on welfare dependency and unemployment. Academics and others took offence. For them, the idea that welfare *caused* the dependence that brought substance abuse and violence ignored a history of the state and its exclusions. Just as important, many anthropologists thought that these critiques targeted land rights. Did critique of living conditions on the homelands aim at undermining government support? Some proposed that what outsiders thought was poverty was in fact cultural difference.[16]

The voice that emerged in opposition to opinion writers and representing anthropologists was the Centre for Aboriginal Economic Policy Research (CAEPR), located at the Australian National University (ANU). CAEPR writers rejected the common critique of a federal government scheme, Community Development Employment Projects (CDEP). These projects provided federally funded part-time employment in communities and had been intended as a constructive alternative to welfare. It was argued that in areas where there were no labour markets the CDEP offered community-based employment compatible with a traditional style of life. Critics responded that the scheme had become no more than welfare and should be replaced by other policy measures that would not produce a 'dependency' likely to contribute to social pathologies. Some of the suggested alternatives involved attacks on land rights; for example, Hughes proposed dismantling land rights in order to encourage more engagement with a market economy. Johns proposed that residents of homelands should migrate to locales with more employment options—as other unemployed do elsewhere in the world. Pearson did not endorse these measures meant to undermine land rights. Nonetheless, he did underline that welfare was 'poison' and recommended that CDEP should go.

This debate was well established when, just before a federal election, the NT government released the *Little Children are Sacred* report (2007) on child sexual abuse in remote communities. The terrible issues that the report raised demanded action on a broad front. To a startled public, the link between so-called welfare dependency, substance abuse and pathology seemed clear.[17] The NT Intervention followed, and then policy change. At least in part, the change involved a shift away from small community-based programs to greater emphasis on inclusion in the larger economy. Nonetheless, the focus was on individual dependency and not on structural disadvantage or the enduring cultural difference that makes that disadvantage hard to address. The best known of the legislative measures involved the management or 'quarantining' of welfare incomes for the care of recipients' children. A major part of welfare payments could only be spent on basic goods—food, clothing and the like—and definitely not on grog. Because the measure applied solely to some Aboriginal communities, the *Racial Discrimination Act 1975* was suspended and remote Aboriginal people were made markedly unequal before the law (see Behrendt 2010). Less well known but equally important, CDEP were disbanded in all but name. This was prompted in part by the fact that federal government could in law only quarantine welfare payments, not a wage. With the cessation of CDEP many residents in remote communities simply reverted to unemployment benefits. Post-Intervention, a further swathe of federal policies was introduced to 'close the gap' between services and outcomes for Aboriginal and non-Aboriginal Australians. On the Territory government's part, departments devised a 'Working Futures' program to improve remote Aboriginal training and employment. However, the gains in services have been modest and no one suggests that the Intervention so far has brought significant advance in remote education, employment or health.[18] In fact, the outlook in these areas is bleak as the public loses interest once again. In the course of Australia's 2010 federal election campaign, Aboriginal issues were barely mentioned.

A culture war or not?

Like the postcolonial critique, the remote communities debate involved issues of cultural difference and inequality. Moreover, there was something of a parallel between the debates, though one critique came from the left and the other from the right. Both groups have argued that anthropology, in its commitment to difference, has been blind to major disadvantage. With eyes firmly fixed on cultural difference, anthropologists have largely ignored poverty, race, or both. Each critique has stressed this point, the left in terms of the history of civil rights that has involved Indigenous people, especially in Australia's coastal regions; the right in terms of remote Aboriginal communities. As a form of analysis and politics, anthropologists have privileged cultural difference over inequality.

In the context of the remote communities debate, critics pressed their case in the face of apparent silence from the universities. With the exception of Peter Sutton and those whom he cited, academics seemed disinclined to address the issues of violence and distress (see Sutton 2001, 2009). Some of the critics read into this a vested interest in consultancies; hence the claim that those who defended homelands were a part of an 'Aboriginal industry'. Other explanations have always been available. Some anthropologists almost certainly felt that to dwell on distress might jeopardise land rights and native title—reforms for which Indigenous peoples had fought long and hard. Moreover, a reified notion of traditional culture produced by land claim research obscured the actual state of communities and the variation between them. Many anthropologists were writing from an intensive engagement with one or two locales and possibly it was easy to say, 'Not in the communities that I know'. Some anthropologists also feared the violation of confidentiality. Only intimate engagement with particular people can bring real insight into social suffering. But do those involved want their distress paraded in a public way? Again, the inconclusive nature of the postcolonial critique put anthropology in a double bind. History and Indigenous studies had criticised the discipline for its focus on cultural difference and its neglect of the history of encapsulation that had brought marginalisation and inequality within the state. At the same time, most academics and many of the public *endorsed* land rights and the maintenance of homelands. The culturally different had found a niche, albeit conveniently remote, in Australia's consciousness. All these factors led to uncertainty and ambivalence: did the reports of distress reflect something real and pervasive, or was this a political campaign to debunk and pathologise a way of life costly to the state and counterintuitive to neoclassical economics?

As debate heated up, a further factor impressed some anthropologists. Broadsheet descriptions of remote communities said little of cultural difference but much about pathology. Accounts of remote Aboriginal life were portraits of far more than unemployment or reliance on government support. They also described drunkenness, personal violence, disease, ignorance and incompetence. When the *Little Children are Sacred* report was released it seemed to confirm an elaborate portrait of pathology that was already abroad in the public domain. Explanations for this condition sometimes went to a 'savage' culture that had passed its use-by date, or to economic deprivation caused by faulty policy that included land rights (see Austin-Broos 2009a:238–258). Sutton's book reflected the view that too much weight in this account had been given to economic factors, and insufficient attention to the collapse of traditional culture. He sought to specify the situation. Other anthropologists watched in consternation as Sutton's efforts to assert expertise, and to express real grief as an Australian land rights consultant, seemed to locate the source of pathology almost exclusively in an exhausted Aboriginal tradition (see Cowlishaw 2003). This circumstance seemed to confront anthropologists with a familiar phenomenon: a readiness to render difference in terms of deviance and deficit alone and push through policy change on that basis (see Austin-Broos 2010b). The moral certainty once created in settler society by the image of the backward savage was provided in this debate by images of entirely pathologised communities. Therefore two collections edited by anthropologists, one soon after the NT Intervention and the other more recently, suggested that the debate about remote communities was a further chapter in Australia's 'culture wars'. Like a previous debate between historians, this one referenced European settlement and the integrity of Aboriginal culture. In the case of homelands, the proposal has been that the war is between a left defending cultural difference and a right beholden to neoliberal policy (see Altman and Hinkson 2007, 2010).[19]

And yet the matter is not straightforward. Sutton broke ranks in 2001. Eight years later, and post-Intervention, his original essay was expanded into a book which, by implication, endorsed the Intervention.[20] Historian Inga Clendinnen supported Sutton's views, just as she supported historian Henry Reynolds in his culture war (Clendinnen 2009). Reynolds clearly came from the left. Many anthropologists identified Sutton's position with the right and proposed that difference or identity politics was the appropriate left position (see Lattas and Morris 2010). Sutton was also supported by Aboriginal leader and anthropologist Marcia Langton (Langton 2009). After the Intervention, Langton made common cause with Noel Pearson, who had been a strong supporter of the Intervention. Endorsing both his views and Sutton's, Langton also became an executive of his Cape York Institute (CYI) for policy research. Langton's theme was poverty, not cultural difference. Again, on the publication of the CYI's *From Handout to Hand Up*, which just preceded the Intervention, Robert Manne, political scientist and staunch critic of Aboriginal child removal as well as Keith Windschuttle's work, voiced his support for Pearson (see Manne 1998, 2003, 2007).[21] In sum, some veterans of past culture wars saw the matter differently from their ostensible allies in anthropology. For these veterans, the issues of distress and poverty seemed to transcend concerns about pathologising homelands.

The NT Intervention focused the remote communities debate on issues of rights and pathology. One position, which many anthropologists endorsed, defended the right to be culturally different and free from racial discrimination. This position pitted itself against a view that the distress produced in communities actually violated other rights of individual women and children. The group rights of a different culture were juxtaposed with the claimed universal rights of individuals. Argument then revolved around whether or not remote communities were in fact pathological at all, and whether or not any such condition justified suspension of the Racial Discrimination Act. This style of debate also presented the matter as a culture war: Aboriginal difference versus the state and mainstream society. And yet some academics demurred because this latter construal is in fact simplistic. In reality, there are no bounded cultures involved; rather, the matter concerns ways in which Aboriginal people can and will reconcile different types of institutional practice that embody very unequal forms of power. Stated plainly, the maintenance of customary ways as they exist today relies on remote Aboriginal people grasping a secure position for themselves within the state and its economy. This is a process that creates conflict within individuals and their communities—not simply between separate cultures. For example, Mathew, as a youth, wished to be both culturally different *and* engage with a wider world; to be a custodian, have congenial work, take an interest in regional politics, and perhaps to travel beyond Central Australia. Rights and the routes to them will always be important for remote communities, not least defending land rights. But beyond the Intervention as an event lies the relation between the right to cultural difference and socioeconomic standing. It is unlikely that culture and its legal status can be defended effectively without more socioeconomic autonomy and this entails, in turn, trade-offs both for individuals and their communities. A debate about the right to be different cannot get to the heart of the matter without an awareness of the way in which economy bears on culture.

This book takes its departure from the observation that in the remote communities debate, the pathologising by opinion writers *and* the denial of distress by some academics were real factors in the debate. Forms of silence marked both sides and reflected fundamental issues. On the one hand was a failure to acknowledge cultural difference and the complexity it brings to policy-making geared to address disadvantage; on the other was a failure to grant that the suffering and the distress brought by marginalisation are not simply defined away by Aboriginal forms of life. As I have suggested throughout this chapter, the issues that concern remote communities would be fairly easy to address if they involved only cultural difference.[22] It is because this is not the case that there is distress of the type now familiar in communities.

An argument and outline

In the chapters that follow, I propose to criticise anthropology in order to defend it. As stated above, my argument is that cultural difference does not override inequality or redefine it as experience.

The prevalence of lifestyle illness, substance abuse, early death and personal violence in communities attests to this. At the same time, inequality cannot be addressed except through the cultural difference of those who live remote today. Routes to literate education and employment need to address and not dismiss the cultural difference in communities, including an inclination not to migrate away from country on a permanent basis. This circumstance also reflects the need for a mix of policy, and not the polarisation that took place in the remote communities debate. If elements of tradition tie remote Aboriginal people to the local, their status as Australian citizens and market participants requires that some among them move beyond the local to negotiate a larger world and its economy as well as regional and national politics. In sum, the identities of remote Aboriginal people are multifaceted today. As such, the reproduction of cultural difference requires non-local solutions as well as local ones.

In effect, my discussion of the two debates involves completing the task of the postcolonial critique. That task involved criticism of the study of cultural difference as a bounded and reified whole. It involved a critique of classical ethnography.[23] Aboriginal people, the critics argued, should be addressed as historical agents. And as such, their experience of inequality in the state is equal in importance to their cultural difference. To this view I add the point that these matters affect the writing of ethnography and its relation to critical thought. How a specifically Aboriginal experience and its significance are defined changes as the context of an account becomes more historically attuned. To make these observations is not to dismiss cultural difference and turn to a focus on inequality, even including race. Rather the issue is that all Aboriginal difference, as it is lived and interpreted today, is difference mediated by the state and its histories of inequality. The task is to understand what difference means within the framework of a state underpinned by the market institutions of a capitalist economy.

Finally, I have written this book as an anthropologist and in significant part about anthropology, but in order to speak to a broader audience of academics and others who are interested in policy debate. Anthropology's tools are important because they are designed to interpret difference. Equally important for Australian research, anthropology needs to enter fully into dialogue with other humanistic social sciences that address Indigenous Australia. This should mean the end of representations of remote Aboriginal life as an exotic, even privileged, 'other' beyond the gamut of historical research and changing, contested experience. The connections between Fitzroy Crossing, Maningrida, Ntaria and Bourke need to be underlined, as well as the differences. In addition, the distance that the postcolonial critique created between anthropology and the other disciplines should be reduced. If anthropology has not addressed inequality as it might have, there is little evidence that policy today actually does come to grips with fostering equality in the context of cultural difference. Not doing better at this task entails the perennial pathologising of remote communities. Australians who are in and beyond the universities share a responsibility to do better.

The book includes three 'background briefings' as part of Chapters 2, 4 and 5. They provide the reader with useful information that helps make sense of the debates. The briefings concern, in turn, traditional Aboriginal culture, the growth of an Indigenous sector, and unemployment in remote Aboriginal communities. Most chapters end with an overview. Chapter 2 involves a discussion of classical ethnography and its strengths and weaknesses. I also sketch the postcolonial critique as it was pursued in anthropology itself. Chapter 3 describes some aspects of the postcolonial critique that was launched by history and Indigenous studies. These include the charge that anthropology is or was a racist discipline. I assess the validity of this critique, both its sound and unsound points. An account of the ways in which this critique both within and beyond anthropology struggled with issues of equality and difference sets the stage for the remote communities debate. Chapters 4 and 5 address that debate as it unfolded through the 1990s and into the 2000s. In Chapter 4, I describe the types of critique fielded by those who opposed what they saw as a 'separate development' for remote Aboriginal communities. They argued that these remote communities had become sites of pathology and suffering. Often they also proposed that cultural difference precludes equality and therefore should be dispensed with. These writers had a range of positions, including those maintained by some Aboriginal leaders. Chapter 5 describes the position of many anthropologists on land rights, CDEP and the NT Intervention. Often these defences were in the form of writing produced or coordinated by CAEPR. Although contributors to these collections did not have a uniform position, the collections have a discernable tenor in support of homelands and outstation life. It was among these writers that the view was put that 'statistical equality' and cultural difference do not always go together. Chapter 6 assesses the debate and relates it to the postcolonial critique. I explain how cultural difference and inequality were in play throughout the debates. I also raise some general points concerning the politics of difference (or identity) and the politics of equality, and the tensions between them. Finally, I instance mainstream education as a policy issue that needs to be understood both in terms of equality *and* cultural difference. I argue that equality in primary education for remote communities is a matter of equal citizenship and a prerequisite today for cultural difference as well. I conclude with an update on Mathew's story.

2
Culture and ethnography

There was much discussion, particularly during the anthropological evidence, about the location of boundaries... The claimants' case was put on the basis that people of semi-desert regions do not conceive of their country as discrete blocks... Rather, it is thought of as an area surrounding a number of 'Dreaming tracks'.

> Justice John Toohey, Extract from Warlmanpa, Warlpiri, Mudburra and Warumungu land claim, Aboriginal Land Commissioner's Report No. 11

The concept of *walytja* can be said to define the moral order of Pintupi society as 'family', in contrast to relations with strangers, which are full of fear, hostility, and suspicion. This view portrays the larger Pintupi society as a group of closely cooperating kin.

> Fred Myers, *Pintupi Country, Pintupi Self: Sentiment, place and politics among wester desert Aborigines*

These epigraphs describe two common continuities in life for most Aboriginal people living remote today. They underline the continuing importance of place and relatedness, country and kinship, to people who also often speak Kriol or an indigenous language in their camps and communities. These three attributes of country, relatedness and a first language other than English suggest why it is difficult, even in propitious circumstances, for remote Aboriginal Australians to leave their region in a one-way movement in search of jobs. They also confirm that many remote Aboriginal people themselves do not wish to be assimilated to a system of private property ownership alone—even if it is a tool of economic development. In short, it is simply not feasible to address the troubling issues in remote communities today without addressing these forms of difference which will not disappear soon. The political moment of land rights legislation, with its corollary in a homelands movement, both responded to this difference and reinforced it in ways interpreted by the state. Moreover, this is the difference of people who have been located by preference *and* by legislation on the margin of a capitalist economy.

It is therefore not surprising that in the 1960s, 70s and 80s Australian anthropologists responded to the demands of land rights with alacrity, pursuing new research on cultural continuity and reinterpreting old research in the light of new ideas and a new policy period. The corpus of classical ethnography today is an amalgam of early research, from the *fin de siècle* to the 1950s, and of more recent work encouraged by heightened public engagement with Indigenous affairs.[1] It is clear that the nature of this ethnography has not been simply salvage or retrieval.[2] Some of it concerns ongoing practice and the task of recording it has been a shared and valued task for those concerned, both Aboriginal and non-Aboriginal.

Nonetheless, it is fair to say that ethnographers have tended to confine their attention to particular customary or traditional practices and to airbrush out, in the name of difference, those practices and contexts that underline the impact of invasion, settlement, raced relations, and new forms of sedentary life. It is not surprising that inequality within the state and Australian society figured little in this research. The facts on which such analysis would be based were generally deemed not part of ethnography. Moreover, the plausibility of this position, which has been discarded in other anthropologies, was reinforced in the context of NT land rights. Ethnographies of continuity were the required thing. This situation was buttressed by a series of generalising texts written both for students and the public.[3] They provided overviews of 'Aboriginal society and culture' in language that was plainer than that used in academic monographs and articles. Where tertiary students were concerned, the texts had a further role: they imbued young researchers with an imaginary in terms of which they might locate their own research focus. Armed with a holistic model, divergences from it were classified as factors beyond the ethnographer's interest. In this fashion, reification of matters Aboriginal became an entrenched affair. New partial and particular ethnography reinforced the holistic model. Albeit unintentionally perhaps, 'difference' screened from the ethnographer's gaze issues of historical experience and the inequality that encapsulation in a state entails.

This chapter does three things: first, it provides this book's initial background briefing, knowledge that is crucial to later arguments in this chapter and the next. In this case, the brief involves a thumbnail sketch of some aspects of Aboriginal culture—as recorded in ethnography. Second, the chapter provides a reason to value this classical ethnography in terms of its importance both to scholarship and land rights. To this end, Aboriginal ideas of country are juxtaposed with John Locke's views about property. These views were seminal for modern liberalism, including Australian neoliberalism. In this context, ethnography confirms the reality of difference. Third, and finally, the chapter considers implied and explicit critique of this ethnography from within anthropology. The discussion focuses on three writers—Gillian Cowlishaw, Jeremy Beckett and Elizabeth Povinelli—who raise different but related issues concerning race, welfare colonialism and the state. Hence this chapter begins with classical ethnography and cultural difference. In its latter part it shifts to critique, and to issues of inequality.

A background briefing: Traditional Aboriginal culture

Migration, language and economy

The forebears of Aboriginal Australians migrated to a once unpeopled continent probably on various occasions and by more than one route both through South-East Asia and New Guinea (Mulvaney 1975; Blainey 1997:15–31). In time, a growing population fanned out across the continent to build forms of regional association and long-distance chains of exchange involving ritual knowledge and/or material goods. Linguists estimate that some 250 related languages were once spoken among indigenous Australians, the majority of which are of a form called 'Pama-Nyungan' today. A smaller and more diverse group of 'non-Pama-Nyungan' languages is located in areas from the Kimberley across to north-eastern Arnhem Land (see Walsh 1993:6; Yallop 1993:16–17). As these Australians moved south, they settled in regions that certainly in the past few centuries have had different climates, producing variations in food production, social institutions and belief. Keen (2004) discerns 'four broad resource regions' for the Australian populace at the time of European settlement: the south-east of Victoria; the south-west of Western Australia; a 'grain belt' of arid Central Australia stretching from western New South Wales through Central Australia to the Kimberley; and a tropical region that includes northern Cape York and northern Arnhem Land. Each harboured different types of staple ranging from grass seeds to cycad-palm nuts and species of yam. Moreover, all these staples were collected seasonally in the absence of plants and animals that could be domesticated. Technology differed to some degree according to environment: watercraft in riverine and lacustrine areas were the only form of transport; grinding stones for seed were used in central arid areas; and skin cloaks were used in the sometimes chilly south-west and south-east. Hand tools were similar across the continent, and included digging sticks, various spears and other missiles including the boomerang. Groups from all regions used fire as their main form of energy conversion. Keen remarks that Aboriginal people intervened more than previously thought in the reproduction of natural species, mainly through the use of fire but also through limited plant propagation, damming and 'small scale irrigation' (Keen 2004:381). Labour organisation across the continent was similar, with most tasks done by individuals or small work groups. Women concentrated on staples and small sources of protein while men sought larger animals and sometimes helped with foraging tasks.

All the regional groups that Keen describes had developed a common pattern of movement: 'People formed home bases (residence groups) from which they made logistical forays and within which they shared their produce' (Keen 2004:382). He notes that the relatively similar technology across varied ecological zones produced quite different carrying capacities in the diverse regions. Density varied between one person to 100 square kilometres in desert areas and one or more persons to two square kilometres in some tropical zones. Clearly this variation in population density would have engendered different forms and frequencies of regional association and seasonal movement, and different incentives to long-range communication. Generally, people searched for food and distributed it within small domestic groups that revolved around a senior man or men and his/ their wives.

Ideology and ritual

If these attributes suggest common ways in which environment was interpreted, there were also other—culturally elaborated—ways in which that environment was known. As Maddock remarks, 'Patterns of human relations to the land would have grown gradually after Australia was settled' (1982:34). Nonetheless, a feature of Aboriginal knowledge continent-wide was an emphasis on 'law' and the imperative to follow it or 'follow it up'. With this imperative came the proposal that what the law described was relatively fixed, even eternal, in contrast to the changing and often ephemeral nature of actual life on the land. One followed the way of ancestral beings in order to 'hold' one's descendents, and their environment, in place.

Beyond this general feature of Aboriginal cosmogony, it is likely that at least two types of knowledge about the land developed in interdependent ways. Forays by a domestic group away from a home base involved at least seasonal movement and cooperation with others in the use of micro-environments, or a 'range' as Stanner (1965) termed it. Even today in Central Australia, women rely on particular people associated with particular locales to give advice on finding bush foods—fruits and reptiles and the like—in particular seasons. A small region dominated by one language group reveals a patchwork of highly detailed knowledge concerning the run-offs from the ranges and the terrain that becomes the plain. Because there has been species degradation and knowledge attenuation with white settlement, it is likely that this patchwork knowledge would have been more elaborate in the past. This knowledge management to facilitate sustenance was largely cooperative. It involved communication across highly permeable boundaries in which the appropriate form was 'to ask' before moving into the vicinity of someone else's terrain (see Peterson 1976; Myers 1986:71–102; Williams 1999). As life stabilised, a second type of knowledge intersected with the first. Forms of association with places and species built distinctive identities within these regions. People were known as 'coming from' a particular place associated with particular species and, possibly, with the locale where forebears had been buried. Over time, these forms of identity came to be socially inherited as well. Moreover, this inheritance was often ritually objectified in the course of both male and female initiation. These developments were the source of an elaborate ritual life concerning ancestral totemic figures—part human, part other species in their propensities—to whom individuals were related via their place of conception or birth, or via inheritance through fathers and mothers. As Ingold observes, the knowledge surrounding ancestral figures and their marks in the land was used to define alienated forms of both individual and group identity. Each identity, in some degree, was differentiated from the identities of other individuals or groups. These groups and individuals, through their particular ranges and levels of knowledge, had specific ritual responsibilities in relation to the land (see Hamilton 1998; Morphy 1991:39–51; Ingold 1986:156). In 'following up the law', Aboriginal Australians were also acting to reproduce through ritual the form and species of their environment. In sum, foraging knowledge for the shared ends of sustenance, and ritual knowledge for specifying social identities, tended to work in concert. The heightened productivity of a region in which people cooperated allowed the elaboration and the differentiation of ritual practice and identity.

Ways of understanding how unoccupied land became ritually interpreted, and mainly managed by men, tend to find a route through the activities of women—who were men's labour force. Hamilton suggests that richer environments, which required less movement in a region, were also ones where fathers would have found it easier to return to their place and pass their knowledge on to sons (Hamilton

1998:104). Povinelli, citing Ronald Berndt, notes that for Aboriginal people, 'The land is a living thing... and the mythic deities who symbolize that land... need to be nurtured' (Povinelli 1993:157). The nurturing, Povinelli writes, came in the first place through women's foraging, sweat and smell; through their everyday intimacy with the land, including the experience of conceiving and giving birth. These women's acts in a particular place marked it as the locale for a vital force; an emplaced ancestral figure that might in time become the patrilineally inherited identity of those who were conceived or born in that place. In short, these writers suggest that identities forged by women's everyday intimacy with the land became the socially inherited ones. Not all Aboriginal societies involved the alienation of totemic identity through patrifiliation. In some eastern and western Australian societies, this identity came mainly through women. Moreover, it was common in a range of societies to have both matrilineal and patrilineal totemism and exogamy.

T.G.H. Strehlow in particular has underlined that practical and ritual knowledges were by no means separate systems. The song cycles that described the travels of ancestral totemic (Dreaming) figures also, progressively, described a slice of landscape and its significant waterholes or soakages where these figures 'spelled' or rested as they moved along (Strehlow 1970). In addition, Strehlow notes that the secret/sacred nature of these places made them forms of refuge for animals in times of drought. (His remarks pertain to Central Australia's arid landscape.) Of Jalpalpa, now Glen Helen in the MacDonnell Ranges, Strehlow notes that it 'remained a game reserve for fish, ducks and all kinds of water bird... [Moveover], many of the finest waterholes in the MacDonnell Ranges provided inviolable sanctuaries for kangaroos, emus, and native animals of every kind' (Strehlow 1965). Again, locals say that 'big places', those of major ritual importance, generally were not located at perennial water sources, but rather in regional proximity to them. In times of drought, this allowed those sources to be available to women and children as well as men. Correlatively, Thorley (2001) reports that sites that were host to large regional gatherings seem to have been ones at which there might have been an adequate regional rainfall only every three or more years. Gatherings, such as those described by Kimber and Smith (1987), would have been spaced in time thereby preventing the total exhaustion of appropriate sites. In addition, such large-scale regional gatherings also occurred close to grass seeds and grinding stones, the source of the major mass staple that was storable—at least for a period of weeks. These grinding stones were the property of women who were kin and cooperated in a region.

This alignment of material and ritual life speaks to an integrated system. Yet, there were ways in which groups and individuals were also distinctive. One concerns the nature of ritual life and the fact that in many societies there were both male and female forms of initiation secluded from each other—though it seems that male rite was the more elaborate. Gendered secrets and blocks to knowledge flows were part of these societies. Many societies had male initiations that were complex cults of masculinity imparting esoteric knowledge in stages over years. Often, but not always, these ceremonies involved 'varying degrees of privation, pain, mutilation and other harsh treatment' (Keen 2004:245). The physicality of these ceremonial forms and the liberal use of blood drawn from either arms or urethras established the 'shock and awe' of these procedures that led initiands and maturing men to respect 'the law'—the mythic teachings and designs, as well as forms of social organisation that defined individuals and groups in relation to each other. For people past food-gathering age, knowledge was a valued resource. Elders held knowledge in order to command a range of services including gifts of meat. Moreover, knowledge that was stratified and also tied to place fostered varieties of knowledge distribution and accumulation. All these factors shaped the elaboration of song cycles and ritual performance. Along with this elaboration came an aesthetic of design in terms of decoration, dance and song performance, and a characteristic personal bearing especially among those who were cognoscenti. These types of achievement were revealed in the increase rites of Central Australia, where men took it on themselves, as the responsible agents, to reproduce the species in their region. In places such as the tropical north, where species reproduction did not seem so pressing, a comparable elaboration of rite was focused on death. Long and socially intricate mortuary ceremonies were maintained among the clans that offered specific roles to structurally significant relatives (see Morphy 1984). These forms of ceremony, some of which endure today, acted both to integrate regional groups and also to distinguish them and their members in terms of both inheritance and achievement.

Kinship and classification

Traditional Aboriginal society was one in which economic and ritual life interpreted the land and its species. This society was also one in which kin or kin-like relations were extended to an entire social universe. Being one form of kin or another—either ascribed through inherited relations or achieved through long-term practice that conferred relatedness—was the only route to a recognised status. In this sense, everyone was classified as one form of kin or another. This meant that marriage partners were also a kind of kin. An Aboriginal society might have twenty commonly used kinship categories, only a few of which could provide a marriage partner—often the preferred one being someone we would describe as a form of 'cousin'. In all Aboriginal societies this role of kinship as a universal classification was marked by terminologies with specific features (see Keesing 1975:101–120). Dating back to Lewis Henry Morgan, these terminologies have been distinguished as 'descriptive' or 'classificatory' ones (see Fortes 1969:9, 12).[4] Indigenous Australian terminologies are mostly classificatory. A common feature of these terminologies is the 'equivalence of siblings', whereby a mother and her sisters and a father and his brothers are called by the same term. Consistent with this, the children of these women and men are also called by the same terms, so that multiple 'mothers' and 'fathers' acknowledge 'children' who are parallel cousins to each other. Keesing describes the outcome of these classifications as one in which 'collateral kin are terminologically equated with lineal kin' (Keesing 1975:148). Cross-cousins, children of father's sisters and of mother's brothers, are identified by other terms generally translated in English as 'cousin', while the parents of these cousins have particular terms sometimes translated as 'uncle' and 'aunt'.

These terminologies had many roles. They could designate potential marriage partners, and mark relations of amity in contrast to authority relations—between grandparents and grandchildren on the one hand, and children and parents on the other. They also marked relatives prominent in ritual roles for a younger generation, for example in initiation and in bestowal negotiations between a boy's fathers and the brothers of his future mother-in-law. Again, these terminologies could signal particular avoidances between and within generations and other etiquettes of interaction. Where marriage is concerned, it is important to understand that these terms defined a category of kin, rather than a single person or a few known specific relatives whom someone might marry. In addition, when the rules proposed that a man should marry a woman in the category of daughter to mother's mother's brother's daughter in the Arrernte case, or a woman in the category of daughter to father's sister in the Kariera case, it was common for this rule to define a preferred option, with other options available. In polygynous societies where competition for wives was also part of male politics, alternative categories, along with marriage to widows, were crucial options for many men (see Hiatt 1965). In most societies, men married late and women married very young, increasing the feasibility of polygyny. Younger men had to wait for their wives. A man with a number of wives became a clansman with links into other clans across a region. Moreover, bestowal could involve designating a young man's future mother-in-law who, with her husband, would produce in time a daughter for him to marry. In this way, an elaborate social system extended both through space and time.

In traditional society, there were also other forms of classification into moieties, sections, subsections and semi-moieties. It was common for societies to have one of these latter forms along with a particular type of kinship classification. Moieties in the form of patri- or matri-moieties divided societies into two. Often they subsumed clusters of patrilineal or matrilineal descent groups and commonly, though not always, these resulting larger groups practised moiety exogamy. This dual form of classification also involved totemic affiliations—eaglehawk and crow is the well-known example—with specific characteristics and obligations (see Lévi-Strauss 1973:117ff; Elkin 1979:123).

Like moieties, the division of society into four or eight classes, called 'sections' and 'subsections' respectively, is a socio-centric form of classification rather than the egocentric form realised in kinship classifications. In other words, while kin classifications are always from someone's (ego's) point of view, moieties, sections, subsections and semi-moieties are comprehensive and impersonal social classifications. Section and subsection systems have often been associated with marriage because it is usual for a preferential rule to locate a man's wife in one particular section or subsection. However, as Elkin pointed out, in a section system, a man's first (cross-) cousin and second (cross-) cousin belong to the same section and, in many societies, while second cousin marriage is preferred, first cousin marriage is prohibited. In a subsection system, on the other hand, there are separate classes for first and second cousins. In short, the marriage rule is defined in kin terms and is part of the kinship system rather than a specific section classification. What this form of classification does do is to delineate adjacent generations, the paradigm being parents and children, who absolutely must not marry (see Elkin 1979:128).

Section and subsection classifications can extend to ancestral figures and even to the estates on which their sites are marked. For example, in the subsection system of the Central Australian Arrernte, an ancestral (totemic) figure, a patri-clan and its estate (or 'country') ideally should all retain the same intergenerational subsection pair—*penangke/pengarte*, or *pwerrerle/kemarre*, for instance. Marriage of the women of these clans sends them and their female descendants on one of two cycles through four subsections each. These cycles are completed after four generations and can be identified by tracing the different paths initiated by a woman and her father's sister. From men's point of view, alternate generations in a patriline take their wives from different classes and different locales within a region. Arrernte women who taught me their system conceptualised it in just these terms and explained that it was because women 'go round like a clock'—across generations and through countries—that people's relatives were distributed in clusters across a region. Over time this process produced options in visiting, foraging, ceremonial and further marriages.[5] Beyond issues of marriage and rite, the role of these systems was to group people into manageable classes that provided kin-based guides to proper behaviour. Accordingly, when a stranger was given a subsection or a 'skin', he/she was provided with a social repertoire of rights and obligations in interaction. At gatherings, strangers were 'fitted in' as if everyone were kin (Myers 1986:111). Subsections seem to be a fairly recent historical development, possibly in the past 200 years (see McConvell 1985a, 1985b; Dousset 2005). Colonisation and its population movements may have increased the need to classify and incorporate strangers. Finally, semi-moieties were a classification based on the subsection system that grouped together the father–child intergenerational pairs of a ritual descent group (as in *penangke/pengarte*).

To summarise, kinship and other forms of classification provided the means for Aboriginal Australians to organise the major spheres of interaction, connect themselves with a broader cosmos, and to allocate a place to a stranger within their known milieu. These classifications informed a remarkable sociocultural system extended through space and time to interpret the environment.

Governance

Traditional Aboriginal society was notable for the fact that there were no centralised governmental institutions either for a region or a language group. Governance was exercised between generations, age-grades and genders and within the confined spheres of residential and ritual groups. Individuals could acquire considerable prestige and influence both within and beyond these groups due to birth order, accumulated practical and ritual knowledge, and through performance skills and esoteric magical powers (see Keen 2004:246). Order was maintained through the device of placing the law 'outside the realm of human action' so that, as interpreted by an older generation, it became non-negotiable for that generation's juniors. Through initiation and the dominance of men over women this law was confirmed sometimes with extreme physical force. Young men suffered in initiation and retribution for women could mean a broken arm or smashed skull. Myers notes that the rupture to relatedness that this force could bring was masked by older Pintupi men. The power and authority they wielded was described instead as a 'nurturance' of the young (see Myers 1986:216–218). Drawing on the work of Merlan, Keen summarises the position of women: 'Although not mere objects, women were mainly reactive to marriage arrangements made by others, though they gained control with age. Men tended to deploy women's sexuality in wider relations, and women occupied a structurally disadvantaged position in ritual life, "more excluded than excluding", and subject to the threat of violent sanctions' (Keen 2004:247). Keen observes that payback feuds could spin out of control until a point was reached where reciprocity was re-established. Women often suffered most in these conflagrations.

The dispersed nature of Aboriginal governance meant that conquest was almost non-existent, although there was revenge and warfare. For all its individual physical harshness, the social world of the first Australians was in fact relatively pacific (cf. Blainey 1997:109–112; Reynolds 2003). No doubt this fostered highly developed resource management, including deployment of knowledge, multilingual interaction—it was common for people to speak three or four languages—and systems of kinship and marriage that are models of social order. It also meant that over time Aboriginal sociality produced a highly cultivated aesthetic in performance and design, and in personal communicative style. The lack of a sedentary life that came with limited domestication created the space for these achievements. This very lack of technological development, however, also meant that 18th and 19th century Europeans, by and large, were unable to see these achievements even when they looked for them—and that was only occasionally. Translating these achievements has been the task of classical ethnography.

The reality of difference . . .

The three characteristics that introduced this chapter—attachment to place, relatedness and a regional language—are indicative of present-day remote communities. To these three one could add a strong sense of kin group autonomy although the significance of this sense has changed.[6] I have gestured to traditional society's complexity in order to underline its longevity, which Blainey also links with slow population growth (1997:114–115). This longevity has particular relevance today. Where hunter-gatherer economies were swept aside by capitalism in south-east Australia, for example, this sociality attenuated rapidly. Those who survived fended for themselves and early on made accommodations to waged work. By contrast, in remote Australia there has been a different trajectory. Until recently, most of these localities had quite limited interest for investors. Governments responded with subsidies for settlements that also discouraged migration for jobs and thereby encouraged continuity with this longstanding past. While settlement and mission stations in particular subdued the violence in traditional life, more intimate and secret aspects of life could and did continue. Encapsulation in the state brought engagement with a market society only to a limited degree. As a result, customary ways mediated by post-settlement history produced the conflicting forms of value that remote Aboriginal people grapple with today.

This situation was reinforced quite recently. Australia's mining boom of the 1960s confronted the state with the dilemma of peoples living remote who were largely disengaged from the economy that mining represents. This was due in part to continuing cultural difference and in part to post World War II social services that seemed generous in terms of the past. For many remote Aboriginal people coming off a previous low income base, social service payments 'eliminated the need to sell labour to survive' or accumulate property (Peterson 1985:97). As remote Aboriginal people entered the late 20th century, many remained disengaged from the precepts of market society. For those familiar with pastoral or mission work regimes, subsequent rising unemployment and the payment of unemployment benefits reinforced or re-established this disengagement. In 1982 the High Court, on appeal from a South Australian case, ruled that land rights were not discriminatory because they were not based on an arbitrary distinction. Rather, they were a 'special measure' to ensure those involved 'equal enjoyment of human rights and freedoms'

(Peterson 1985:98). In other words, the route to equal citizenship possibly could be only through cultural difference—hence land rights. Or so some governments seemed to think. In this fashion, contemporary policy reproduced and elaborated on a cultural impasse already entrenched by prewar practice. In remote Aboriginal Australia, far from cultural difference being just an ancient fact, a history of encapsulation has reproduced it not as an isolate but rather as *a factor in* a conflict that land rights was meant to ameliorate. One way to suggest this cultural distance is to compare John Locke's view of property with Aboriginal ideas of custodianship. Here the ethnographic record can be used to gain a sense of the types of conflict that remote Aboriginal people face.

John Locke knew nothing of Australia, but his writings helped shape 19th century ideas about property, governance and savages residing in or near a state of nature—the mythical baseline for his philosophy. He has also been described as the theorist of 'possessive individualism' par excellence (Macpherson 1962): an early architect of the liberalism that preceded neoliberalism. Locke wrote on rights of colonists with regard to Native American land. Rights of colonists have also been an issue in Australia where the doctrine of *terra nullius* was based on a distinction between conquered and settled colonies. In British legal thought, conquered colonies were ones that had been occupied previously, while settled colonies were ones established on vacant land. The previous law prevailed in a conquered colony until a new sovereign changed it. Settled colonies, where no previous law obtained, were immediately subject to English law. Uninhabited or uncultivated territory became a settled colony—as New South Wales was deemed in 1889. Maddock remarks that Australia was 'inhabited,' if not 'cultivated'. Nonetheless, Australia was treated as *terra nullius* because peoples lacking cultivation were deemed to be savages and thereby 'incapable of intelligent transactions with respect to land' (Maddock 1982:17; Hiatt 1996:13–14, 30). As Australians know, it would take more than 100 years for this view to be legally overturned in the Queensland Mabo judgment (see Brennan 1995).[7]

What did Locke have to say that bears on Australia? He proposed that in a state of nature, it is labour that initiates property. It is only through labour on a piece of land that a person truly occupies it. Explicating Locke, Stephen Buckle writes 'To occupy is to seize or take hold of something, and the Roman principle is that such taking establishes a right where there is no prior claimant. But what must one do in order to take hold of a thing . . . ? This is the problem [that] Locke's labour criterion is designed to answer' (Buckle 2001:257).[8] Labour 'takes hold' of land. The point is striking in view of the Aboriginal English idiom that a custodian 'holds' a country. At site hearings in the course of land claims it is common to hear the question put: 'Who holds this country?' This 'holding' rests not on labour leading to cultivation, but rather on knowledge of a ritual type that proves domain over a place and species. Aboriginal Australians took hold of country in terms of knowledge that interpreted the land. Holding was the ability to ensure reproduction of a locale and species through rite. As ethnography makes clear, this law informed and stabilised a social system of both inclusion and ritual exclusion which allowed a foraging people to make effective use of their regional resources.

Buckle notes that in Locke's time, European landed property was even less uniformly cultivated than the Britain of today. However, this is not to say that, in Locke's view, uncultivated land was not property. Labour was not, in fact, the sole criterion. Labour bears on the 'beginnings' of property, which thereafter is secured through political society. This form of society is the precondition of the rule of law 'created through the institution, and separation, of . . . legislative, judicial and executive powers' (Buckle 2001:252). Moreover, this political society becomes truly civil society when these institutions are public and serve that interest rather than a sectional one (Buckle 2001:253). In Locke's view, Native Americans did not have political or civil society because they did not have this form of institutional separation that served public interest. Nonetheless, they did have law and governance designed for mutual protection and for the delineation of hunting territories. This view seems to modify Locke's description of the 'in-land vacant places of *America*', so like Australia's *terra nullius*. Possibly there was and is New World property.

But there is more. A third criterion also bears on property—need. In Locke's view, alienation of the land should be 'limited by what one "can use the Product of"'. In other words, people who are property holders by a previous legal agreement 'have no right to exclude [others] from [a] natural bounty' (Buckle 2001:270). Buckle argues that this principle would have led Locke to question the ostensibly large tracts possessed by Native Americans or, likewise, Aboriginal Australians. However, it also would have led him to condemn the colonial land grab of New South Wales. From a Lockean perspective, the colonists acted illegally but, nonetheless, Aboriginal Australians had no right to exclude them from the land's natural bounty (Buckle 2001:270). Although he does not argue it, Locke's remarks suggest that, in the New World context, issues concerning land should have been negotiated and settled legally, possibly by the respective parties coming together in a political society.

In the context of early colonial Australia, ethnography presents a reality check to this line of reasoning. For a foraging people with limited technology and a spatially extended social system, what would count as an unreasonably large tract of land? What would count as a natural bounty and how should we interpret the 'need' of the colonists, and that of indigenous people?[9] Moreover, given the initial inequalities of technological power, what would count as a civil agreement transcending sectional interest? And what forms of practice would be deemed to demonstrate 'holding' the land? With reference to the ethnographic record, Locke's notion of property could not apply to Aboriginal Australians except by a gross distortion of their ways. Aboriginal Australians were not gardeners but foragers, interpreting the land through extensive knowledge systems and through extended but kin-based forms of social organisation. Status was located in the ritual domain which authorised custodianship of sites rather than neatly bounded areas. These custodians and their sites embodied an acephalous system of regional power unlikely ever to produce a 'team' that might have negotiated with the British. Notwithstanding, all these features of Australian life meant that Australians, *in their own terms*, had a sense of ownership, proprietorship, custodianship and authority over land. Moreover, normative procedures for gaining access to someone else's place have been recorded extensively in ethnography (see Williams 1999). Aboriginal people identified with and held themselves responsible for these countries which they came from and to which they wished to return at death. Aboriginal Australians did not have the European legal sense of property. However, by virtue of their knowledge systems they did indeed 'hold' countries, and not merely 'occupy' them—as much as Europeans held their landed properties under the law of their society.

The comparison of Locke's view of property with this sketch of an Aboriginal system underlines the coherence of both as they might have been at point of contact. It also provides a window onto the sense of longevity regarding their system that many Aboriginal people still have, albeit an altered and attenuated sense. Finally, this account suggests the type of cultural distance that remote Aboriginal people still need to negotiate, not in the form that it was once, but translated by the state. This is the impasse that classical ethnography helps us understand; the awkward clash that now pervades homelands life. Yet classical ethnography can make this contribution only when its findings are contextualised by accounts of encapsulation and the marginalisation which that process brought.

. . . and of inequality

One would have to lack a sense of irony not to note that, in order to give classical ethnography its due as a tool of specification and comparison, the previous two sections have themselves produced an imaginary or ideal type. Yet without this analytic exercise, it would be difficult to show why there ever was a Land Rights Act—for a colonised people within the state—and why that act and its social corollaries have proved problematic for critics of remote communities today. The Land Rights Act does acknowledge an ownership at odds with private property just as the state usurped Aboriginal land in the name of this property when settlement first occurred. The issues have not gone away. To provide a model of a culture, though, should not be to assume the reality of just that bounded whole, either in the present or the past.

To do so would be to treat a culture just like 'race' or the inheritance of 'blood'—as a concrete and bounded essence. Culture then becomes something that a person has in degrees, making him or her fully Aboriginal, or partly, or barely so (Cowlishaw 1987). Citing Maddock's *The Australian Aborigines*, Cowlishaw notes his decision to confine himself to 'living tradition' but to reference 'what is dead' where required in order to explain the surviving parts (Cowlishaw 1987:31). The problem with this understanding is that nothing is taken to be Aboriginal beyond the bounds of this notion of tradition. Maddock's position ignores the fact that Aboriginal people have had historical trajectories quite unlike those of other Australians, and specifying for them today. These trajectories are influenced by their 'traditions' but also by their negotiation of new capacities and constraints within the state. His stance denies the specification of Aboriginal people by post-settlement history and the inequalities that encapsulation brought.

Originally, Cowlishaw made her remarks with reference to Aboriginal people in New South Wales. She was concerned that classical ethnography privileged remote Aboriginal Australians as really the only indigenous people continent-wide (see Cowlishaw 1988). Nonetheless, her critique of the way in which classical ethnography reifies cultural difference also applies to people who live remote. These are groups that Maddock described in a fashion that airbrushed out a significant part of their daily lives. This was done in order to focus on particular continuities that were deemed not only 'different' but also significant for sociocultural comparison. Cowlishaw's initial research as a student of anthropology was in southern Arnhem Land, not too distant from the erstwhile pastoral station where Maddock did his research.[10] Her account, published in 1999, shows quite another aspect of this milieu. Cowlishaw notes that 'labour relations . . . were also race relations' in which a station manager liaised with a protector who in turn liaised with a Native Affairs Branch in Darwin (later the Welfare Branch of the Northern Territory) and/or with Native Affairs in Canberra.[11] All Aboriginal workers were recorded in terms of their tribe, age and wage, and according to their dependents as deemed by the whites in terms of their own concept of a family.

Pastoralists were licenced to be employers and licences could cover men alone, women alone, or 'male and female aboriginals'. In this particular matter, the pastoralists were answerable only to the Director of Native Affairs, a long way away. Therefore it is not surprising that white individuals, and later the Northern Territory Pastoral Lessees' Association, felt that they were and should be the sole authority on the value of Indigenous labour. How different to the conditions of other workers in Australia at the time (Cowlishaw 1999:108–109). Towards the end of the 1940s, the federal government committed to funding rations distributed to the registered dependents of Aboriginal workers. The view was that these workers should be able to command their pay as individuals, although that pay was still managed by a protector. At this time, the standard wage of 5 shillings a week was raised to 1 pound for experienced workers—a wage that was still only a quarter of a comparable white worker's pay (see Cowlishaw 1999:123, 314–315).

These aspects of a micro-management of Aboriginal people, which produced the experience of race, extended into personal life, including child removal and the control of marriages between 'half-caste' or non-Aboriginal men and Aboriginal women. Cowlishaw tells the story of Tex Camfoo's protracted petition to marry Nelly, who did eventually become his wife. Many years later, Tex, who was well versed in 'blackfella' and 'whitefella' law, remarked:

> Sometimes they call me a black bastard. I just laugh at it, I just say, 'I'm proud of it.' I say, 'You're a white bastard too. What's the difference?' Sometimes it sort of makes me shame . . . I always say, 'You're to blame for it. You've been knocking round with my mother, that's why I come out a bloody yella-fella. That's your blame.' And he just shut up like a book then. (Cited in Cowlishaw 1999:185)

Cowlishaw proposes that comparable forms of management by the state continued into the land rights era. She describes the homelands movement from Mainoru station to Bulman in terms of 'betrayal', 'imagined communities', 'fantasies of progress' and the 'ventriloquism' of whites as they sought to prop up their idea of progress in an ostensibly self-managing Aboriginal community (see Cowlishaw 1999:202–220, 221, 222, 233).

In her 1999 work, Cowlishaw wrote about governmentality.[12] Elsewhere, she recorded numerous life histories (e.g. Camfoo and Cowlishaw 1995). In this, she followed Jeremy Beckett, who had first worked with autobiography or 'oral history' in the 1950s when he pursued research in Wilcannia, NSW. It is not an accidental matter that anthropologists like Cowlishaw and Beckett employ life histories, or the analysis of social dramas, as a method in their research (see also Austin-Broos 2009a). A person's life, or a telling series of events, shows the way in which unequal power and conflicting institutions bear on experience. Methodologically, the shift is away from a cultural whole and towards the cultural or interpretive capacity of agents. Beckett's earliest venture in the genre was published in 1958. The initial study found its culmination in his 1978 account of George Dutton, an Aboriginal drover. Later, Beckett would produce Walter Newton's 'history of the world' and Myles Lalor's 'oral history'. Dutton's is a story of itinerant labour and indigenous knowledge; Newton's, an eschatological story both Aboriginal and Christian. Lalor's is a story of labour and race relations, the 'testimonial' of an accomplished but nonetheless marginal man. With these publications Beckett secured a significant new genre for Australian ethnography (Beckett 1978, 1993; Lalor and Beckett 2000).

Here is Beckett describing his developing relationship with George Dutton:

> As time went on . . . I was still eager to learn what I could about tribes that had gone undescribed, but I was becoming interested in the man himself and ready to let him take his own course. The culture was dead, but its exponent was alive and accessible. Much of his talk was about the country which he knew both in its mythological associations and as a drover. I had to send for large-scale maps to follow the tracks that the dream-time heroes—the *muras*—and he had followed. In the arid back country, both Aboriginal and stockman must be able to recognize landmarks which to others seem nondescript, and they travel slowly enough for each feature to make its impression on them. I have heard drovers in bars rehearsing

each step of a route, remembering what had happened here and
there along the way, as though they were Aborigines 'singing the
country'. The country provided the link between George Dutton's
life as a stockman in white society and his life as an initiated man
in black society. For him at least it seems to have mediated the
conflict between two worlds. (Beckett 1978:4)

For Beckett, Dutton's description of life as a travel story evoked Russell Ward's portrait of the 'nomadism' of white rural workers (see Ward 1958). On Beckett's account, this was the culture that Dutton moved to, away from an Aboriginal culture that had died. In fact, Dutton uses travel as a homology to link the passage of Aboriginal groups, as they 'followed up' the law, to the nomadism of pastoral labour. The travel story constitutes a bridge between these two domains. Cultural difference is reproduced in the use of travel stories but also rearranged in a changed milieu (cf. Sansom 1982). That these Aboriginal men in New South Wales were the ones who changed the most reflects their inequality before the law and in their working lives.

Possibly Beckett is best known for his structural account of this inequality in terms of welfare colonialism (see Beckett 1987:12–18; Paine 1977). Beckett notes that although the term 'colonialism' is usually applied to overseas territories, it can also be applied to a relation between people who reside 'within national boundaries . . . and to the indigenous populations of colonies of settlement, such as Australia' (1987:13). He notes that the marginalisation of Australia's Indigenous peoples has been and remains heavily mediated by the state so that 'the political mode has been dominant' (1987:12) A better formulation would be that, in Australia, the state has managed economic marginalisation with a plethora of legislation that, both in the past and present, has done as much to entrench as to ameliorate that position. This has occurred in part by providing remote Aboriginal people with modest but sufficient means to disengage from market society, its modes of consumption and orientation, while not equipping them to avoid the panoply of ill-health and distress that comes with marginalisation (see also Peterson 1998). In Beckett's view, these internal colonial relations stand opposed to the full rights of citizenship which Australia was slow to grant to Indigenous peoples:

> While governments have readily committed themselves to citizenship for their indigenous minorities, the implementation of this goal, particularly in its socio-economic implications, has proved to require more than just the passing of legislation. Nor can the problems be solved simply by making them eligible for the regular benefits provided by the welfare sector to all citizens. (Beckett 1987:16)

In short, the dismantling of this colonialism requires both astute legislation and careful and sustained implementation of a type seldom seen in Australia—not least because the people involved in the process also need to grasp it as their own.

Beckett writes that given the competing demands on the state, government action came in conjunction with an identity (or difference) politics. While the practical response was in terms of welfare and other government support, 'at the ideological level the "native", who once stood in opposition to the "settler" and outside the pale of society, undergoes an apotheosis to emerge as its original citizen' (Beckett 1987:17, 1988:12–13). The romance of the Dreaming that a land rights movement brought has been indicative of such an apotheosis. Beckett's comments reference the Land Rights Act and the homelands movement that addressed in turn an 'honourable status within the nation' and a supposed new route away from marginalisation. This involved reinventing small, domestic, bounded economies within the framework of the welfare state. To the extent that the latter remained a welfare measure, and not a step towards autonomy, Beckett's welfare colonialism has continued (see also Peterson 1985:97).

Clearly these accounts of race and other inequalities amount to anthropology's own postcolonial critique of classical ethnography.[13] They underline that difference exists within the state of inequality. This incipient critique took another turn with Elizabeth Povinelli's *The Cunning of Recognition* (2002). Even more directly than Cowlishaw and Beckett, and in ways that they might contest, Povinelli criticised Australia's land rights legislation and the ethnography that it summoned. She argued that, at the point of contact, Aboriginal and British cultures were incommensurable. In other words, they were fundamentally unassimilable one to the other without some major damage to, and misrepresentation of, one culture by the other (Povinelli 1995). In Povinelli's view, this magnitude of mistranslation began with the rendering of ritual acts in terms of a modern and moralised notion of 'sex' that made these acts indicative of savagery, so-called. It continued with inaccurate accounts of totemism in the conceptual shadow of Judeo-Christianity. This mistranslation found its culmination in the view that inheritance through patrilineal descent is the paradigm of Aboriginal land tenure. In short, throughout the 20th century, anthropology sanitised and simplified Aboriginal culture for a mainly British audience. The outcome was that 19th century notions of jural inheritance, through the father and grandfather, inhabited the Land Rights Act. Povinelli argues that the highly contextualised practices involved in walking across the land and foraging on it forged material, sensory and cognitive–emotional relations in which the land itself became personified. In addition, each major site supported a wide range of relations with variable levels of engagement and knowledge that involved women as well as men. Nonetheless, the courts have required judgments of ownership that are 'incontestable, certain, concrete [and] decontextual—in short monumentalising abstractions', and with a preference for patrilineal descent (Povinelli 2002:227). Just as important, Povinelli documented the rehearsals required of Aboriginal people prior to a land rights hearing—the loss of authenticity called for in order to seem authentic to the courts. She traced this 'repressive authenticity' through two major anthropological studies (Povinelli 1993, 2002; Wolfe 1999:169–214). The 'cunning' of the state's recognition lies therefore in the fact that the state, by virtue of its power, can assimilate in all innocence. In this fashion, Povinelli argued, anthropology has served the state.

An implication of Povinelli's work could be that there was no point in land rights. Her position might seem similar to that of historian Patrick Wolfe, who proposes that the 'superorganic' models of culture, abstracted from economy, that classical ethnography produced contributed to the repressive authenticity of land rights. In turn this legislation, argues Wolfe, denied an indigenous identity to Aboriginal people in regional and urban Australia, a concern that Cowlishaw also voiced (see Wolfe 1999). This is a difficult critique to sustain *tout court*, not least because most remote Aboriginal people would not agree with it, not to mention Indigenous leaders all over Australia.[14] Their support for land rights reflects that Aboriginal people themselves change once they are encapsulated and come to interpret their own traditions in ways that are influenced by the state. Minority difference engenders inequality and, in turn, inequality engenders other forms of difference as Indigenous peoples take control of their own circumstance. The land rights movement demonstrates this.

Classical ethnography has had both strengths and weaknesses. Its major strength has been to document the continuities that made a land rights movement possible. In so doing it has also recorded the source of continuing and transforming types of difference that endure in communities today. To truly understand remote communities, and the orientations of those who reside there, some recourse to classical ethnography is required. This fundamental point has been overlooked by many academics and opinion writers who remark on remote Aboriginal life. At the same time, the acknowledgement of cultural difference is only useful if it is located historically. The contexts I have in mind are encapsulation in the state and the ways in which capitalism has positioned individuals and groups. The legal and economic constraints that these contexts impose also bring inequalities that influence culture and the trajectory of cultural difference.

In this context, change is neither mere loss nor the free creation of Indigenous peoples. Change is a structured process that also involves the impact of inequality on cultural continuity. Lack of attention to this process has been classical ethnography's major weakness. This weakness has been magnified by the unexamined contexts in which ethnography has been practised from time to time. One such context was late 19th century evolutionism, a factor I discuss in Chapter 3. More recently, classical ethnography was practised in the context of a land rights process. Where the former context encouraged ethnographers to assume that change would bring cultural demise for all Aboriginal people, the latter context tended to encourage an optimistic focus on continuity to the neglect of change and its challenges. Neither emphasis adequately grasped the historical nature of Aboriginal culture. Again, the limitations of classical ethnography become more marked when it assumes a totalising status as the sole form of research, or of valuable research. This point has been made before by arguing for more research, and regard for it, in urban and rural Australia. Yet the issue is not locational as such but rather conceptual. It involves conceding that cultural difference is a historical phenomenon and, in this case, mediated by the state and Australia's capitalism. The intersection of economy and law positions Aboriginal people in a stratified order. And with this positioning comes the experience of inequality. If this was the message of anthropology's internal critique of classical ethnography, it was put more strongly still in the postcolonial critique launched by history and Indigenous studies.

3
A postcolonial critique

> A responsible anthropology should expand its scope so as to take in the total social process in which it participates. Rather than silencing anthropology, this project will give it more to say.
>
> Patrick Wolfe, *Settler Colonialism and the Transformation of Anthropology: The politics and poetics of an ethnographic event*

No one should overlook the legacy of 19th century ideas in present-day views about remote communities. The contrast between civilisation and savagery, between the settlers' self-image and their view of 'Aborigines', has lived on in recent debate. Initially, these arguments referenced Christianity and its superiority or otherwise to traditional Aboriginal life. With the reconciliation debate came a tendency to invoke ideas of Europe's civilisation as a gift. Why should elderly missionaries, for instance, apologise for purveying their belief and practice in the outback? Such talk entered public discourse in the early 1990s.[1] Later, with the NT Intervention, the target was not savagery as such but a thoroughgoing pathology—a new form of deviance and deficit that could not be countenanced in civilised society. Let there be no mistake: child sexual abuse and other forms of personal assault are against the law. Perpetrators of these acts should be charged, convicted and punished. This is beyond dispute. However, media portraits of remote communities commonly identified their specificity *only* as pathology. They invoked the idea of pathological communities *per se* that should be changed forthwith. For the public, these portrayals brought a moral certainty just as surely as notions of the savage comforted the consciences of settlers. In the period of the *fin de siècle*, some of Charles Darwin's work gave such views his imprimatur. They have been resilient since.

For this reason the postcolonial critique, as conducted by historians and practitioners of Indigenous studies, has both value and relevance today. It provides a genealogy of popular and academic ways of thinking about remote Aboriginal people that has lingered into the 21st century. Yet this critique does more than discuss the use of 'civilisation' and 'savagery' as terms of commendation or abuse. It also names anthropology as the discipline most responsible for spreading these ideas. As the discussion below will show, this is a charge that carries some validity, but also invalidity as well. To assess anthropology's role requires discussion of the range of texts involved and exactly what they did. Moreover, although this postcolonial critique concerns anthropology done mainly prior to 1960, the case that is made against the discipline is, by and large, a comprehensive one—for all times and places (see for example Wolfe 1999; Gray 2007). At least some postcolonial critics have come to bury anthropology, it seems.[2] Yet, if this means burying the study of cultural difference, then their project is a misguided one. A grasp of difference as well as inequality is still crucial in the present. This chapter therefore has two aims: to underline the strengths of a critique of false forms of thought about Indigenous Australians, but also to confirm that studies of cultural difference can be done in postcolonial ways. This task is crucial for an understanding of the histories of, and present-day conditions in, remote Indigenous communities.

Below I discuss some writings drawn from the work of Russell McGregor and Patrick Wolfe. Both have been committed to an examination of anthropology's focus on cultural difference as it was defined initially—in terms of an engagement between civilised Europeans and savage Australians. The discussion is focused on three portrayals of Aboriginal people which these critics judge offensive, and the product of anthropology. Attention to these representations allows an assessment of this postcolonial critique. It also provides a basis for proposing a new approach to cultural difference in the context of the state's inequality. To this end, I call on Martin Nakata's work and integrate some of his suggestions with my own.

The doomed race

For those interested in social analysis, one of the most intriguing features of Charles Darwin's work is the different types of approach he brought to his study of evolution as speciation, and his study of humankind. Where one process of evolution manifested itself as proliferating species, the other—human evolution—involved passage along a shared path, at different rates, that would witness over time the survival of those more fit and, simultaneously, the extinction of the less fit (McGregor 1997:28–30). Darwin chose one evolutionary path ('progress') to civilisation, whereas anthropologist Franz Boas chose diverse histories that produced different cultures (see Stocking 1982:202–206).

'Race' and Darwin's indecision about the concept were at the centre of his approach. Darwin's commitment to monogenetic theory stood in a tension with his view of race as possibly a form of sub-speciation. Sensing the tension, perhaps, he proposed that the differences between races were mainly inconsequential. He sought to explain differences of phenotype and perceived moral and emotional development in terms of a 'sexual selection' and the development of institutions including, for instance, agriculture and governance. In this respect, Darwin was a Lockean (Darwin 2008 [1871]:261–264). On the other hand, Darwin endorsed survival of the fittest and saw hunter-gatherer groups as doomed:

> Extinction follows chiefly from the competition of tribe with tribe, and race with race. Various checks are always in action . . . such as periodical famine, the wandering of parents . . . the stealing of women, wars, accidents, sickness, licentiousness, especially infanticide, and, perhaps, lessened fertility from less nutritious food, and many hardships . . . and when one of two adjoining tribes thus favoured becomes more numerous and powerful than the other,

the contest is soon settled by war, slaughter, cannibalism, slavery, and absorption ...

When civilised nations come into contact with barbarians the struggle is short ... We can see that the cultivation of land will be fatal in many ways to savages, for they cannot, or will not change their habits. New diseases and vices are highly destructive ... until those who are most susceptible ... are weeded out; and so it may be with the evil effects from spirituous liquors, as well as with the unconquerable strong taste for them shewn by so many savages. (Darwin 2008 [1871]:281)

Notwithstanding, Darwin was exceedingly cautious in his remarks on races as equivalents to species. He did not embrace a polygenic view. Rather, he sought to underline the primitive nature of early man:

> [T]here can hardly be a doubt that we are descended from barbarians. The astonishment which I felt on first seeing a party of Fuegians on a wild and broken shore will never be forgotten by me, for the reflection at once rushed into my mind—such were our ancestors. These men were absolutely naked and bedaubed with paint, their long hair was tangled ... They possessed hardly any arts, and like wild animals lived on what they could catch; they had no government, and were merciless to every one not of their own small tribe ... For my own part, I would as soon be descended from [the] heroic little monkey, who braved his dreaded enemy ... to save ... his keeper; or from that old baboon, who ... carried away ... his young comrade from a crowd of astonished dogs—as from a savage who delights to torture his enemies, offers up bloody sacrifices, practices infanticide without remorse, treats his wives like slaves, knows no decency, and is haunted by the grossest superstitions. (Darwin 2008 [1871]:332)

Darwin promoted humanity's place in speciation by pathologising savages. Though 'the link' between man and other species remained illusive, savages were the likely candidate. In Australia, Darwin's ideas prepared the ground for views that endured for generations, and among them was that branch of pseudoscience known as eugenics, that did embrace polygenic views.

In his discussion of the early anthropologists who were active in Australia, McGregor cites in particular A.W. Howitt, John Mathew and Baldwin Spencer. Howitt and Mathew (1899) fielded contemporary accounts of the racial origins of mainland residents and the Tasmanians. Howitt concluded that initially the Australian continent was populated by 'frizzly-haired Melanesians, such as the Tasmanians' but with 'a strong infusion of some other race, probably a low form of Caucasian Melanochroi'. The latter term was one used by T.H. Huxley to describe dark-skinned Caucasians (see Mathew 1899; Howitt 1996:31; Baum 2008). Howitt suggested that Australians and Dravidians from southern India could have been 'two tribes co-descendants from a common . . . stock' (1996:30). In his view, this group overran the autochthonous people who were forced back to Tasmania. Moreover, these events occurred prior to the rise in ocean levels that formed the Bass and Torres Straits (Howitt 1996:24). Howitt's sometime co-author, Lorimer Fison, was less engaged with issues of migration and human types. His concern was to reconcile social evolution with both science and the Bible. Therefore he was keen to establish that the evolution of the Australians should begin from a state of 'innocence' rather than degenerate civilisation (Fison and Howitt 1991:162). Fison treated it as plain that:

> [T]he human race started from a very low point in the social scale; that certain races have made a continuous advance; nation after nation dying as men die, but always leaving their heirs behind them; that others, after making considerable progress, came to a halt and remained stationary; while others again, who, at the very beginning fell out, or were driven out, from the line of progress, are found in the present day at a point lower than that from which the start was made; degraded, therefore . . . but certainly not degraded from a civilization to which they never attained. (Fison and Howitt 1991:163)

This third path had been the one followed by Australians.

These remarks were made by men who published prior to or concurrently with Baldwin Spencer, foundation professor of biology at Melbourne University and, subsequently, highly influential evolutionary ethnographer. Spencer corresponded with Howitt but more importantly was mentored by James Frazer, who circulated his work with Frank Gillen among Europe's intellectual elite. As director of the National Museum of Victoria, Spencer relegated Aboriginal Australians to the museum's natural history display. As McGregor notes, Spencer's intent was not to classify indigenous Australians as animals. Rather, he counted 'the Aboriginal' and local fauna as equally primitive versions of their respective species (McGregor 1997:41). Spencer made this clear in his 1927 preface to the revised edition of his Central Australian work with Gillen:

> Australia is the present home and refuge of creatures, often crude and quaint, that have elsewhere passed away and given place to higher forms . . . Just as the platypus, laying its eggs and feebly suckling its young, reveals a mammal in the making, so does the Aboriginal show us, at least in broad outline, what early man must have been like before he learned to read and write, domesticate animals, cultivate crops and use a metal tool. It has been possible to study in Australia human beings that still remain on the cultural level of men of the Stone Age. (Spencer and Gillen 1927:vii).

Spencer's remark evokes a particular type of *fin de siècle* evolutionism. Higher and lower stages of culture were attributed to the capacities of their bearers, who were seen, respectively, as more or less developed organically. These spurious ideas gained currency at a time prior to modern genetics. Not Darwinian as such, the view invoked a biogenetic 'law' that 'ontogeny recapitulates phylogeny' and is reflected in different phenotypes (Langness 1975:12). In other words, the more or less developed stages of a society are reflected in each stage's component human beings. Furthermore, variations in external appearance were seen to be indicative of supposed organic variations between different human types.

The standard version of this view involved a sequence from savagery through barbarism to civilisation. Lewis Henry Morgan broke this down into seven more specific stages. Each people, nation, culture or society was assumed to move along a developmental path, not always through the exact same stages, but nonetheless in a shared direction. And as societies changed, so too did the organic nature of the concomitant human beings (Morgan 1877; Stocking 1982:116–119). In addition, the assumption was that some, and especially Western Europeans, had transitioned through these stages more readily than others. In his 1899 publication with Gillen, which followed the Horn Expedition to Central Australia, Baldwin Spencer exemplified this school of thought. He drew a parallel between forms of social practice and organic development. He was writing of the Arrernte of Central Australia:

> [I]t seems that in the evolution of the social organisation and customs of a savage tribe, such features as those which we are now discussing are clearly comparable to the well known rudimentary organs, which are of great importance in understanding the phylogeny of [animals]. (Spencer and Gillen 1899:109).

The first Australians were identified as savages and, in a more Darwinian mode, as possibly representative of the link between humankind and its predecessors. In this view, Aboriginal people were indicative of Western Europe's past—as the child might be to the adult. It was also assumed—and Darwin did—that juxtaposed in the same time-space, the 'adult' would eclipse 'the child'.

Two important points contextualise these early anthropologists. First, they had contemporaries who did not share their views. For instance, Carl Strehlow, German Lutheran missionary to the Western Arrernte in Central Australia, was clearly aware of these ideas when he wrote in 1921, 'And these people with such mental capacities should form the "missing link"? Never' (cited in Kenny 2008:7). This comment came in the wake of Strehlow's mastery of Arrernte language, his copious recording of indigenous myth and his Bible translations—working in conjunction with Arrernte men. His conclusion mirrored that of German émigré to the United States Franz Boas, who repudiated the comparative method of evolutionary ethnography and promoted particularism and a plural culture concept. For Boas, regional historical specification, not morphological stages, explained human social variation (Boas 1940: 281–289; Stocking 1982:195–233). Germany at the time was not the rampant imperial power that

Britain was; nor did biological science as opposed to history and linguistics bear so heavily on its ethnology. Less accomplished than Carl Strehlow, but nonetheless an eager anthropologist, R.H. Mathews researched and wrote between 1893 and 1918, when he died. His writings were mainly in the form of articles published in Australia, the United States and Europe. Like Strehlow, but for different reasons, Mathews had little contact with British academia and therefore with Darwinian views. Schooled at home, he grew up on his father's property, worked as a drover, and later became a land surveyor for a time employed by the NSW Government Railways. He had a lifetime of contact with Aboriginal people. Mathews concentrated on firsthand observation and more modest generalisations—whether or not he could always defend them (Thomas 2007). Notwithstanding their strengths as well as their weaknesses, Baldwin Spencer excoriated both Strehlow and Mathews. He pushed them to the margins of academic debate.

A second point regarding these evolutionary ethnographers is a more challenging one. Notwithstanding their adherence to false theory, Fison and Howitt, Spencer and Gillen, and W.H.R. Rivers as well, produced early research that laid foundations for later studies of kinship classification, social organisation, cosmology and ritual performance for the entire Oceania region.[3] For example, Spencer and Gillen's maps and text, which trace the topography around Alice Springs and note the unfolding of ancestral myth to explain the natural features of the land, foreshadowed modern understandings of the Dreaming (see Morphy 1997:37–38). The heated debates about moieties and marriage, including the nature and role of sections and subsections, in time brought a better understanding of Aboriginal sociality and its organisation in space and through time (see, for example, Strehlow 1965; Elkin 1979; and later McConvell 1985a, 1985b and Dousset 2005). These observations of the early ethnographers were the building blocks for contemporary social analysis. As McGregor remarks, perhaps this work's most notable feature was dense and precise ethnographic observation—revolutionary for its time—linked nonetheless to race-based evolutionism (McGregor 1997:35–36; Morphy 1997). How to explain this paradox? Status was involved. Given the prominence of Howitt and Spencer in Australian academic circles, and Spencer's initial training as a biologist, it is likely that this framework gave legitimacy to their research in a period when evolutionary biology was seen as a paradigm of science, at least in the English-speaking world. This anomalous setting for the practice of ethnography bears on the Boasian view that grand theory and social research are uneasy partners. All too easily, facts can be digested as a prevailing discourse. And yet, as we know, paradigms do change and discourse with them. Therefore, it cannot be theory or position alone that defines the value of research.

These two points not only contextualise the early ethnographers but also sound a caution regarding the postcolonial critique. Hot on the trail of words like 'race', and relatively unversed in social analysis, the enthusiast can easily ignore the ethnography in *fin de siècle* research. In an otherwise exemplary work, McGregor approaches this excess when he conflates two categories of writer—evolutionary ethnographers and early 20th century eugenicists. Among the latter, Dr John Wild from Victoria presented an initial paper to the anthropology Section G of the Australasian Association for the Advancement of Science (AAAS) in 1888. He advocated anthropology as a 'strictly scientific' pursuit that could reveal 'our remote ancestors slowly toiling up towards ... civilisation' (McGregor 1997:34). Sydney-based Dr Alan Carroll, who specialised in the treatment of children, convened the Royal Anthropological Society of Australasia and published its journal between 1895 and 1913. Carroll was a eugenicist who thought that humanity comprised different species. For British people to breed with Aboriginal Australians would be degenerative, in his view (see McGregor 1997:46).[4] Again, in 1898, Edinburgh-trained pathologist Dr W.L. Cleland presented a paper to the Royal Society of Adelaide that drew parallels between the 'two races' of orang-utan in the Malay and 'the Aborigines of Australia' (cited in McGregor 1997: 47). Finally, Dr William Ramsey Smith, trained in pathology and president of the Anthropology Section of the AAAS in 1913, proposed of Aboriginal people that 'Centuries ago, nature "side-tracked" a race in Australia' (cited in McGregor 1997:38). Unlike Fison and Howitt, Strehlow, Mathews, and Spencer and Gillen, these men were mainly medical doctors hypothesising not on the basis of ethnography at all but rather on the basis of morphological fantasy. Cressida Fforde records a gruesome case in which Ramsey Smith and Cleland shared between them the preserved head and penis of an Aboriginal man declared insane before he died (Fforde 2004:42). Whatever the sins of the ethnographers, they were not these.

As McGregor may have meant to underline, in the public mind there was little distinction made between eugenicists, who dignified themselves as 'physical anthropologists', and the early ethnographers with their race-based ideas but also their engagement with social and cultural fact. 'Doomed race' and 'culture with its own moral order' were the competing legacies of this initial engagement with difference. It would take some time to sort them out (see also Morphy 1996:183–185).

Intelligent parasites

The status of savage accorded to Aboriginal people seemed to entail the rapid extinction of both their culture and physical being. Perceptions that indigenous women became less fertile following contact with settlers were used to support the idea that the constitution of indigenous Australians could not withstand or adapt to civilisation. Moreover, their ruin was seen to be moral as well as physical and the product not simply of engagement with Europeans, but also with Chinese or 'Asiatics', especially in the north Australian settlement of Darwin. Federal inspectors observed that free interaction between blacks and Asiatics had 'debased and rendered [the blacks] vicious, cunning and untrustworthy'. Traditional practices were 'dying out' (cited in McGregor 1997:70). In the first decade of the 20th century, Charles Darwin's premonitions seemed to be realised.

Yet as protector of Aborigines between 1912 and 1913, Baldwin Spencer assumed a more hopeful stance. He proposed that the federal government adopt a policy of 'preservation and uplift' (McGregor 1997:72). Spencer recommend that both 'full-bloods' and 'half-castes' be isolated on reserves, kept apart, and offered separate and appropriate forms of training. He justified this on the basis that 'though the half-castes belong neither to the aboriginal nor to the whites', generally they became a part of an Aboriginal community (cited in McGregor 1997:81). Therefore they should be on reserves but, unlike full-bloods, separated from their mothers. Then they might begin to learn white ways. For Spencer, policy and science should work in tandem to protect Aboriginal people and record their disappearing world (see also Wolfe 1999:155).

As the 20th century turned into its second and third decades, the 'doomed race' theory proved inadequate. Increasingly, the state's view was that something definite needed to be done to manage remote Aboriginal people, especially those drawn to camp around white settlements. Wolfe remarks, '[T]he romance of the dying race steadily gave way to the spectre of "the half-caste menace"' (Wolfe 1999:30). More complex than Wolfe suggests, much policy discussion concerned the appropriate but different routes for half-castes on the one hand, and full-bloods on the other. Moreover, the view of half-castes changed over time as notions of hybrid inferiority gave way to the idea that a quantum of white blood made half-castes superior to full-bloods (McGregor 1997:139). This shift occurred in the inter-war years and paralleled the rise to prominence of A.P. Elkin, Anglican cleric and professor of anthropology at Sydney University from 1933 to 1956. While Adelaide-based J.B. Cleland, son of W.L. Cleland, and Western Australia's A.O. Neville advocated biological absorption via the route of half-caste child removal, Elkin began to focus on assimilation and a *social* form of absorption (see also Anderson 2003:225–252).

Nonetheless, Elkin's thought was definitely transitional between biology and the sociocultural. Although he came to focus on the social, in the 1930s and 40s elements of a race-based view of Aboriginal people lingered in his writing. In 1932 he could still remark that the 'smaller brain capacity of aborigines as compared with that of the bearers of the new culture suggests at least a handicap' (cited in McGregor 1997:197). Moreover, many years later Elkin did not discard his textbook's introductory remarks on racial types and a 'stone-age' culture (Elkin 1979:1–11). Still, his focus on assimilation opened new vistas. With fieldwork extending across Australia, Elkin developed a 'firmer faith' in Aboriginal Australians' capacity to advance themselves (McGregor 1997:186).

In Elkin's publications, the best known statement of these ideas came in his essay, 'Reaction and Interaction', published in the *American Anthropologist* (Elkin 1951). It was in the course of this discussion that he coined the term 'intelligent parasitism', referring to a complex of behaviour often described today as Aboriginal 'dependency'. The latter usage has been adopted by a number of contemporary writers, including Pearson (2000) and Sutton (2009a). By 'dependency', they mean the apparent inclination to live off a system without participating in it. Elkin's version went like this:

> Parents leave their children at the mission school to be fed while they themselves move about on tribal affairs—only to take them away, if they can, when it suits them, especially when initiation or marriage requires them in tribal life. And the natives on the Trans-Continental Railway line ply a well-developed art of 'preying' on the passengers, most of whom have not seen bush Aborigines before. Donning tattered garments, and borrowing babies if they have none of their own, groups of men and women visit the train stopping places to sell their own few artefacts, to amuse and to beg. The provision of clothing and ration depôts and the work of missions have failed to prevent this active, successful, interesting, and new form of 'hunting'.
>
> Thus, in these various ways a stage of *intelligent parasitism* and of equilibrium is built up in the marginal regions. Adaptation, which was formerly to nature . . . is now to the settler and other persons and institutions. (Elkin 1951:168)

Elkin first used the terms 'parasites' and 'parasitism' to describe a hunter-gatherer economy. He depicted Aboriginal man as 'a parasite on nature; that is, he did not assist nature to produce his sustenance either by tilling the soil and sowing seed, nor by domesticating and breeding animals. He was subservient to nature' (cited in McGregor 1996:119). Nonetheless these hunters and gatherers *deliberately* lived off the land. Elkin explained that 'nomadism' was not 'biologically founded' but rather involved an intentional practice integral to a particular type of economy. Moreover, this was an economy geared to consumption rather than production and this consumption was directed to 'specific socio-cultural ends within a kinship-dominated system'. Post-settlement, this style of distribution of food and other things to kin was maintained 'by transferring . . . dependence from the resources of nature to the goods in the station store' (Elkin 1951).

During the 1930s, Elkin tended to characterise Aboriginal relations with white society as ones of 'utter dependence'. In like vein, when he began to use the concept of 'parasite' to describe Aboriginal relations with non-Aboriginal people, he used it in the sense of an abjection: 'Because of ignorance, hopelessness, selfishness and even callousness, on the part of some of us—the responsibility of us all—the Aborigines were disinherited and bewildered; they were made parasites, and were faced with extinction' (cited in McGregor 1996:121). Five years later, though, Elkin wrote of parasitism in a new way. He continued to underline the 'forced' nature of Aboriginal adaptation. At the same time, he stressed two other things: first, that though constrained, this adaptation was intelligent, knowledgeable and skilled; and second, that with it Aboriginal people limited their investment in white society and thereby sustained their kinship and ritual life. He observed, 'this adaptation is external and means a double role—economic parasitism on the white man, and [a] social and spiritual role within the [tribe]' (cited in McGregor 1996:121).

'Intelligent parasitism' was just one stage of adaptation in Elkin's scheme, but it was a crucial one (Elkin 1951:178). People would transition from hunter-gatherer society, through parasitism, to an appreciation of capitalism and its social order. In his view, those Aboriginal people on the south-east coast who had become mere 'paupers' would find this transition harder. Parasitism in fact provided a 'short cut' to assimilation. Elkin came to this conclusion during World War II when he observed the participation of Arnhem Landers in Australian army camps (McGregor 1996:122–124, 1997:186–187). In his view, assimilation would work best for Aboriginal people who retained a fairly integrated culture. Parasitism on remote white settlements had allowed the maintenance of this integration.

Elkin's analysis was wrong. In fact, traditional life was not parasitic on nature. Rather, it rested on extensive and detailed knowledge organised between groups in ways that commanded a region. The ritual 'work' of senior men ensured the reproduction of species so far as these men and their wives and children saw it. Minimally, this world of rite and its stratified knowledge diversified relations between groups and distributed economically relevant knowledge among far-flung peoples. The interaction between human beings and environment was a slow-moving one because this form of society and culture responded to and shored up a limited technology. Nonetheless, it was an order assiduously worked at. This intersection of ritual and mundane knowledge was undermined by sedentary life. To begin with, the new form of living rested on a complex technology mysterious to those who lived remote. They began to see their own system as the less powerful one. In addition, sedentarism brought a centralisation of sustenance that undermined the previous practice without providing new routes into a different social system of production with its own forms of knowledge and practice. The condition that Elkin described as 'intelligent parasitism' was in fact the dependency created by becoming sedentary and then marginalised in a more powerful socioeconomic order. In increasingly elaborate ways, state and law confirmed this status. One must stretch the meaning of 'dependency' almost to breaking point to apply the term to hunter-gathering *and* to marginalisation in a capitalist society. It is more illuminating to point to the gap in productivity between hunter-gatherer and agricultural—not to mention industrial—economies; and the consequent gross mismatch between hunter-gatherer forms of social organisation and those of late industrial capitalism.

Elkin endorsed assimilation as both required and inevitable. The only question was by what route to attain it. To him, a route through parasitic dependency seemed promising. Many disagreed. They included Baldwin Spencer, Donald Thomson, Olive Pink, Norman Tindale and W.E.H. Stanner, who recommended 'preservation by reservation' (Stanner 1979 [1963]:191). Reporting on his 1936 Arnhem Land research, Thomson advocated 'absolute segregation' on the grounds of psychology, culture and physical health:

The fact must be stressed that the difference between a nomadic race with its peculiar and specialised adaptations and social organisation, and a gardening people, with an established village life, is more than a matter of environment, it depends on deeper factors, and has a definite psychological basis. (Thomson 2003:118–119).

Olive Pink also advocated a 'secular sanctuary'. Her views were influenced by contact with the Warlpiri in Central Australia and a comparison with the Arrernte of the Hermannsburg mission. Pink hoped that the Warlpiri could avoid the destiny of the missionised Arrernte. Therefore she recommended:

[A] place for them where they can call both their souls and bodies their own. For the full-bloods only—not half-castes. So they will not then be play-things of Europeans—clergy and laity alike—with as aim their being 'labour fodder' which can be exploited. Let us help them to be *developed 'black' men and women* and proud of it. Not sham Europeans whose 'destiny' . . . is to be (immorally) 'absorbed'. (Cited in Marcus 2001:147, emphasis in original)

Of these advocates, Stanner was perhaps the most ambivalent. He proposed that policy should be aimed at securing 'survival' first and only then 'civilisation'. In the early years he leaned towards separate development. In 1939 he recommended that 'ample funds' be supplied to reserves in order to stop malnutrition and the 'population drift' to white settlements (see McGregor 1997:224–225). In 1958 he voiced his displeasure at federal minister Hasluck's assimilation policies in his seminal essay 'Continuity and Change'. Fifteen years later, and following his Boyer Lectures, Stanner would support Northern Territory land rights as social justice. Nonetheless, he expressed some uncertainty about the separatism implied by some versions of self-determination. In 1974, he and H.C. Coombs proposed that

[P]olicy be directed to ensuring that Aborigines are not forced by economic and social pressures to accept a European style of life if they would prefer a simpler or more traditional style: i.e. that Aborigines be allowed and helped to adapt freely of their own requirements and circumstances such white Australian practices as they consider of value to them. (Cited in Hinkson and Beckett 2008:13)

Maintaining a 'choice' between the options of 'staying out' or 'coming in'—presumed to be culturally different paths—became anthropology's position.

Timeless dreamers (and unproductive)

The progression from doomed race to assimilation and/or separation captures the transition from biological to social and cultural notions of difference. As Elkin's ideas about parasitic dependency show, this transition did not in itself supersede the inclination to pathologise. A fear that encouraging mainstream capabilities meant discouraging others as inferior or even pathological raised the heat of postwar debates about assimilation. Nonetheless, there were marked advances in knowledge, not least in Elkin's own corpus, and there were 'arguments about Aborigines' among the anthropologists.[5] Notwithstanding, historian Patrick Wolfe has suggested that Australian anthropology will inevitably bear the imprint of colonialism. His views meet those of Povinelli's at various points and also diverge from them (Povinelli 2002).[6] Wolfe's position is exemplified in his discussion of the Dreaming as an icon of difference for Australians, both Indigenous and non-Indigenous (Wolfe 1991). In Wolfe's view, not only does this icon stand for Aboriginal difference in Australia, it also locates Aboriginal people as an 'other' beyond Australian capitalism; as beings beyond economy. In his critique of anthropology's account of the Dreaming, Wolfe rehearses a more general argument about settler colonialism and anthropology's complicity in it (Wolfe 1999).

The article in question is entitled 'On Being Woken Up' (1991). Wolfe's focus is the Arrernte word that Baldwin Spencer transcribed as 'alcheringa' and translated as the 'Dream times' on the advice of his field associate Frank Gillen. Later anthropological accounts of this phenomenon, and especially Stanner's mid-20th century rendering of it as an 'everywhen', would produce a related term: 'the Dreaming' (see Stanner 1979 [1953]). Today this term is used to refer to the experienced world or cosmos of traditional Aboriginal people. Many non-Indigenous Australians assume that most or all Aboriginal people who still live remote also live in a world that is best described comprehensively by this term. Reference to an Aboriginal 'spirituality' evokes the Dreaming: an acceptance that the ancestral beings, part human and part other species that shaped the earth and sky, are also a continuing and unseen presence in daily life. The Dreaming, in other words, is everywhere and for all time.

Wolfe's intent is not to provide his own account of the Aboriginal ideas and experience for which Spencer and Gillen provided English terms. Rather, his focus is on the nature and dynamics of the translation process. He is not interested in the phenomenon referred to by the Arrernte or other Aboriginal peoples, but rather in the name given to this phenomenon by British settlers and their descendants, and its connotations. Wolfe sees a specific process of change between the context of Spencer's initial translation at the *fin de siècle* and the later context in which Stanner wrote. The similarity and the differences between these contexts and the usages involved—as the 'Dream times' became 'the Dreaming'—are central to Wolfe's argument. Importantly, the second of these contexts, from the 1960s to the present, has been the one in which numerous Northern Territory land claims were settled under the Land Rights Act.

He associates the initial translation with the period of evolutionary theory in early anthropology discussed above. In particular, Wolfe links this period with the work of writers such as Adolf Bastian and British evolutionist E.B. Tylor (see Tylor 1903; Köpping 1983). Tylor and others proposed that the source of primitive ideas about causality was an animated or enlivened view of nature which he called 'animism'. He argued that the context for these ideas came not simply from intimate contact with the natural environment but also from dreams which were treated as continuous with waking life. Dreams suggested vital interactions in a world beyond mundane experience. The natural world which men inhabited was animated by unseen forces that also were present in dreams. Wolfe argues that Tylor's account of magic and natural religion encouraged Spencer's view of the Aboriginal past as 'vague' and 'Dreamy' and, according to Wolfe, definitely pre-rational (Spencer and Gillen 1927:592; Wolfe 1991:203). Moreover, the idea that savages were pre-rational beings 'provided a bridge between the animal and the human'—the missing link once again—for Spencer and the evolutionists who influenced him (Wolfe 1991:206).

Wolfe connects this usage with another one from rural popular culture: the rendering of Aboriginal mobility across a region as 'walkabout' (Wolfe 1991:210–211). 'Jack's gone walkabout' could have been a remark in the white Australian outback up to and including the 1970s. Such an observation would have implied unpredictable and aimless wandering that made Aboriginal people unreliable employees and therefore deserving of payment that was well below the white award. This rural terminology became urban in the popular Australian magazine *Walkabout*, published from 1935 to 1972. Designed for restless urbanites, *Walkabout* was replete with images of the outback Aborigine used to romanticise Australian rural life. Wolfe argues that the 'Dream times' and 'walkabout' both contributed to a 'theme of precolonial somnambulance' which white settlers and their descendants ascribed to the first Australians. And in this pre-colonial milieu, as rendered by white settlers, 'land was but a spatial condition' rather than a force of production to be both valued and owned (Wolfe 1991:211). The impact of these representations, in Wolfe's view, was to locate Aboriginal people in a time-space of unproductive life prior to European settlement. Productive civilisation only began with the arrival of the British.

In Spencer and Gillen's original usage 'the dream times unequivocally referred to the past' (Wolfe 1991:212). From the late 1950s, however, and in the work of Stanner, Elkin and others, increasingly the view was that the Dreaming was not just past but also ever-present. This reinterpretation came with the intensification of research in remote Australia that preceded and then accompanied the land claims period. Wolfe notes that (classical) ethnography produced a portrait of Aboriginal life consisting mainly of ritual and kinship, which involved points of striking difference with a European world. Yet, he remarks, 'the great majority of anthropological data was collected from people who were dependent upon the settler economy' (Wolfe 1991:213). Maddock had acknowledged this in his text when he wrote that 'Rite and myth—and the information stored in them—can stay alive long after the hunter-gatherer economy has collapsed' (Maddock 1982:29).

However, that 'collapse' was of no concern to Maddock. As we have seen, Maddock's account excluded all those factors that Cowlishaw's (1999) account included: Aboriginal involvements with the state and with cash and forms of employment. In Wolfe's view these exclusions meant that Aboriginal people became 'ritually constituted entities' in classical ethnography. Wolfe would describe this representation as a 'superorganic Aboriginality' (Wolfe 1991:213, 1999:178). Equally important, even in the 1970s and 80s much ethnography seemed to suggest that the time-space of this ritualised and unproductive life was not only past but also present in remote northern and Central Australia.

Wolfe's conclusion is that, as translations, a common feature holds the 'Dream times' and 'the Dreaming' together. Both versions underline aspects of Aboriginal life that have little connection with the post-settlement economy on which both settlers and Aboriginal people came to depend. Either as 'precontact idyll' or as ever-present 'otherness', these representations of Aboriginal life became estranged from the 'economic realities' (Wolfe 1991:214).

There are some major errors and elisions in Wolfe's argument. To begin with, a considerable range of Aboriginal languages have terms which map out a semantic field comparable to the Arrernte one that Spencer and Gillen recorded (Morphy 1996:177). The rapid spread of 'Dream times' among other anthropologists is therefore not surprising, though initially such translations may have been based on slim evidence. This does not mean that they were wrong. In addition, the polysemy of the relevant terms in Arrernte and in other Aboriginal languages includes those juxtapositions of meaning that so offended Wolfe. Spencer's *alcheringa* and related terms carry both the sense of past times and of dreaming while asleep. Through dreams, Arrernte people, for instance, connect with the ancestral realm which is both past and ever-present. This is not a European imputation about irrational 'dreaminess' but rather a real feature of Aboriginal experience for many people past and present. Language reflects this (see Dussart 2000:139–176; Green 2007). Again, the shift between Spencer's and Stanner's rendering of this indigenous phenomenon was not simply a reflex of changes in Australia's socioeconomic conditions. It also reflected conceptual developments in the practice of ethnography. Morphy remarks:

> Anthropological discourse has progressed by . . . shifting the meaning away from 'dream' and 'time' towards a more generalized conception of the relationship between cosmology and society. The connotation of a simple past time was rebutted through the development of phrases such as the 'eternal dream time', and there was a shift from *time* to *place* to *event* signified in Stanner's 'Everywhen' and away from *dreaming* in [the] 'ancestral past' . . . Discourse over such terms became a means of modifying the concept of the Dreamtime: not merely as a term of art in Western anthropology but as a reflection of more sophisticated and detailed understandings of phenomenological meaning to Aboriginal people. (Morphy 1996:179)

Finally, Wolfe makes no clear distinction between popular usage and disciplinary analysis, treating both as aspects of popular culture. Consequently, the 'Dreaming complex' and 'walkabout' are given the same status, though one is integral to sustained research and the other is *just* a popular usage. For this reason, in Wolfe's hands ethnography becomes no more than an artefact of a popular and dominant discourse (Morton 1998:368–369). While history remains above the fray, anthropology becomes intrinsically an invalid enterprise (see also Morphy 1996:169). Wolfe creates his own conditions for this position by reading very little 20th century ethnography except where the texts support his position.

Wolfe treats classical ethnography roughly and unfairly. Yet there is something to gain from two of his more general positions. The first I have noted already: his account of the product of classical ethnography as a 'superorganic Aboriginality' that masks the fact of dependence on, but limited engagement with, a capitalist economy. This position is equivalent to Asad's initial postcolonial critique of African ethnography that bounded and reified colonial subjects (Asad 1973). Likewise, only part of an Aboriginal subject is allowed to appear in Australia's classical ethnography. And contrary to Maddock (see above), the ritual life of Aboriginal people could not be sustained unchanged and intact once the indigenous economy 'collapsed'.

Integral to this position is Wolfe's perception that the invasion of Australia is in fact 'a structure not an event' (Wolfe 1999:163). In other words, the inequalities established by the imperialism that came to Australia—as capitalism and the state—have been reproduced and at best ameliorated. On this point, Wolfe's analysis meets Povinelli's when they both underline that even land rights proceed on the state's terms because the possibility of other terms is lost (see Povinelli 2002). Furthermore, Wolfe's account of the 'repressive authenticity' in land rights that limits the scope of Aboriginality and those to whom that status might apply echoes points made by Cowlishaw as early as 1987. With his usual overstatement, Wolfe is ready to suggest that land rights therefore are no more than domination. Merlan (1997) has contested this in terms of the experience and aspirations of Aboriginal people themselves.

Wolfe's second point bears directly on my critique, which is also a defence of anthropology. It concerns his view of anthropology and the ethnographic task as such. Alone among the disciplines, Wolfe assumes that anthropology's empirical records and its analysis of them will always be infused with notions of difference dictated by the more powerful culture from which the anthropologist (often) comes. Anthropology will speak for the other, misrepresent the other, and not be aware of it. Wolfe has sought to demonstrate this with his discussion of two foci in Australian anthropology—the Dreaming and Aboriginal nescience concerning procreation (Wolfe 1991, 1999:9–42). 'Dreaminess' and false notions of 'virgin birth' have stood in contrast to the productive and science-based society from which the anthropologist generally comes. This is Wolfe's way of suggesting that there is an insurmountable problem at the heart of rendering difference. In order to interpret cultural difference, anthropologists must take their own culture as the reference point and thereby skew analysis, often in potent political ways. As Max Weber once observed, what is *interesting* and value relevant tends to reflect the interpreter's position. Weber wrote:

> Order is brought into this chaos [of causes] only on the condition that in every case only a *part* of concrete reality is interesting and *significant*

to us, because only it is related to the *cultural values* with which we approach reality. Only certain sides of the infinitely complex concrete phenomenon ... are therefore worthwhile knowing. They alone are objects of causal explanation. And even this causal explanation evinces the same character; an *exhaustive* causal investigation of any concrete phenomena ... is simply nonsense. (Weber 1949:79, emphasis in original)

Weber's comment is in fact tough-minded. He proposes that there will be no accounts in a social science that are not value relevant. Ordered analysis can proceed only on the condition that particular values (and not some others) are in play. Nonetheless, there can be debate about what is 'interesting' and what forms of value relevance should be brought to an analysis.

The postcolonial critique has in fact been such a debate. It needs to be vigorous and far-reaching and from time to time renewed. Nonetheless, it does not obviate the need for or the viability of comprehending forms of cultural difference—especially in Australia. Below I argue that a better integration of historical and ethnographic method can assist in this task.

Beyond pathology and stereotypes

The argument of the preceding section does not deny that colonialism has been both a powerful and negative force in the lives of Indigenous peoples. In his account of the 1898 Cambridge Anthropological Expedition to the Torres Strait, Martin Nakata notes some ways in which *fin de siècle* evolutionism distorted the findings of science (Nakata 2007). His account shows why the descendants of the Islanders might place shadow quotes around the word 'science' as it was deployed among them in the 1890s. In addition, Nakata demonstrates the manner in which the fact of this research, whether or not it is read today, acts to interpolate a people. As a consequence, their own critique of the society and state of which they are now a part struggles for salience. Nakata's task is to 'savage the disciplines' that described his forebears as 'savages'. A significant part of his discussion concerns W.H.R. Rivers, trained as a psychologist and, once in the Torres Strait, intensely interested in kinship terminology and in the sociological study of relatedness. In anthropology, Rivers is regarded highly, notwithstanding his flawed scientific accounts of so-called savage sensory abilities and his 'histories' of marriage and other forms of practice. Like Spencer and Gillen, Rivers presents the confronting paradox of gross error juxtaposed with insight.

Rivers and his colleagues arrived in Torres Strait determined to test the visual and aural acuity of Islanders. These tests would be followed by others concerning 'taste and cutaneous sensations', blood pressure and the like (Nakata 2007:43). Nakata's account points to the use of measurement to render Islanders as native subjects of a European science (see also Anderson 2003:229–244). He also underlines the elaborate ideological context of this measurement, ostensibly worthy but also hedged about with European ambivalence: 'The first task . . . was to counter claims that native people were closer to animals than they were to civilised people. Only after this was incontrovertibly established could these scientists proceed to show precisely how the savage mind interpreted the senses.' The logic behind this research was that the natives could be similar to the civilised but not their equal. Faced with inconsistent results, Rivers resorted to *ad hominem* argument (Nakata 2007:43–47). Nakata is less convincing when he discusses Rivers's kinship research and its significance. His notes Rivers's propensity to describe the kinship terminology of Islanders as 'complex'—to the outsider, Nakata suggests, but not to a Torres Strait Islander child (Nakata 2007:109–112). This is true of most classifications, kinship or otherwise. Forms of classification that we take for granted and can use 'without thinking' are seldom used so readily by those from another culture. Moreover, Nakata nowhere allows that there was something more to Rivers's interest in this terminology. Rivers developed a 'concrete' or empirical method of recording genealogies from a number of related individuals. With it, he was able to confirm Lewis Henry Morgan's point that terminologies are in fact indices of normative practice. In his own words, Rivers sought to demonstrate 'the close connection between the terminology of the classificatory system of relationship and forms of social organisation' (Rivers 1914:5). These forms of social organisation were conceived, after Morgan, as social systems that were more than mere domestic life. In sum, Rivers's work was a major early contribution to a comparative sociology. He stood midway between the work of Morgan and Radcliffe-Brown in the growth of an understanding of small-scale, stateless societies.

Yet Rivers's contribution did come amid spurious theories of evolution and diffusion. In his history of ethnology, American anthropologist Robert Lowie wrote of this aspect of Rivers's work, 'From beginning to end it rests on pure fantasies ingeniously interwoven' (Lowie 1937:175). Meyer Fortes, professor of anthropology at Cambridge from 1950 to 1973, was equally critical. He remarked at length on 'the preposterous theories' involved in Rivers's *History of Melanesian Society* (Fortes 1969:27). I cite these two critics within anthropology because they came well before Langham's book-length and discriminating appraisal of Rivers in 1981, and Stocking's more succinct but revealing account in his essay 'The Ethnographer's Magic' (Langham 1981; Stocking 1992). None of these sources are cited by Nakata. Rather, the impression he leaves is that anthropology accepted the entire corpus of Rivers's work, which was of uniform, negligible significance. This failure of scholarship obscures the more important parts of Martin Nakata's book.

In its second section, Nakata demonstrates the adverse legacy of early missionary and scholarly writing on educational policy for the Torres Strait Islands. Post World War II decolonisation across the Southern Hemisphere brought changes in ideas about Indigenous Australians and the pedagogic task. Nakata traces a shift from early racist ideas to ones concerned with disadvantage. Still, this apparent advance brought its own problems. Islanders came to be seen almost solely in terms of disadvantage and deprivation (Nakata 2007:158). Time passed and ideas of cultural difference began to supersede those of disadvantage. One outcome was that '[previous] pedagogical practices were recognised as culturally inappropriate and incongruent with Islander learning styles and cultural ways. The use of English as the language of instruction was questioned' (Nakata 2007:159). Parallel curricula were devised for the teaching of history, language and culture. As well-intentioned teachers sought to become culturally relevant, they also inscribed their pupils with their own ideas of difference. Worse, the preference of Torres Strait Islander parents for a mainstream curriculum in schools was interpreted by these teachers as a desire for a 'white' education (Nakata 2007:160–161). Nakata is right to be angry about this succession of failures, bequeathed in part by colonialism. The crucial feature of formal education in English is not its imagined 'white' status. Rather, the crucial feature is its role as a tool of knowledge and power within Australian society, the milieu of which Islanders are now a part. Nakata confirms that Torres Strait Islanders desire this tool for their children.

His discussion implies that analyses in universities can have a bearing on policy. The humanistic social sciences need to have a positive and not a negative influence on public domain knowledge. Therefore they should avoid the migration of both reification and naïve relativism into the policy domain. To this end, Nakata proposes forms of analysis framed historically and not as simply bounded accounts of 'others'.[7] He suggests that, henceforth, research on the Torres Strait Islands should take 'the Cultural Interface' as its focus. By this term Nakata intends a move away from approaches that present portraits of cultural wholes located in a distant past. Rather, the starting point should be the engagement that began with colonisation; a set of relations between groups. Nakata employs the term 'trajectory' to underline that Islanders, rather than being specified by a timeless culture, are instead specified by a structured process of historical engagement. The trajectories that different Islanders pursue articulate and re-articulate the relations between Torres Strait society and regional and global milieus. Nakata proposes to 'give primacy to the Islander lifeworlds as a complex terrain of political and social contests. In this terrain we have developed a reading of ourselves at the interface of colliding trajectories; we continue to maintain our values as a people of tradition; we have actively shaped new practices and adapted our own to deal with the encroaching [world]' (Nakata 2007:197). Given his own account of a Torres Strait history of change and cultural continuity, Jeremy Beckett would probably agree (Beckett 1987:18–23).[8] I would simply add to Nakata's formulations that histories of difference within the state will inevitably be mediated by histories of inequality in which minorities—Indigenous and non-Indigenous—work to supersede hegemonies and assert their own agency. This is a social, economic and political progress as well as one of representation. It bears on the cultural continuity produced. A scholar who is not an Islander or Aboriginal will quite likely write from a standpoint or an interest somewhat different from Nakata's, although not necessarily so (Nakata 2007:214). Either way, forms of value relevance, as Weber termed them, can be argued about, and are, and will continue to be. This is the nature of humanistic social science.

What has the postcolonial critique achieved and what is its significance as a debate principally within the universities? For the purposes of my argument, two achievements are especially significant. First, the critique offered by history and Indigenous studies has provided a genealogy of the discourse of pathology in Australia regarding Indigenous peoples. From discussions of the savage as missing link, to parasites, dreamers and the intrinsically disadvantaged, this literature distils the legacy of popular culture and some scholarship for debates today. McGregor's writing is seminal in this regard. Second, Wolfe and Nakata also provide valuable comment on the present. Wolfe underlines the marginalisation of remote Aboriginal people in Australia's capitalism and the way in which land rights were as much a bounded welfare measure as they were restorative justice or equalitarian politics. His critique of anthropology is, in fact, a critique of the classical ethnography of the land rights period which, by virtue of its positioning, could not fulfil his request to address 'the total social process' of which it was a part (Wolfe 1999:178). As an educationist, Nakata's critique fastened on issues he knows well. His discussion of schooling and curricula underlines that though Torres Strait Islanders may occupy a space of difference, they are also located within an Australian society. As citizens, Islanders require an education that provides them with the capabilities to be autonomous agents rather than mere clients of the state. Noel Pearson has had similar concerns for remote communities. Wolfe and Nakata reintroduce a politics of equality to the account of communities that for some time has been beholden only to a politics of difference. In this, their writings are consistent with the broader thrust of the postcolonial critique, which has placed the emphasis on Indigenous peoples as historical subjects rather than as timeless icons of difference. Their positions confirm that Indigenous Australian difference as recorded in ethnography has always been a difference mediated by the state and capitalism's inequities.

I have described the postcolonial critique as a debate within the universities because it has been in major part a war of position between disciplines. This has been especially unfortunate for anthropology. A critique of the discipline as a colonial one was launched by some who played with the possibility of superseding it. As I have sought to show, the arguments put by both historians and practitioners of Indigenous studies have been overstated. At the same time, other important points have not been carried through. It is unfortunate, for instance, that Wolfe's critique of the way in which classical ethnography has masked economic marginalisation did not take up more specific critiques written by Peterson and Beckett (see Peterson 1985 and Beckett 1987, 1988). In particular, Peterson's observation that the communal property of land rights is anomalous in a capitalist society and therefore needs some explanation as a political and policy fact received little attention from Wolfe. Again, there has been little comment, if any, about the convergences between Wolfe's work and Povinelli's critique of the state (Povinelli 2002). Both have proposed that representations of Aboriginality have been mediated by the politics of state. Above I remarked that Wolfe's concept of 'repressive authenticity' could apply equally to Povinelli's account of the 'cunning' of the state's recognition.[9] This lack of analytical follow-through on the part of anthropology itself has also applied to the work of Cowlishaw and Beckett. Both anthropologists have worked in remote Australia as well as in the south-east. Each has theoretical points to make that are not specific to a region but rather to the practice of ethnography generally. Yet their forms of anthropology have not been trialled in a serious way for research in remote Australia.

As a result, although classical ethnography has been rejected as anthropology's sole method, it has remained ensconced in research devoted to the homelands. Historians and practitioners of Indigenous studies have been disengaged from this field of research—which has been seen as a focus that involves enthnographers in the main. Where anthropology itself is concerned, classical ethnography has continued to supply the descriptions of communities that homelands consultancy responds to. Therefore, anthropology was poorly equipped, both conceptually and politically, to address a new round of pathologising used to highlight inequality at the expense of difference. Anthropology's reified account of cultural difference would prove very hard to defend in the remote communities debate.

4
Opposing separate development

[T]he Aboriginal struggle has to wake up to the fact that our belated citizenship in 1967 gave us two things. Firstly, it gave us land rights and increasing recognition of our human rights—and this has been a good thing. Secondly, it gave us passive welfare as an economy—and this has been disastrous.

Noel Pearson, *Our Right to Take Responsibility*

I am not convinced that the long-term sustainability of small remote communities with low income levels and poor health is necessarily... desirable.

Bob Gregory, Between a Rock and a Hard Place: Economic policy and the employment outlook for Indigenous Australians

Writing that shaped the debate about remote communities began to appear in the early 1990s and continued through to the NT Intervention in 2007. This debate in the public domain was concurrent with the postcolonial debate within universities, which began in the 1980s and extended into the 2000s. One debate was a scholarly one and the other a debate about policy. One occurred within the universities and the other in the public domain. One concerned a range of academics, and the other, opinion writers who mainly sidelined the academics. Yet there was an intimate link between these debates that was significant for anthropology and humanistic social science generally.

The remote communities debate concerned the condition and the future of outstation or homeland communities in northern and Central Australia. Especially in the context of the Land Rights Act, some opposed and some defended the proliferation of these small communities described by critics as pathological or as too impoverished to be encouraged further. Anthropologists, by and large, defended these communities and the policy direction that had shaped them. The leading voice in this defence was the Centre for Aboriginal Economic Policy Research (CAEPR) at the ANU in Canberra. By no means all its members were anthropologists, though Jon Altman, its head and founder, was. Opinion writers in a number of venues opposed CAEPR's policy positions and were given editorial support by *The Australian*, the national daily, and by *Quadrant* magazine. Both these publications had strong links, formal or informal, with News Limited, headed by media magnate Rupert Murdoch. Other organisations supported these critics of the homelands movement. They included the Bennelong Society and the Centre for Independent Studies (CIS).[1] The *Little Children are Sacred* report and the NT Intervention brought this debate to a head, and the critics prevailed. The policy response from the federal Coalition was in large part confirmed by the Labor government that followed it.

The postcolonial critique shares a striking feature with this policy debate about remote communities. Critics in the former debate proposed that classical ethnography had frozen Indigenous peoples in time and focused only on bounded tradition. Patrick Wolfe described the matter in terms of an anthropology that produced a 'superorganic' portrait of culture. In his view, this anthropology did not address the fact that most Aboriginal people had lost their previous economy and had been held on the margins of society. He criticised the romanticism of classical ethnography, and its impact on the less traditional, who were made to feel they were less authentic Aboriginal people. The remote communities debate involved a comparable theme. The proposal was that anthropology, and the universities generally, had romanticised remote Aboriginal communities. A politics of difference and separatism had pursued group rights premised on the view that there were viable futures in the homelands, even at the smallest outstation sites. The writers who opposed this form of 'separate development' contested this view. In their more dramatic remarks, the romance of the Dreaming was juxtaposed with the pathology and distress that was present in communities. Critics came to dominate the views expressed in Australia's media.

The counterpoint to this critique was put by anthropologists and others. Those who defended the homelands proposed that Aboriginal people lived according to their own institutions only partly mindful of market values. As Peterson noted in 1985, many remote Aboriginal people were disengaged from the modes of consumption and work practices that other Australians embraced. In the place of these values were forms of status, knowledge and mundane pleasures concerning kin and country, both in their social and ritual dimensions. The continuation of Aboriginal song and the flowering of a fine art movement were indicative of this milieu. In this defence of homelands, there was also an implication that what seemed like poverty to an outsider was in fact a difference of meaning for remote Aboriginal people. Clothing (often second-hand), shelter (often makeshift) and food (a mix of the foraged and shop bought) were common examples. These items of consumption might look second-rate to the outsider, but it was a different matter among Aboriginal people themselves. Likewise, larger items including motor vehicles and houses were not treated as private property. Rather, their value lay in their shared use by kin. Therefore depreciation was rapid, consequent on heavy use. Supporters argued that often this fact mattered less to remote Aboriginal people than it would to some others. Nonetheless, an outsider could 'read' this cultural difference as inequality and that would be the outsider's mistake. Evidence for this interpretation came in the fact that homelands people valued their land rights and showed no inclination to migrate to areas with more employment, notwithstanding their remote conditions. Cultural difference mattered more than social inequality as the latter might be perceived by other Australians.

In sum, both debates raised issues concerning cultural difference and inequality. Moreover, either explicitly or implicitly, both debates addressed the issue of cultural reification. Were remote communities bounded wholes or were they variable, changing, and 'fractured' by encapsulation in the state and by their marginal economies? Put more bluntly, does culture count in these communities or not? In this chapter I discuss the positions of the anti-separatists. They included John Reeves QC, Peter Howson, Peter Sutton, Noel Pearson and Marcia Langton and, finally, Helen Hughes, Gary Johns and Bob Gregory.[2] Discussion of their writings is ordered in a rough chronological sequence. The writings are also grouped according to some other characteristics: land rights factors, issues of pathology, the perspectives of Aboriginal leaders, and those who emphasised economy the most. Not all those who opposed separatism can be termed 'neoliberal'. Therefore, at the conclusion of this chapter, I also define a neoliberal position and its relevance to issues of culture and government support.

A background briefing: Trouble in the Indigenous sector

The background to this debate is not a corpus of scholarly work in the style of classical ethnography. Rather, the background is a set of events and emerging conditions that marked the policy period of self-determination from the late 1960s to the early 2000s. Two developments were notable. The first was the growth of an Indigenous sector concurrent with the land rights and homelands movements (see Sanders 1985). The second was the social suffering in communities caused by economic marginalisation, poor service delivery and, as some proposed, the collapse of Aboriginal culture into pathology (see Sutton 2009a). Where supporters of remote communities applauded growth of the Indigenous sector, critics saw it as a retrograde step. Where supporters of homelands proposed that suffering—where it existed—was due mainly to service delivery failure, critics argued that the suffering was due to economic marginalisation and a consequent growth in personal pathology. Others blamed Aboriginal culture itself.

NT land rights were a flagship project of the self-determination policy period. Once the *Aboriginal Land Rights (Northern Territory) Act 1976* became law, large tracts of the Northern Territory were transferred as inalienable land into Aboriginal hands. By 1998,

42.3 per cent of the NT land mass had been passed to Aboriginal Australians (Reeves 1998:v). Though some of this land had considerable commercial appeal either as the site of mineral deposits or as national park, much of it was of little immediate worth in market terms—hence its previous unalienated status. Many people, Aboriginal and non-Aboriginal alike, underlined that country was significant, and enriching, for reasons quite beyond market value. This cultural fact encouraged increasing federal support for a homelands movement that built houses and provided vehicles for newly acknowledged traditional owners to return to and reside on their land. The homelands movement became a social corollary of NT land rights and provided a model for aspirations elsewhere in Australia.

These developments had an administrative counterpart. In 1973, Prime Minister Whitlam had established both the federal Department of Aboriginal Affairs (DAA) and a much smaller National Aboriginal Consultative Council (NACC) to advise the DAA on policy. There followed a National Aboriginal Conference (NAC) in 1977 and, in 1980, an Aboriginal Development Commission (ADC) with a focus on economic issues. Beyond the DAA and its state equivalents, the Northern Territory was also a major site of organisations specifically designed to represent Aboriginal interests. The land councils, and especially the Northern and Central land councils (NLC and CLC), had considerable impact on NT politics. At times they assumed the role of an opposition to incumbent government and were seen by some to represent a block to NT development and subsequent statehood. As these arms of bureaucracy expanded, along with the number of Indigenous corporations—Rowse estimated roughly 3000 in 2002—opposition to the sector grew both within and beyond the NT (Rowse 2002:178). Critics called it the 'Aboriginal industry'.

In 1989, the roles of the DAA and ADC were merged in the Aboriginal and Torres Strait Islander Commission (ATSIC), subsequently decommissioned in 2004. ATSIC and its Community Development Employment Projects (CDEP) came to be seen as the core of the Indigenous sector, designed to serve Aboriginal and Torres Strait Islanders in a distinctive set of regional, territory/state and federal institutions. As Sanders and Morphy relate:

> The CDEP scheme arose in the mid 1970s in response to the increasing payment of unemployment benefits in remote Aboriginal communities with few formal labour market employment opportunities. This payment was seen by some as unhelpful and inappropriate in these circumstances. So an alternative was developed whereby the Commonwealth's Aboriginal affairs administration, rather than social security administration, made payments to Aboriginal communities roughly equivalent to community members' unemployment payment entitlements, in order for communities to employ their members on a part time basis. (Sanders and Morphy 2001:1)

A scheme that began in 1977 with just twelve communities would grow to involve around 300 organisations and more than 30,000 Indigenous people by 2000 (Sanders and Morphy 2001:1).[3] Projects within the scheme were community-based and administered with provision for on-costs and some infrastructural spending. Where employment was concerned, a keynote was 'flexibility' and 'choice' across different regions.[4] In sum, NT land rights, the homelands movement in remote Australia and their support by an Indigenous sector marked a response by society and state to Aboriginal cultural difference. Along with the Mabo case and native title provisions Australia-wide, the NT developments were a paradigm for the period. Moreover, from the outset this politics of cultural difference drew both strong support and opposition (see Goot and Rowse 2007).

The debate was intensified by reports of social suffering in communities.[5] Possibly Colin Tatz (1990) raised the relevant issues first for the Northern Territory. As a South African political scientist, he came to his Australian research with an anti-racist position and a considerable engagement with anthropologists. Ideologically, he had no particular links to the critics of separatism. His views were based on visits to 70 Indigenous communities across Australia.[6] Time has proven his observations apt. He described 'stark realities' of ill-health in remote communities coincident with high unemployment. Tatz remarked of CDEP that 'Aborigines are working, at times in a tokenistic and artificial way . . . There are few real jobs with real wages' (1990:250). He listed other serious issues. These included a 'great deal of personal violence'; a 'great deal of child neglect';

'violence and damage committed in sober states'; a 'marked increase in Aboriginal deaths from non-natural causes'; 'destruction of property'; attacks 'on white staff'; 'the vast quantity of alcohol consumed'; and the tendency among 'Aborigines [to] externalise causality and responsibility for all of this' (1990:250).

A recent report by the federal government's Productivity Commission on causes of Indigenous avoidable death in the NT and three states suggests overall a steady state of affairs in these matters (see SCRGSP 2009:7.31).[7] At 10 per 100,000, the Indigenous rate of death from personal assault is ten times higher than the non-Indigenous one. Indigenous deaths from diabetes stand at 95 per 100,000 and from kidney disease at 27 per 100,000. These rates are respectively almost eighteen and more than sixteen times higher than those for non-Indigenous Australians. Although only five times higher than the non-Indigenous rate, in fact the greatest killer of Indigenous people is ischaemic heart disease (SCRGSP 2009:7.31). A standard reference describes risk factors for myocardial ischaemia as age, smoking, high cholesterol, diabetes and hypertension. These and other lifestyle-related deaths are entirely consistent with those reported by Trovato (2001) for Canada, the United States and New Zealand. They mark common forms of Indigenous distress that coincide with marginalisation.

In 1991, papers from a workshop convened by Jon Altman for the Academy of the Social Sciences in Australia (ASSA) had spelt out the structural factors behind this social suffering. The workshop had been called to address the fact that the Hawke Labor government's 1987 call for Aboriginal employment equity by the year 2000 was simply unattainable.[8] Prime Minister Hawke's goal entailed, conservatively, the creation of around 48,000 jobs spread across urban, rural and remote Australia (Australia 1987a, 1987b, 1987c). The ASSA workshop found that pervasive unemployment would endure well into the 21st century—especially in rural and remote Australia. Altman and Sanders (1991:9) summarised four factors that pointed to an intractable position. They were the *long term exclusion* of Aboriginal people from mainstream institutions generally; a *demographic structure* in which there would be an unanticipated very rapid growth of working-age

Aboriginal people through the 1990s; *marked locational disadvantage* for remote Aboriginal people; and the exacerbation of this in Australia by a long-term decline of semi-skilled and unskilled rural employment, especially for males.[9] The intersection of a demographic explosion and a dearth of jobs created a dire prospect (Altman 1991:171–172; see also Tesfaghioghis and Gray 1991:53, 60–61). These matters have come to pass, and place in context the deployment of CDEP as a damper on unemployment. A decade later, Taylor and Hunter reported that, even counting CDEP employment, '33,000 jobs are required nationwide to achieve equity with the non-Indigenous unemployment rates.' If all those who want to work were to be employed, including discouraged job seekers, 'then policy makers [would] need to find work for another 30,000 or so people' (Taylor and Hunter 2001:102–103).

Finally, Altman and Sanders listed a different type of factor. It concerned the '*cultural inappropriateness*' of employment equity programs in remote communities. They remarked, 'Aborigines, particularly in remote areas, may choose lifestyles that are substantially different from those of other Australians. We take this to be a positive theme... reflected, for example, in the growth of the Aboriginal homelands movement' (Altman and Sanders 1991:10). Altman proposed that for a group in remote northern Arnhem Land, still immersed in a hunter-gatherer life, there would be a 'lifestyle' preference away from conventional employment (Altman 1991:162–163). Among such people, pursuit of employment equity could only be a denial of cultural difference.[10] His position was consistent with the support of land rights as such. As Peterson had noted some six years earlier, it seemed that for remote Aboriginal people possibly the only route towards equality might be through the support of cultural difference. Here was the making of a debate (Peterson 1985:98).

Land rights and the Reeves Report

John Reeves QC, a Darwin-based lawyer, was commissioned by the Howard Coalition government to conduct a comprehensive review of the Land Rights Act, which he pursued over nine months between

November 1997 and July 1998. He presented his report, *Building on Land Rights for the Next Generation*, to the minister of Aboriginal Affairs in August 1998. On Reeves's own account, at least three factors influenced the exercise. These were, first, socioeconomic conditions in Aboriginal settlements and outstations where 'reliance on social security payments for basic needs had become entrenched'; and second, the advent of self-government in the NT and the growth of the Territory's population and economy. (The Reeves Report proposed that the NT government should have the right to compulsorily acquire Aboriginal land for the common good.) Third, and finally, Reeves proposed that media communications would soon lead Aboriginal people themselves to change their 'needs and aspirations' as members of Australian society (Reeves 1998:1–3). A further issue of significance was that land claims under the Act were drawing to a close. The Act contained a 'sunset clause' related to the finite amount of unalienated Crown and other claimable land in the Northern Territory. Reeves was proposing that once land claims were concluded, Mining Royalty Equivalents (MRE) derived from Aboriginal land should be used in other ways (Reeves 1998: 216–217, 367–368).[11]

The recommendations that Reeves made were intended to change land rights.[12] He proposed to abolish the two large land councils and put in their place a network of eighteen smaller regional councils. In each region and council, traditional owners and Aboriginal migrant residents would be recognised equally. The authority position of traditional owners under the Act would go. Moreover, titles assigned to the existing land trusts, formed with each successful claim, would be reassigned to the regional councils. Having dispensed with traditional owners and the large land councils, Reeves proposed a new 'central institution of governance'. This was a Northern Territory Aboriginal Council (NTAC), appointed entirely by the federal and NT governments, at least at the outset. The council would have oversight of NT land rights, including the administrative and financial functions of the regional councils. It would also administer the assets and the liabilities of Aboriginal royalty associations and all MRE previously administered by the Aboriginal Benefits Reserve (ABR). The NTAC would become the 'banker' to the regional councils and also assume all NT funding programs maintained by ATSIC at the time. In sum, government nominees to the NTAC would control all financial and administrative matters of a decentralised group of small regional councils. The focus would be on development. In addition, the Reeves Report proposed that miners should be given easier access to Aboriginal land. Reeves anticipated the NT Intervention by almost ten years when he proposed that permits to enter Aboriginal land should be abolished.

On 15 July 1999, Ian Viner, a previous minister of Aboriginal Affairs in a Coalition government, posted his opinion of the Reeves Report on the internet. In part it read: 'Governance of Aboriginal land will be centralised in a superordinate non-traditional Aboriginal institution ... Whilst control over Aboriginal land would on a superficial level be decentralised to Regional Land Councils, the actual political and financial power would be centralised in the NTAC and the Northern Territory government' (Viner 1999). Amid uproar in the wider community, the Reeves Report was referred to the House of Representatives Standing Committee on Aboriginal and Torres Strait Islander Affairs. At that time, the committee was chaired by Liberal MP Lou Liebermann. Members agreed to consider the report with reference to some common 'shared principles or values'. These included the proposition that there be no diminution in Aboriginal land rights and no undermining of the rights of, and opportunities for, Aboriginal Australians to determine their own lives. The committee rejected the Reeves Report as a basis for legislation.

Although it was thwarted as a political initiative, and a legislative one, the Reeves Report is instructive as an example of anti-separatism. In it, the tension between cultural difference and inequality looms large. More precisely, it was Reeves's view that employment opportunity was simply more important than cultural difference in the longer term. His assessment of NT Aboriginal disadvantage rested in significant part on issues of location and education. Twice in his report, he cited a passage from a CAEPR discussion paper (Reeves 1998:88, 571). The passage makes three points: first, the production of exports in remote areas, be they materials or services, tends to be capital- rather than labour-intensive, and subject to market fluctuation. In other words, activity in mining, tourism and pastoral ventures offers little employment. Second, if further employment is to be generated, it is more likely to come from 'import substitution' activities, including local services in construction, commerce, land management, media, transport and the like. Third, and now I cite from the paper: 'Short of any sustained migration for employment away from such localities . . . [these factors suggest] a continued need for public subvention along with flexibility and realism in the drive for increased private sector involvement' (Taylor and Roach 1998:21). In sum, on most Aboriginal land returned under the Land Rights Act, prospects for private sector employment are poor, and most employment is local and service-oriented, and will be supplied through CDEP. With reference to this situation, Reeves noted that remote NT Aboriginal people were less educated and received less benefit for their education than Indigenous Australians beyond the Territory, as well as non-Indigenous Australians (see also Hughes and Hughes 2009).

He came to two conclusions: first, that in view of the fact that less skilled rural employment was contracting all over Australia, the future both for young Aboriginal men and women lay in education. Reeves remarked, 'Far more important modern sources of economic progress than the possession of land are the possession of productively useful skills, technology and capital of the kind in demand in the mainstream Australian economy' (Reeves 1998:571). Second, he proposed that MRE should be deployed to stimulate more investment and job creation, and better education for children who live remote (Reeves 1998:324–326).[13] These conclusions were either disputed or opposed by many who responded to Reeves. I discuss these responses in Chapter 5.

Cultural difference as pathology

Between the time when Tatz wrote and debate around the Reeves Report tapered off, evidence of Indigenous violence and substance abuse was mounting in Queensland (see Atkinson 1990; Memmott and Stacey 1999; DATSIPD 2000). Boni Robertson, chair of a Queensland-wide women's task force on violence, painted a startling picture:

> The degree of violence and destruction in Aboriginal and Torres Strait Islander Communities cannot be adequately described. The Task Force found evidence of all forms of physical, psychological, cultural and structural violence . . . Appalling acts of physical brutality and sexual violence are being perpetrated within some families and across Communities to a degree previously unknown in Indigenous life. Sadly, many of the victims are women and children, young and older people who now in many cases are living in a constant state of desperation and despair. (Robertson in DATSIPD 2000:12)

The task force surveyed urban, rural and remote communities in Queensland. It cited a range of 'causes and contributing factors'. These included previous child removal and community and family disruption, substandard living conditions, health, education and welfare payments. Critical failures in service delivery were noted, along with the impact of the 'sly grog trade'. The report found that resulting trauma was passed from generation to generation (Robertson in DATSIPD:13, 45ff).

This report was taken up by Peter Howson, the former Coalition minister of Aborigines, the Environment and the Arts, 1971–72. Howson had become a contributor to *Quadrant* magazine as well as a leader of the Bennelong Society. In a piece he published in *Quadrant*, Howson cited the task force report along with Tatz's 1990 article. He also referenced Rosemary Neil, a journalist with *The Australian*, who would later write a book citing Judy Atkinson on child sexual abuse in Queensland (Atkinson 1990; Neill 2002). Howson turned the focus onto Aboriginal pathology. He wrote:

> The state of barbarism which is now ubiquitous in every remote Aboriginal community in Australia is best described in the words of Thomas Hobbes in *Leviathan:* 'where every man is enemy to every man . . . wherein men live without other security than what their own strength . . . shall furnish them. In such condition, there

is no place for Industry . . . no account of time; no Arts; no Letters; no Society; and which is worst of all continual fear, and danger of violent death; And the life of man, solitary, poore, nasty, brutish, and short.' (Howson 2000:22)

Howson also cited Reeves, noting his emphasis on the 'economic cul de sac' that was the circumstance of remote Aboriginal people in the NT. With this situation, Reeves wrote, came 'loss of self-reliance, and the build-up of . . . dependency' along with 'hopelessness, despair and anti-social behaviour' in conjunction with 'contempt and hostility' (cited in Howson 2000:21). To these socioeconomic factors, Howson added the effects of 'ill-advised' policies. These included '[all] land rights; the rhetoric of black suffering and white guilt; the promotion of Aborigines as perpetual victims . . .; the support for self-determination in international fora; and the encouragement of Aboriginal separatism' (Howson 2000:23).

Two characteristics of Howson's article stand out. First, the account is a blanket one. This is the condition of all Aboriginal peoples who, on that account, should not be indulged with land rights of any type. Second, the principal focus in Howson's analysis is the pathology of tradition. By quoting Hobbes, Howson shifted the focus from current conditions to arcane hunter-gatherer culture: 'Australian civilisation has far, far more to offer Australia's Aborigines than the hunter-gatherer life which their forebears endured' (Howson 2000:24). His point was reinforced by other writers in the *Quadrant* and/or *The Australian* group. Roger Sandall, former editor of *Quadrant* and retired anthropologist, remarked a year later, 'If your traditional way of life has no alphabet, no writing, no books and no libraries, and yet you are continually told that you have a culture which is "rich", "complex", and "sophisticated", how can you realistically see your place in the scheme of things?' (Sandall 2001:4, 14). Later again, in 2005, Christopher Pearson for *The Australian* was still underlining the 'perverse' elements of hunter-gatherer culture, including 'violence, witchcraft, necromancy, fatal curses and the belief that . . . mortality is due to malign, human intervention and demands payback'. As a practising Roman Catholic, Pearson did not put his own beliefs to the test—apostasy, original sin, transubstantiation, virgin birth and the like. Sandall and Howson also rounded on anthropology. In Howson's words, 'These remote Aboriginal communities have to be dissolved. They are lawless, anthropological prisons; civilisation has been banished from them and the inmates live lives of unspeakable horror' (Howson 2000:22).

Among these writers the contrast was between civilisation and the pathology of a remnant savage life. They would be reinforced in their views by independent historian, and later *Quadrant* editor, Keith Windschuttle. In his discussion of the early years of settlement, Windschuttle painted the Tasmanians as barely more than beasts: '[T]hey usually slept in the open. They rarely stayed in one place more than a day or two. Settlers who came across their abandoned campsites found them strewn with the rotting remains of the animals they had eaten, and the faeces deposited close to the fires where they slept' (Windschuttle 2002:377).

In 2001, linguist and land rights consultant Peter Sutton published his inaugural Berndt lecture, 'The Politics of Suffering'. He was not as tough on the anthropologists as Howson was (Sutton 2001:142–143). Nonetheless, he was moved to speak out, and forcefully, about the violence and suffering in remote Aboriginal communities. As Australia's leading land claims consultant and with wide experience across a range of different communities, his words carried considerable weight, especially when he recast his original lecture as a book (see Sutton 2009a). Sutton's target was the politics of difference and the 'Aboriginal industry' as it was sustained by a 'liberal consensus' within and beyond universities. In his view, almost all explanations for current conditions in remote communities went to histories of invasion and marginalisation, and to issues of political economy (see also Austin-Broos 2010a, 2010b). Instead Sutton sought to specify the matter in terms of Aboriginal culture at odds with mainstream mores or modern individualism. He cited the following Aboriginal practices and values as problematic: 'socialisation of children, or the "demand sharing" of resources, the pervasive importance of kinship, a high stress on personal autonomy, long patterns of internecine feuding, resistance to delegating authority, the blaming of deaths on out-group sorcerers rather than on those involved in episodes of drink-driving or wife-bashing, for example' (Sutton 2001:140). Later he would stipulate: forms of traditional power that created 'dependency'; 'family loyalties' that supervened notions of the common good; traditional beliefs that blocked 'preventative health'; the 'minimal hygiene practices' of 'an originally semi-nomadic economy'; practices of 'self-redress during conflict'; and finally 'a deep and old philosophical tradition of assent to the tragic terms of human life' that renders 'notions of general social progress deeply alien' (Sutton 2001:148–149).

It seems likely that Sutton's focus was influenced by issues of criminal assault in the community he knew best—Aurukun in Queensland. Like David Martin, he underlined that high rates of violence in communities are due not simply to poverty but also to factors of pathological tradition. These include issues of male competition and notions of autonomy (see Sutton 2009b:40; Martin 2008). Similarly, Sutton, like Martin, was sceptical of Noel Pearson's proposals for community mobilisation (which I discuss below). In Sutton's view, kin-based conflicts had already split communities apart (Martin 2001; Sutton 2001:134–135, 2009a:48, 64–68). Sutton sought a 'forensic' path to treatable causes of distress. His analysis produced three issues: a failure to generate new authority structures after the departure of missions and the like; extreme alcohol dependence; and intimate inherited aspects of gender relations, ego formation and anger management among men. He suggested that not much would change without a restructuring of personal psychologies in the early years of life (Sutton 2009a:135, 138). While inequality might be the 'trigger', for Sutton cultural difference as it weighed on personal pathology was the major cause of distress.[14]

Leaders speak out

Noel Pearson had published his seminal statement *Our Right to Take Responsibility* in the year 2000. It is not surprising that, as an Indigenous leader, Pearson endorsed land rights.[15] Moreover, his list of the ways in which communities were 'dysfunctional' moved beyond both personal and cultural pathology. He listed an average Aboriginal life span twenty years shorter than that of other Australians; the worst health in Australia, including diseases not found elsewhere and new threats such as HIV; very poor education; a vastly disproportionate prison population; and Australia's most violent communities (Pearson 2000:15). Pearson isolated two major causes: one was alcohol abuse, which he described as a 'psychosocially contagious epidemic', and the other was 'welfare dependency'. He also noted that these factors acted to corrupt traditional culture and to undermine local authority structures. At no point did Pearson propose that traditional culture is dysfunctional *per se*. Moreover, he argued that passive welfare is connected to an 'economic circumstance'—the lack in many Indigenous regions of a 'real' economy (Pearson 2001:24–25). Pearson noted that during the course of colonisation, usurpation of the land reduced Aboriginal people to 'beggars'. Their subsequent position, of participating intermittently at lower levels of the 'white economy', was disrupted from the late 1960s on. He proposed that equal wages and decreasing rural jobs ushered in reliance on welfare (Pearson 2001:29–30). Pearson remarked:

> We share many problems with rural Australia generally, such as the decline of rural industries and the lack of infrastructure. When these difficulties are compounded by our social disintegration, our lack of resources and education, and by the low expectations the larger community has of us, it is difficult to see how a real market economy could replace this passive welfare economy. (Pearson 2001:28)

In sum, structural circumstances that remote Aboriginal people share with others are intensified by the specifying nature of Aboriginal history. It is only Indigenous people who have been encapsulated in the state and comprehensively disadvantaged in market society on account of race.

Pearson's views on an appropriate response were nothing if not hard-headed. He began his discussion with an acknowledgement of the racism that had pushed most Aboriginal people to the margins of a prosperous society. However, he also noted that racism is a resilient part of Australian society and hard to change within a generation's span. Economy, on the other hand, can be addressed, albeit within confined parameters (Pearson 2000:36–37). Pearson was keen to sketch these out. He noted that enduring economic conditions reduce the likelihood of dramatic change in 'most country towns'. As a consequence:

> [W]e are stuck with government being the provider of basic resources. One focus must therefore be on how we can change the nature of welfare, as well as trying to get economic development going. Together with improving our engagement in the real economy, we must also change the *nature* of the welfare economy in which we are destined to live for the foreseeable future. (Pearson 2000:55)

'Leeching' the 'poison' from a welfare economy became the focus of Pearson's position. He drew attention to 'servicing'—in fact an over-servicing that made remote Aboriginal people passive clients of the state; to the tangle of departments involved in servicing; and to the stifling of local leadership that the Aboriginal industry involved (Pearson 2000:37–49). An integral part of this governmentality was education that imposed on Indigenous children highly localised curricula that could not equip them for a larger world (see also Nakata 2007). Pearson made proposals that he hoped would strengthen local communities against a state bent on micro-management through service delivery (2000:67–82). With regard to economy, he proposed a four-pronged plan. It involved foraging activity where it was appropriate, CDEP-style support reorganised as 'reciprocity programs', local small business, and capital investment in the mainstream economy. Later, he would also stress vastly improved education in English literacy, numeracy and other academic and vocational skills (Pearson 2009a).[16] Nonetheless, Pearson made clear that actually getting beyond an economy dependent on government support and extensive servicing would be very difficult; hence *Our Right to Take Responsibility* and his appeal to individual initiative.

Noel Pearson and Marcia Langton offered the 'Dr Charles Perkins AO Memorial Oration' in successive years at the University of Sydney, Pearson in 2001 and Langton in 2002. Foundation chair of Indigenous Studies at Melbourne University, Langton concurred with Pearson's analysis, but focused on the economic dimension of his argument and gave it a further twist. Citing Andre Gunter Frank, she located Aboriginal poverty in the context of the radical forms of marginalised localism that a global capitalism creates.[17] In addition, she proposed that this Aboriginal localism within Australia also had an enduring context: a two-tier wages system directly tied to race. Langton noted that prior to the 1970s, limited Aboriginal employment and below-award payments were camouflaged as 'training allowances' (Langton 2002:3, 5–6). In her view, the introduction of CDEP in the 1970s simply rebadged this two-tier system (Langton 2002:10–18). Like Pearson, she argued that Aboriginal groups should pursue capital investments beyond their immediate locales, implying, like Reeves, different uses for NT land rights royalties. In addition, Langton demanded 'economic justice' from the federal government:

> A generous investment in the Aboriginal sector, by which I mean at least several times the annual budget in Aboriginal affairs, targeted towards industry research and development, genuine labour market strategies, employment, education and training initiatives, and infrastructure investment would substantially transform the poverty trap of Aboriginal dependence on government transfers, CDEP and social security. (Langton 2002:19)

Langton described it as a 'new deal' for Aboriginal Australia. Economist Helen Hughes would also propose a 'new deal', though not one that relied on government support.[18]

Market economics, more or less

Polemic reached new heights when Helen Hughes entered the debate. She dramatised her own position by describing land rights and the homelands movement as a form of 'apartheid' that was also a 'socialist' plan devised by H.C. Coombs (see Hughes and Warin 2005:2, 4).[19] An erstwhile governor of Australia's Reserve Bank, Coombs was widely taken to be the instigator of the homelands movement, supported in the early days by anthropologist W.E.H. Stanner (see Coombs et al.

1983; Rowse 2000:84–86). Hughes's proposal was to replace a failed 'socialist utopia' with a 'new deal' for remote Aboriginal people. She juxtaposed portraits of extreme pathology with her proposals for policy change. In an early statement with Jenness Warin, the description went like this:

> Adults in remote communities are overwhelmingly illiterate and innumerate. They do not have enough English to express themselves. They cannot read the instructions for simple do-it-yourself jobs. They cannot read food labels, medicine instructions or cleaning material warnings. People do not know their fortnightly, monthly and annual incomes and expenditures. Digitalisation of CDEP and other welfare payments has exacerbated the difficulties of protecting incomes from communal obligations and 'book-up' (buying on credit)—both typical of traditional and poor communities. Very low literacy and numeracy makes banking a nightmare.

Hughes and Warin's account of Aboriginal houses also focused on pathology and lack:

> In many instances, a single bedroom can house a family of six to eight people. Foam rubber mattresses cover the floor. There is no room for furniture. There are no tables, no chairs, no wardrobes and no cupboards, let alone desks for children's homework. A young girl is lucky to have an airline bag for her clothes and toothbrush. (Hughes and Warin 2005: 6, 10)

Hughes identified a comparable pathology embedded in CDEP. The system was simply welfare:

> In the 'homelands' CDEP payments are made to teaching and health aids, for office work and administration, for the maintenance of public spaces and tracks, rubbish collection and for building and housing maintenance. But overwhelmingly these are 'ghost' positions that are known as 'sit-down' money. In the smaller settlements schools are hardly ever open, medicine in health centres is severely restricted (sometimes with only Panadol available), rubbish is not collected and buried, and grass is not cut, and there is no building and house maintenance. In the larger 'homeland' settlements (and in fringe settlements and ghettos), where CDEP funding supports

Indigenous assistants to non-Indigenous staff, the situation is often worse. (Hughes 2007:71–72)

Similarly, education is a disaster:

> So-called 'Indigenous bilingual' programs that mandate education only in natal languages during early years of schooling only pretend to be bilingual. They are responsible for most children leaving the so-called bilingual schools after years of schooling, unable to read, write or count in any language. (Hughes and Hughes 2009:9)

In Hughes's view, these factors produced an appalling state of being:

> Violent DVDs tend to be the main source of entertainment. Boredom and lassitude are broken by bouts of frustration and resentment (especially when mainstream lives are glimpsed) ... Overcrowded derelict housing, bouts of hunger, malnutrition and ill health are their daily lot. Fishing, hunting, food gathering and traditional ceremonies are at best intermittent. They do not provide the rewards of mainstream work and incomes. Instead, drinking, smoking tobacco and marijuana, kava parties, sniffing petrol and using methamphetamines fill the vast spaces of ennui created by the joblessness and isolation of the 'homelands'. (Hughes 2007:28–29)

Again:

> The neglect of children by mothers and fathers in the throes of alcoholism, drug abuse and domestic violence is a damning indictment of 'living museum' societies ... the high incidence of paedophilia [may be due] to neglect so dire that children are seeking love. (Hughes 2007:32)

This is the form of writing that Marcia Langton, after Jean Baudrillard, described as 'War Porn' in the remote communities debate (Langton 2008:145). Its pertinent feature was total disregard for forms of cultural difference or even mundane local competence. In Hughes's account, every individual in every community is a bundle of mere lack. The polemic worked, in some quarters at least. When it was published by the CIS, *Lands of Shame* (2007) soon sold out.

What were Hughes's policy proposals? First, she advocated repeal of land rights legislation, and native title legislation as well; second, she advocated rescinding government support for homelands residence; and third, rapid development of mainstream, English-language education for all remote Aboriginal children. In addition, Hughes proposed that health, law and order, and Indigenous community administration be mainstreamed (Hughes 2005:9–16). Hughes's support for repealing land rights rested on the view that 'the institution of private property rights has been central to the development of productive economies and rising standards of living throughout the world' (Hughes 2005:10). As I discuss in Chapter 6, at least where Aboriginal communities are concerned, a spectrum of opinion disagreed with Hughes (see McDonnell 2005:32–33; see also Johns 2009:10). Development economist Roy Duncan also proposed that 'individual rights to the land in some form' are most 'likely to lead to the largest gains in welfare' for remote Aboriginal people. However, Duncan underlined that such rights can be pursued through forms of leasehold rather than undermining communal ownership of the NT type (see Duncan 2003:316; see also Dalrymple 2007). Later, Hughes's focus turned to remote schooling and to a critique of the teaching profession and public education. Accordingly, she supported remote independent schools where possible and recommended that governments rigorously monitor public schools. Where it is necessary, she proposed, families should move to larger population centres for their children's schooling, or have their children bussed or boarded (Hughes and Hughes 2009:viii). Possibly Hughes's most influential suggestion has been her proposal that there be 'core' remote Aboriginal towns, where service and administrative provisions to homeland residents can be centralised and improved. The Territory government's designation of twenty Territory Growth Towns (TGT) in the Northern Territory seems to conform to this plan. Hughes proposed that cost efficiencies to government would come from the TGT. This was a more modest claim than her initial suggestion that her policies would prove cost-neutral to governments (Hughes and Warin 2005:18).

Along with Hughes, Gary Johns of the Bennelong Society and the Menzies Research Centre became prominent in the debate in the mid-2000s.[20] His two major reports have been *Aboriginal Education* and, more recently, *No Job, No House* on remote Aboriginal housing (Johns 2006a, 2009). These policy statements were preceded by an edited collection, *Waking Up to the Dreamtime* (2001). Generally, Johns has been less confident than Hughes that local economies can be built in rural and remote locales. Therefore, he has been an advocate for Aboriginal migration to job centres elsewhere. At a *Quadrant*-sponsored seminar in August 1999, Johns observed that education was in fact a 'migration by stealth' policy. In 2006, he argued that transitions to better mainstream education 'will be better managed if educators and governments understand that education is essentially an instrument in economic integration'. More provocatively, he observed that 'educators and governments should understand that western education cannot and should not preserve Aboriginal culture' (Johns 2006a:4). Regarding housing, Johns proposed that permanent rental housing should only be available to those who comply with 'the standard responsibilities attached to tenancy agreements and social security benefits'—'no job, no house' (Johns 2009:34). With reference to remote Aboriginal welfare and royalty incomes, Johns remarked on the 'recreational lifestyle' of an Aboriginal 'leisure class' that allowed families to travel their region using incomes and resources for which they had not worked (Johns 2006b). In his view, only strict market incentives can address this circumstance. Both Hughes and Johns have proposed radical free market solutions for remote Aboriginal conditions. Both have portrayed remote community distress in terms of the pathology that comes with impoverishment. In their view, that poverty has been caused by government indulgence of cultural difference in the policy period of self-determination.

Finally, Bob Gregory has written on remote Aboriginal issues as a professional economist and without the polemic that has been the hallmark of Howson, Sutton, Hughes and Johns. (Where polemic is concerned, generally non-Aboriginal writers have far outstripped their Aboriginal counterparts, who have been more considered.) Four of Gregory's articles are of interest, one of them co-authored with Anne Daly (Gregory 1991, 2005, 2006; Gregory and Daly 1997). In the two earlier articles, Gregory compared the circumstance of Aboriginal Australians, and especially those in rural and remote

Australia, with African and Native Americans in the first case (1991) and, in the second, with Native Americans alone (Gregory and Daly 1997). The comparisons show that employment–population ratios among the Australians have dropped more rapidly than they have for either of the American groups. Yet, mainly through welfare and labour market policies, Australians have experienced rising incomes while American incomes dropped. These income rises, mainly due to social security and CDEP, hardly suggest prosperity, though. In 1997, Gregory and Daly wrote: 'Changes at the bottom of the income distribution are the most worrying. The long-run well-being of Aborigines cannot improve with ever shrinking employment levels and increasing dependence on part-time CDEP employment in return for unemployment benefits' (1997:118). Gregory also noted that increasing government support that brought no significant improvements in employment would probably become a political issue. This came to pass and was reflected in the writings of Pearson, Langton, Hughes and Johns in the early 2000s.

Gregory continued to track matters in remote communities with increasing unease. Aggregate data produced by CAEPR for the whole of Indigenous Australia suggested employment growth. Disaggregated, though, Gregory argued that the data told a different story. While expansion of the Indigenous sector had increased middle-class jobs, matters had grown worse for most Aboriginal residents of remote communities, who were semi-skilled or unskilled (Gregory 2005). Gregory noted that the decline in non-CDEP Indigenous employment had continued through the 1990s, that only the 'elite' sector had grown, and that categories of Indigenous full-time and private sector employment had suffered marked declines (Gregory 2006:128–130). In sum, the remote Aboriginal workforce was retreating back into small communities and reliance on CDEP. Gregory was sceptical about these developments. He wrote: 'remote communities as isolated enclaves depending largely on welfare payments and few links to mainstream employment outside the community will be [unable] to provide health outcomes and living standards closely approximating that of the Australian community' (Gregory 2005:149, fn 2 and passim). He noted that 'to leave a remote community successfully and earn income to remit, it is necessary to obtain a well paid job. However, this is where Australian policy seems to have failed most. We have failed to create an environment in which Indigenous Australians, unskilled in labour market terms, can successfully outmigrate' (Gregory 2005:135).

Gregory had more to say on the conditions required for outmigration. He remarked that the trend in federal government policy was to encourage welfare recipients into work wherever possible. Yet Aboriginal job seekers were 'extremely poorly qualified', with low educational levels and low levels of English competence. Moreover, even the very best assistance programs, 'that focus on skill development and job-finding skills for adults', seemed to have little effect among remote Indigenous participants (Gregory 2006:134, 137). Gregory posed a crucial question: When normal human capital policies fail, is there something different about remote Aboriginal communities, and about their youth? He noted that we need to know 'the extent to which Indigenous people want to be employed in the mainstream economy but cannot find jobs . . . and the degree to which the low employment level is the result of the impact of traditional values and/or financial incentives' (Gregory 2006:131). Among the latter, one would count royalties, CDEP, social security and the like. Gregory's remark raised the prospect of a situation in which cultural difference and government support intersect to turn remote Aboriginal youth away from seeking jobs—a disengagement from the labour market. With this in mind, Gregory remarked on CDEP as the main policy option at the time:

> If there is a significant long-run rejection rate of mainstream jobs because of CDEP, this must be against the long-run economic interests of the Indigenous community. On the other hand, if CDEP is a scheme where community life is made better for people who really have *no* employment alternatives, then we should be less willing to restrict its further growth. (Gregory 2006:134, emphasis in original)

Generally committed to labour market policies, Gregory left the door open for a community-based approach if Aboriginal people would not move, even in the face of unemployment. In Gregory's view, perhaps the matter was culturally specific and not simply market-driven. On these matters, the Labor federal government did not wait to learn more. CDEP was abandoned as a community employment scheme in 2008, although it retained a training role (see Altman and Jordan 2009).

Across the decade of the 1990s, public unease grew concerning remote Aboriginal communities. At first, the focus in the public debate was on issues of Indigenous land rights and native title. Through the 2000s, though, the focus turned to welfare dependency, cultural pathology, substance abuse and violence. Where Howson, Sandall, Christopher Pearson, Hughes and Johns were concerned, there was virtually no acknowledgement of genuine and continuing issues of cultural difference in remote communities—issues that might challenge those who actually lived remote as well as those who formulate policy (see Sanders 2008). Rather, the matter was presented in terms of the pathologies either of traditional culture or poverty. And even in the latter case, degraded culture was often cast as a significant contributor to the poverty involved. These portraits of pathology created moral certainty in the public domain, considerably reinforced when the NT government's *Little Children are Sacred* report was released in 2007. Writers had three routes to the issue of pathology. One was through 19th century political liberalism and ideas of progress, civilisation and savagery. Images popular in the early 20th century reappeared with renewed vigour. Howson, Sandall and Christopher Pearson followed this route. Another route was Peter Sutton's, which noted the pathology not of hunter-gatherer savages, but rather of a degraded tradition in the present. Clearly Sutton came to this position in some distress, but did he ask what else there was of worth in communities? Finally, Hughes and Johns took the route of contemporary neoliberalism, based on neoclassical economics and ideas derived from Friedrich Hayek and the Chicago school of economics.[21] In the context of the remote communities debate this position meant a strong stance against government-supported CDEP (considered as mere welfare); a correlative support for market institutions including private property and competitive labour markets; and finally, an implicit view of human motivation that assumed universal and invariable notions of market value. Bureaucratic interference in market institutions was seen to shore up cultural difference which, in turn, exacerbated poverty. Hughes in particular underlined the dire consequences of persisting in this course. Whatever the route to the issue of pathology, its airing in the media discredited issues of cultural difference and promoted rapid policy change.

Undoubtedly, these neoliberals wrote to debunk what they saw as romanticised ideas about remote Aboriginal communities. Moreover, their approach was economic and concerned with social inequality. However, here they diverged in a radical way from the postcolonial critique. Where the latter addressed the inequalities conferred on Indigenous people by encapsulation in the state and the elaboration of a capitalist economy, neoliberalism focused on disruptions to a universal market dynamic. Their position was one of true believers in an economic and political milieu infused with these ideas. This was reflected in the Manichean way in which they approached the debate.

The anti-separatist position was not, however, a uniform one. Other writers shared some views with—and also diverged from—the neoliberals. Sutton acknowledged structural factors, including an economic marginalisation fuelled by conflicting institutions, of kinship and 'political economy'. Yet he also saw these as constants unlikely to change. Therefore his focus went to cultural pathology. Noel Pearson endorsed land rights and acknowledged the role of the state and race relations in shaping marginalisation. Nonetheless, his focus was on welfare dependency and the social chaos it seemed to engender. He placed his emphasis on alternative routes to employment, including mainstream education, and on Aboriginal capital investment outside the homelands. He also underlined cultural revitalisation based on families and communities. He did not rule out government support. Langton underlined structural disadvantage and the role of government in correcting it. Reeves's report proposed a model of land rights administration antagonistic to traditional culture and with political implications. Where inequality was concerned, his major focus was on using Aboriginal royalties to foster better health and increased employment in remote communities. Although his report described a bleak economic future for outstation life, it did not pathologise Aboriginal people. Gregory was also pessimistic concerning the future of small outstations. Yet, unlike Reeves, his suggestions worked around land rights and not against them. Over time, his analysis also sought to address cultural difference.

In sum, the anti-separatists presented a range of positions on inequality and economic policy. Only a minority, however, acknowledged cultural difference as an enduring and significant factor for remote communities. In Chapter 6 I assess the major proposals of the anti-separatists, along with those of the CAEPR group. It is to those who defended homelands that the discussion now turns.

5
Defending the homelands

Given the degree to which Aboriginal employment problems are intractable, the pursuit of statistical equality is, we believe, both inappropriate and likely to fail.

> Jon Altman and Will Sanders, Government Initiatives for
> Aboriginal Employment: Equity, equality and policy realism

In Australia, different social science disciplines have framed [the 'problem' at the] heart of Indigenous affairs policy in different ways and correspondingly have put forward different policy proposals. For instance, whereas anthropology dwells on cultural difference and presumes that difference to be a social good, economics dwells on socioeconomic inequality and presumes that difference to be the legacy of historical exclusion . . . The [latter] emphasises the need for socioeconomic equality, the [former] sees potential incompatibility between such a policy goal and Indigenous cultural differences and choice.

> Jon Altman and Tim Rowse, Indigenous Affairs

In 1990, the Centre for Aboriginal Economic Policy Research (CAEPR) was established as a response to Aboriginal issues, including those that faced the homelands. CAEPR was located at the Australian National University (ANU), which would soon have the largest concentration of researchers on Indigenous Australia in the society or overseas. Anthropologist Jon Altman was the source of inspiration for the centre; he directed it, recruited staff, and attracted diverse funding. The centre had a dual role as a policy research group and as consultant to organisations, both government and non-government. In the course of ATSIC's life, CAEPR was a crucial, autonomous resource. A published overview of CAEPR's work underlined the broad scope of its research on social and economic policy issues (see Rowse 2002). The CAEPR group was interdisciplinary and included academics trained in social policy, demography and economics. Others had at least one degree in anthropology. In his role, Altman drew on a first degree in economics and field experience as an economic anthropologist in northern Arnhem Land.[1] From time to time, he also worked in association with Tim Rowse, a former Australian Studies fellow at Harvard, biographer of H.C. Coombs, and advocate for the Indigenous sector.[2] Rowse's training was in political science and anthropology, and there is a strong historical bent to his writing (e.g. Rowse 1998a).

In his CAEPR-related work, Rowse saw the Indigenous sector not merely as an administrative vehicle but also as a political vanguard. Consequently, he valued the Indigenous sector most for its role in building 'legal and political capacities' (Rowse 2002:231, 2001, 2005). By contrast, Altman was more concerned with remote and very remote Aboriginal employment. He supported CDEP as policy 'realism' for remote communities. As noted in Chapter 4, he took this position in response to the Hawke federal government's Aboriginal Employment Development Project (AEDP 1986/87). Altman stated his position in the course of an Academy of the Social Sciences in Australia (ASSA) workshop on Aboriginal employment equity (see Australia 1987a; Altman 1991). In contrast to the neoliberal view, Altman and his CAEPR colleagues thought that remote Aboriginal communities would require major federal government support for the foreseeable future.[3]

This chapter discusses writing from the CAEPR group in the main. Throughout, the intention is to distil a public position indicative of CAEPR that has also been supported by many anthropologists. Almost all the material discussed comes in the form of edited collections in which Altman and/or CAEPR played a major part. The first is a collection published to defend the Land Rights Act against the critique of the Reeves Report (see Altman, Morphy and Rowse 1999). The second involves the proceedings of a conference on CDEP held as the remote communities debate took shape (see Morphy and Sanders 2001). I also indicate how Altman's views developed following this publication. The third is a collection published in response to the NT Intervention that drew on both Indigenous and non-Indigenous contributors from within and beyond universities (Altman and Hinkson 2007). A fourth collection was published recently and produced separately from CAEPR (Altman and Hinkson 2010). I do not discuss it here.[4] These four collections reflect a position embraced by many anthropologists. It is not the position, however, of all contributors to the collections. Some have different views.[5] Nonetheless, as is the privilege of editors, introductions and conclusions to the collections have distilled particular themes. These include defence of land rights and its cornerstone: traditional ownership of Aboriginal lands. The corollary of this support is the position that, if they so desire, Aboriginal people should have the choice to live on their land. A reluctance to migrate is taken as indicative of this choice. To this end, CAEPR supported approaches to unemployment that were local and in which CDEP schemes figured prominently. These were promoted strongly in preference to labour market strategies.[6] When the remote communities debate culminated in the NT Intervention, CAEPR's anthropologists and others seemed disinclined to dwell on social suffering or distress as a part of homelands life. They proposed that the so-called crisis in communities was not one of violence but rather of culture clash or even 'culture wars'.[7] The target of this contention was writers who were seen to merely pathologise Aboriginal communities. At times, this position was supported by a view that what seemed like poverty to outsiders was really a matter of cultural difference.

In sum, I will argue that if the failure of some anti-separatists was to pathologise difference altogether, the failure of those who defended the homelands was reluctance to acknowledge distress and the salience of poverty. In order to underline this issue, the final section of this chapter recounts CAEPR member David Martin's critique of Noel

Pearson's initial stance. Ironically, Martin's critique of Pearson was one of very few CAEPR publications that acknowledged major distress in communities.

A background briefing: Aboriginal unemployment

In 1987, the Hawke government's policy statement on employment equity (AEDP 1986/87) divided the Aboriginal population between 53 per cent residing in 'cities, larger towns and small country towns' with total populations of 1000+; and 47 per cent residing in 'remote areas, small multi racial townships and town camps' (Australia 1987b, 1987c).[8] The criterion for this division was access to a labour market. It was assumed that in areas with a population over 1000 there would be such access, therefore requiring a conventional human capital approach to unemployment. This involved governments providing better education, skills, job-search training and the like, especially to unemployed youth. In rural and remote areas of sparser population, however, no such labour market could be assumed and therefore additional human capital would be unlikely to have much impact on job seekers. In other words, education for high-level English literacy and numeracy had limited returns for employment in areas that lacked a labour market.

The 1990 ASSA workshop supported this position. From various perspectives, writers confirmed that labour market policies in the form of improved education would only have a limited impact in areas where there was little employment of any type. At least three papers presented to the workshop put arguments that education of this form—and, therefore, human capital theory in general—had limited relevance for remote Aboriginal employment (see Jones 1991:37–38; Miller 1991:87; Chapman 1991:138). Gregory proposed that improved education should be seen as necessary but not sufficient to reduce inequality (1991:151). In his discussion of Aboriginal migration, Taylor addressed a second theme that shaped the CAEPR stance. He noted that there was little evidence in the 1970s and 80s to suggest that remote Aboriginal people were engaged in labour migration—out-migration in search of work (Taylor 1991:70–72). Taylor proposed that the approach for remote communities should be community-based and in fact 'migration-inhibiting' (1991:73). Finally, Ron Morony, formerly of DAA and familiar with the early homelands movement in Central Australia, provided an optimistic account of Community Development Employment Projects (CDEP). Although the prospects for achieving full employment were low, the scheme would allow communities 'to define "work"' as they saw fit and contribute to 'social and cultural cohesion' (Morony 1991:105–106).[9]

Therefore, at sites with populations of more than 1000, a human capital approach to unemployment geared to labour markets should prevail. At sites that were remote or very remote, the approach should be community-based. The centrepiece of this latter policy response would be CDEP—federal government supported schemes administered through Aboriginal rather than welfare agencies, providing part-time employment and some infrastructure funds.[10] Jon Altman emphasised the need for this difference between a human capital approach and a community-based one that relied on government. He instanced a group in remote northern Arnhem Land where adults spent on average 3.6 hours each day in subsistence foraging and producing artefacts for sale. Their activities amounted to an average working week of 25 hours per adult or a labour force participation of 100 per cent. In terms of more conventional measures, these Aboriginal people would be deemed unemployed or barely so. In their own terms they were fully occupied. Altman underlined that these types of informal activity went hand in hand with land rights and should be seen as a social, cultural and political phenomenon separate from, and possibly antagonistic to, economic development. He thereby sketched an alternative 'lifestyle' for remote Aboriginal Australians that did not involve conventional employment (Altman 1991:162–163, 165). At a later date, Altman presented an interesting variation on his theme. He argued that fine Aboriginal art was a significant Indigenous industry. The production of this art required a milieu that could sustain something of the cultural sensibility involved in that art's production—at least close engagement with country and with a specific social–ritual milieu. It was this sociocultural context that actually made the art unique and therefore valuable in market terms (Altman 2006:4; Morphy 2005). Once again, though, government support would be required to maintain this milieu. Both these arguments proposed that material wellbeing, as well as a social, ritual and aesthetical wellbeing, depended on a local and separate domain in remote Aboriginal Australia. It is important to note, however, that Altman's proposal was not the standard relativist position derived from Polanyi's work—that for remote Aboriginal people economy is embedded in society and culture (see Polanyi 1944). By virtue of government support, this could not be the case. All remote communities were encapsulated in the state and relied indirectly at least on a capitalist economy.

Altman acknowledged differences between remote communities, though he gave no examples of other types of activity mix, and no estimation of the distribution of communities along a spectrum from the more to the less traditional. Neither did he discuss the actual mix of activity—or expectations—in the community he instanced. Perhaps understandably, his focus was on the cultural difference that other social sciences tend to dismiss or overlook. For this reason, CAEPR's defence of homelands focused on 'choice', an issue underscored by Rowse in his review of CAEPR research (Rowse 2002).

Rowse identified 'a speculative model of Indigenous motivation running through CAEPR writing about education and the labour market'; one that proposed that low school attendance and low rates of labour market participation meant that remote Aboriginal people were not motivated by 'monetary return'. He described this as the phenomenon of exercising choice to live in a culturally different way. Rowse went on to observe, however, that CAEPR research also supported a different account. This second story, Rowse wrote, pointed 'not to Indigenous people's choice but to their vulnerability'. People were 'put upon', rather than simply choosing their position. Their motivation might well be to join the labour force, but they were frustrated by low skill levels and other factors. These other factors included a lack of experience in a workplace with consociates other than kin; and unease with impersonal forms of individual competition (Rowse 2002:54–55, 58; see also Austin-Broos 2006). In addition, Rowse listed racism: the felt indifference or contempt of others on the basis of colour and culture that makes employment unattainable or a workplace more or less demeaning (see also Hunter 2005, 2009a). Rowse proposed that this mix of market, cultural, and structural constraints led remote Aboriginal people to confine their aspirations to the homelands. In this second story, then, a lifestyle choice regarding cultural difference was only part of the picture. This picture also involved common issues of market capacity and social inequality. Nonetheless, Rowse, like Altman, became an advocate for the community-based approach rather than a human capital one. Among CAEPR writers, a position on education relevant to labour markets remained undeveloped (see for instance Schwab 1999, 2005; Fordham and Schwab 2007). The costs of mainstream schooling were underlined, rather than the benefits (see Rowse 2002:59–63). Furthermore, CAEPR writers seemed to reject out-migration—even for the adventurous youth who might choose that path (e.g. Altman 2007a:317).

One could assume, therefore, that CAEPR writers regarded 'inequality' simply as a misinterpretation of cultural difference (Altman and Rowse 2005). On this view, motivations to remain remote were not due to past state intervention or to current government support that provided incentives to stay; neither was the central issue a lack of market capacities. Rather, loyalty to kin, locality, language group and the like were the pre-eminent factors. People *chose* to be remote and within the bounds of a known culture—notwithstanding economic disadvantage.

Yet CAEPR writers did draw attention to one marked inequality in remote Aboriginal life: the massive shortfalls in government servicing, especially as these pertained to the NT government. In response to the Intervention, Taylor wrote:

> [E]ven the largest of remote communities do not have the full range of services and infrastructure, with notable shortfalls in hospitals, primary health care centres, pre-schools, secondary schools, aged accommodation, women's refuges, child care, youth centres and above all, housing. Indeed, if we focus on the category of communities included on the Commonwealth's intervention list . . . we see

that the vast majority are substantially deficient across the entire range of selected services. (Taylor 2007:178)

Signally damning was Taylor's account of the way in which poor school attendance in remote communities condemned those pupils who did attend to funding some 50 per cent below the average spent per capita elsewhere in the Northern Territory (Taylor 2007:178).[11] The implication of these remarks was that inequality does exist in remote Aboriginal life, but equal or more adequate servicing can address the matter. As Noel Pearson noted, the emphasis was on service delivery, not individual capabilities (see Pearson 2000:37–49; also Sen 1993).[12] The CAEPR view seemed to be that the state via the Indigenous sector would hold remote communities in place. As Aboriginal people, individuals would benefit most from this approach. In the remaining sections of this chapter I discuss four notable moments in the defence of the homelands.

Defending the Land Rights Act against the Reeves Report

The Reeves Report raised the issues of inequality and cultural difference in a dramatic way. As Reeves saw it, he was proposing major changes to the Land Rights Act in order to promote greater economic opportunity for remote Aboriginal people. His report elicited a swift response. CAEPR and the Australian Anthropological Society (AAS) moved jointly to convene a conference on the report. Papers presented at the conference were published subsequently by CAEPR as *Land Rights at Risk? Evaluations of the Reeves Report* (Altman et al. 1999). Two issues addressed in the collection were especially pertinent to the remote communities debate: first, the way in which traditional owners were defined in the Act and the way in which Reeves proposed to change that definition; and second, the changes that the Reeves Report proposed to the management of Mining Royalty Equivalents (MRE) paid by mining companies and others via government to Aboriginal people for the use of their land.

One of Reeves's concerns was inequities between Aboriginal people that stemmed from the Land Rights Act. In his view, the Act gave traditional owners too much power to the detriment of other

Aboriginal residents in remote communities. He argued that this was reflected in the fact that the large land councils attended to regional land rights politics but were less responsive to the issues that concerned rank and file who were not traditional owners in the places where they resided. Reeves's response involved collapsing the owner/resident category into one, and breaking up the larger land councils (the NLC and CLC) into eighteen regional groups supervened by a single NT one (see above, Chapter 4). The anthropologists who discussed the issue were Peter Sutton, Howard Morphy and Nicolas Peterson. They focused on the likely effects of the change that Reeves proposed.

Sutton noted that 'Aboriginal tradition usually makes a clear and quite profound distinction between traditional affiliations to countries and residential associations with settlements or districts.' As they intermarry with established owners, immigrants may be granted custodian status in relation to land. Still, they remain an 'interference' in the traditional system (Sutton 1999:41).[13] As such, immigrants are seldom granted equal status on historical grounds alone. Sutton was gesturing towards the fact that even intermarriage generally requires that a former stranger acquire ritual and practical knowledge of a place as well, something that is done over time and with a fair amount of personal effort. In Sutton's view, Reeves's proposals, if instigated, would have brought strong objections from Aboriginal people and marked conflict between them. Regarding regions, Morphy described their numerous dimensions and dynamic nature. He rejected the idea that legislation could collapse ownership and use rights into one category (Morphy 1999:34). Morphy also showed that groupings according to descent could be cut in different ways, for different purposes and at different times, with different names provided. 'The fact that there are [many] groups recognised by different names does not mean that all groups . . . have equivalent rights in a given area of land' (Morphy 1999:35). Morphy granted that with the advent of European settlements, mining royalties and land councils, new dynamics would develop. Moreover, he foreshadowed a time when regional organisations might assume the administrative roles of an ATSIC or the NT government. Nonetheless, his view was that such organisations should emerge rather than being imposed, and that mining royalties should remain the province of the land councils with their commitment to traditional owners (Morphy 1999:37–38).

In these remarks one notes the tension between Reeves's desire to constitute a market individual for the purposes of regional development, and the anthropologists' defence of an Indigenous subject constituted through kin relations and traditional rights in land. There is little doubt that, at the time, the matters about which these anthropologists wrote were important to remote Aboriginal people, and remain so today.

For this reason, Peterson's remarks on the nature of land rights institutions were, and are, significant. He rejected the idea that in selecting forms of institution to administer land rights the sole criterion should be the fit with traditional forms. Peterson observed that land rights institutions inevitably have two roles. One is to replicate traditional forms as closely as possible within the state's own legislation. The other, however, involves representing Aboriginal landed interests to the state and thereby 'facilitating the beneficial consequences expected by the wider community' (Peterson 1999:28). One role addresses past and present cultural difference; the other involves representing Aboriginal people and brokering their relations with an encapsulating state. Peterson's argument provided a basis for a limited Indigenous sector charged with the role of mediator between Aboriginal people and government. Nonetheless, he saw complexities in this situation. He remarked:

> The difficulties that face [anthropology] in making a contribution to [the success of the Land Rights Act] are those that usually face it in contexts of change in the lives of the people it works with. It is frequently conservative, protective of existing arrangements, concerned about what cannot be done as much as about what can be done, supportive of organic development rather than radical change, and lacking in a clear practical vision of what should happen ... These factors can make a coherent position difficult and result in such apparent paradoxes as that of many anthropologists arguing for the recognition of indigenous arrangements that foster inequality while Reeves argues for collective ownership and redistribution.

> On the grounds of fairness, justice and equity, I think there is an apparently good case for community title and regional bodies of the kind proposed by Reeves. This is because it would be a great deal more equitable among people who are all equally poor and disadvantaged if they could all be treated as having exactly the same property rights...
>
> However, in judging whether it is possible to easily ride over the notion of traditional owner, everything we know anthropologically... makes it seem that this is unlikely. (Peterson 1999:29–30)

Peterson implied that a change away from tradition and traditional ownership alone could be desirable in many communities. Nonetheless, he underlined that such change might be more difficult to realise than Reeves thought. The nature of this dilemma was demonstrated further by the CAEPR position on MRE.

John Taylor set the scene with a general remark. He questioned whether or not economists' accounts of disadvantage actually applied to remote Aboriginal people. He instanced common views on locational disadvantage, often seen by economists as a poverty trap, especially for parts of rural Australia. He noted the expansion of homeland sites that had occurred under the Land Rights Act and with DAA and ATSIC support. He also noted the self-respect and local community involvement that this development had brought. What was disadvantage in a non-Aboriginal world might be advantage in an Aboriginal one. What economists saw as inequality and poverty, Taylor saw as cultural difference. Aboriginal subjects, in his view, and contrary to neoliberalism, were not market individuals (Taylor 1999:105–106).

Justice Woodward's initial formula had been that 30 per cent of MRE, mostly from mining, should go to incorporated traditional owners in the affected areas; 40 per cent to land councils for their recurrent costs; and a remaining 30 per cent to an Aboriginal Benefits Trust Account (later called the Aboriginal Benefits Reserve (ABR)). The 30 per cent of royalty funds paid to the ABR was earmarked for 'investment or wider distribution' by NT Aboriginal organisations (see Altman 1983, 1999:111). Some of this investment could be in local initiatives or in enterprise beyond the homelands. At the time of the Reeves Report, 50 per cent of royalty equivalents were used for land council recurrent costs, with ministerial concurrence. The 30 per cent to affected groups was paid to traditional owners, who in turn tended to distribute monies among individuals in the relevant custodian groups. This meant that only 20 per cent of annual total funds could be spent via the ABR on investments for community wellbeing or for financial return either in or beyond the homelands.

Views on whether or not Woodward's formula was appropriate rested in part on whether these monies were seen as private rental income or as public compensation under statutory law. Phrased differently, were royalty monies forms of private income to individuals or were they monies dispensed by government for community development purposes? In effect, Woodward had treated monies as a mix of private income and public compensation. Reeves proposed that *all* such monies should be regarded as public compensation—hence his interest in the defined status of NT traditional owners. If 'owners' were redefined as all Indigenous residents on Aboriginal land, then the divide between private rental income and public compensation would be less marked. Peterson's comment on the 'equally poor' invoked this situation. Virtually all the residents of homeland communities were poor according to criteria that non-Indigenous Australians would use. All required some improvement in their circumstance. In effect, Reeves was asking: Might not this improvement come from universalising traditional owner status, and a changed deployment of the MRE? He proposed his own distribution of royalty equivalents: 29 per cent for land councils' administrations, 20 per cent for investment under the ABR, and 51 per cent 'earmarked for an economic and social advancement program' (Altman 1999:117). The proposal was not a disinterested one. The large reduction in funds for land councils, which in Reeves's view had little left to do, would undermine their power to support the homelands and an Indigenous sector.

Jon Altman and Robert Levitus addressed the issue of MRE paid under the Land Rights Act. They both opposed Reeves's proposal on two grounds: first, that the shift in emphasis from private to public monies involved the use of private Aboriginal income to fund what should be public- (government-) funded services;[14] and second, that the Reeves Report ignored the benefits that came to communities when royalty income underwrote traditional ways—funding sorry camp, attending ceremony and visiting relatives, for instance. In short, and unlike Reeves, CAEPR writers proposed that the maintenance of cultural difference was at least as important as reducing inequality. As Taylor had remarked, what seemed like disadvantage to an outsider was in fact advantage in remote Aboriginal life. Both Altman and Levitus opposed Reeves's proposal that a substantial amount of MRE should be used to promote health, employment, education and the like. Levitus called it 'social engineering' because it took away Aboriginal choice (see Levitus 1999:123, 128).

In sum, Sutton, Morphy and Peterson argued that the culture that defined traditional owners was far too strong to allow that status to be redefined in a way that (a) made it universal for Aboriginal people living on homelands and (b) made the status of traditional owner more compatible with the notion of a market individual. In their professional view, major conflict in communities would result from such a manoeuvre. On behalf of CAEPR, Altman and Levitus argued for a strict separation between land rights–derived royalties and development investment as such. The former were private income and the latter was a responsibility of government. Like Taylor, Altman and Levitus thereby implied that Aboriginal people were not market individuals except perhaps in trivial consumer-oriented ways. By their arguments, all three continued to suggest that locational disadvantage, poor education and the like did not have the same significance in remote communities that they have elsewhere in Australia.

Defending CDEP and the hybrid economy

In 2001, two documents on Australian welfare encouraged CAEPR to convene a large conference on the CDEP for Indigenous Australia. Noel Pearson's *Our Right to Take Responsibility* came in the same year as the federal government's *Participation Support for a More Equitable Society* (2000), also known as the McClure Report. Both emphasised reciprocal relations or 'mutual obligation' between welfare recipients and government. Pearson argued that whether or not Aboriginal communities continued to receive government support, the sense of dependency that came from almost lifelong welfare had to be 'leeched' from communities. The McClure Report was the Australian equivalent of reforms elsewhere and especially in the United States, where, in a period of rapid economic growth, the emphasis was switched from unemployment income support to income assistance for those who worked in poorly paid jobs. The *Personal Responsibility and Work Opportunity Reconciliation Act of 1996* was introduced in the latter part of President Clinton's first term (see Harris 2005:84). Although public spending on the poor did not decrease, various US state governments reported sharp declines in the number of their welfare recipients. This period of heightened optimism regarding free markets and the private sector brought a moral tenor to the debate, linked with neoliberalism: any individual could get off welfare if he or she so wished, and to do so was in the individual's interests. In addition, the view was that if people remain dependent on the state by virtue of being welfare recipients, they should do something in return. In short, 'mutual responsibility' should be encouraged. In comparison with the US measures, the McClure Report was a tempered document. Notwithstanding, it carried a distinctive message of 'self-sufficiency, paying your dues, and team effort' meant to promote responsibility among the unemployed (see Harris 2000; see also Altman 2001).

Ironically, CDEP had its beginning in a notion of reciprocity comparable to that implied by 'mutual obligation'. With the advent of unemployment benefits in the 1970s, Aboriginal elders had asked for local employment schemes that would involve more than 'sit down money' for their youth (see Sanders and Morphy 2001:1). Notwithstanding, criticism of CDEP as a mere welfare measure soon gathered force in the media and among some organisations including the newly formed Bennelong Society. The criticism concerned issues that the elders may not have been able to predict. The scheme involved many participants who were confined to part-time, low-waged and often unskilled work indefinitely. Moreover, 'no work, no pay' rules varied in success from site to site, especially where remoteness was a factor. Proper supervision of far-flung projects involved issues of training, authority and cost. In a remote environment, the temptation, especially among youth, was therefore to treat CDEP payments as if they were a welfare payment with no reciprocity involved (see Austin-Broos 2001, 2009:150–151, 236–237). These conditions were signalled by the fact that very few participants actually passed from CDEP to full-time waged employment (see Shergold 2001; Gregory 2005).

In Pearson's view, the welfare-like impact of CDEP was also signalled by the demoralisation, substance abuse, illness and violence that burgeoned in remote communities (see also Brady 2004). He developed his position in subsequent writing on the 'welfare pedestal' (Pearson 2009b:282–291). As noted in Chapter 4, Pearson's point concerned two events: the rise in Aboriginal incomes from a low base that social services had brought, and the decline in full-time rural work that had affected remote communities (Peterson 1985, 1998; see also Gregory and Daly 1997). An outcome that Peterson had described in 1985 as disengagement from market society had, in Pearson's eyes, become the pathology of substance abuse and consequent social suffering. Men in particular drank because they were unemployed and bereft of authority frameworks. The issue was not so much cultural difference but rather disadvantage.

The implication of the emerging policy position was that CDEP and other community-based schemes should be deemed successful only if they brought full-time jobs or were the conduit to full-time employment in a community or elsewhere. The position overruled the idea that a community-based approach was sufficient for remote communities. Notwithstanding, it was Altman's view that the dearth of employment in remote communities meant that federal government support was the only realistic response to a daunting issue. The CAEPR conference on CDEP produced an edited collection (Morphy and Sanders 2001). I consider the contributions of four CAEPR personnel: Sanders, Taylor and Hunter, and Altman.

Sanders noted the scheme's success in terms of its expansion across a period of twenty years. He also noted that, according to the 1997 Spicer Report on the scheme, one-third of all participants were not working (Sanders 2001:49). The issue was not simply supervision.

In the late 1980s an 'all in/all out' provision had been tried whereby communities could have CDEP or unemployment benefits but not both. In many places where CDEP was introduced, there was simply insufficient work for participants. The provision was discontinued though it took some time to shift inactive participants off CDEP and onto unemployment benefits again. In this context, Sanders addressed the workfare/welfare policy divide (Sanders 1993, 1997, 2001:47–48). He traced the way in which a policy had begun as a specifically Indigenous workfare one and was now being absorbed into a different and more general domain of social security. As a consequence, he noted, CDEP was becoming more work-focused but also turning more unemployed towards conventional welfare payments (Sanders 2001:50). His remarks suggested that the scheme was already in decline as ATSIC's centrepiece.

Taylor and Hunter went to demography. They pointed to the disastrous impact on Indigenous unemployment figures were the CDEP to be stopped, or participants reclassified as unemployed (Taylor and Hunter 2001:98–99). If discouraged Aboriginal workers were counted as well, the figures would be even more embarrassing politically. They recommended CDEP as the *least worst option* in many remote and regional areas where 'the scheme is the only source of employment and, in the absence of mass migration to more developed labour markets, there is little alternative for increasing the economic activity of local Indigenous residents' (Taylor and Hunter 2001:104).

Altman endorsed the views of Taylor and Hunter concerning remote Indigenous unemployment. He also observed that a reason why CDEP, as an arm of ATSIC, had grown so rapidly in remote communities was that it provided *some* employment and also some administrative experience in a context of limited alternatives. He noted that the McClure Report promoted local government 'partnerships' of the small business type and yet lacked an account of protocols for implementation (Altman 2001:128). With reference to Noel Pearson's proposals, he sounded a note of caution concerning the ability of communities to link readily with the mainstream economy. Altman wrote:

> When opportunities arise in mining, tourism, or cultural industries, where Indigenous people may have special leverage based on land rights or native title, or a clear competitive advantage, these should be grasped. But so often such opportunities are forgone because of political complexities at the community level, or an absence of appropriate development agencies, or for cultural reasons [of a distinctively Aboriginal kin-based kind]. (Altman 2001:129)

Notwithstanding, Altman concluded that 'the crucial objective of the CDEP scheme' should be to improve the economic status of those involved. Increasingly, he emphasised its economic role rather than a political or diffuse sociocultural one.

In the years that followed this collection, Altman developed his ideas using a notion of the 'hybrid economy' (Altman 2005, 2006). Increasingly, he also included some labour market strategies in his community-based approach. Possibly, this shift was influenced by the demise of ATSIC in 2004, and the absorption of CDEP into the mainstream bureaucracy. Altman's notion of the hybrid economy underlined a crucial point: that remote Aboriginal people could participate in market transactions and receive government support without undermining their right to choose a lifestyle that involved cultural difference and an attachment to tradition. This hybrid economy would consist of customary, private (or market) and public (or CDEP) sectors that overlapped at many points. He instanced many forms of activity that involved elements of all three sectors. These included CDEP support for wildlife harvesting, the products of which participants consumed; direct exchange of regionally produced goods and services; and subsidised employment in local small businesses. The paradigm of these hybrid activities was the production and sale of fine Aboriginal art with 'state, market and customary' inputs. Altman stressed that these forms of hybrid activity could be flexible between regions and invite various forms of regional and government partnership. The industries he emphasised most included wildlife harvesting, fine Aboriginal art and natural resource management. The latter included care of national parks, coastlines and at-risk environments both on and off Aboriginal land. Altman also raised the issue of national security. Was it wise for Arnhem Land, Cape

York and the Kimberley to become less populated (see also Dillon and Westbury 2007:30–49)?

In short, Altman's idea of the hybrid economy focused on regionally specific activities that he hoped would allow at least some Aboriginal people to be employed and remain on their land. He also sounded a cautious note:

> [B]ecause the hybrid economy sits within kinship dominated societies, it remains an economic form that generates limited material accumulation and little long-term saving and investment in conventional terms—it is at odds with the ideology of the market-based dominant society. This... feature is also structural as in many situations the mix of inalienable land and community housing undermines incentives and opportunities to materially accumulate, although some individuals do manage. (Altman 2005:125)

Altman here acknowledged that, in remote communities, the weakness of some market institutions—private property, individual saving and investment—had an impact on the growth of local economies. Cultural difference and the weakness of these institutions combined to maintain forms of value at odds with a desire for the personal accumulation that propels many other Australians out to work for increasing wages.

These essays show some movement on policy matters. Sanders acknowledged that, whatever the initial aims of CDEP, the scheme was being pulled towards social security and welfare and away from a workfare role. Notwithstanding, Taylor and Hunter argued that the scheme remained the best worst option for Aboriginal people who had no desire to migrate for work and often lacked appropriate skills for that course in any case. Altman focused on forms of hybrid employment for remote and very remote communities. All acknowledged either explicitly or implicitly that community-based development also needed some engagement with labour market strategies. Yet consideration of those strategies was limited.

Come the Northern Territory Intervention

Debate about these matters was fast and furious in the mid-2000s. In some anthropological circles, it was proposed that while economists (at their best) were concerned about disadvantage, anthropologists were focused on cultural difference (cf. Austin-Broos 2005 and Altman and Rowse 2005).[15] It was proposed that so-called statistical equality was not necessarily good or compatible with cultural difference (Altman and Sanders 1991). Labour market approaches, including education for human (market) capital, were identified with the push for statistical equality. Community-based approaches with their hybrid industries were identified with defence of the homelands. And while one side frequently pathologised communities, the other—in defence of cultural difference—tended to look beyond what was seen as a pseudo-crisis. The release of the NT *Little Children are Sacred* report in the run-up to a federal election short-circuited this debate and was used by the Howard government to trigger the NT Intervention on 16 June 2007 (see Wild and Anderson 2007).

A state of emergency was declared, troops were sent into more than 60 communities, health checks on children were proposed, and new policy was foreshadowed. Initial legislation came in the form of a Northern Territory National Emergency Response Bill (2007) and two ancillary bills that dealt with social security and family and community services. In addition, the Racial Discrimination Act was suspended in order to facilitate income management (quarantining) only of NT Aboriginal welfare recipients. New directions in schooling were declared, including greater emphasis on English literacy. Later, CDEP was dismantled. Proposals for new forms of leasehold on the homelands were canvassed. The latter were intended to facilitate the construction of public housing that also might become transactable as private property at a later stage. Under a new federal Labor government, a suite of policies was styled as 'closing the gap in life expectancy and life opportunities' for Indigenous Australians. The NT government's partner initiative was 'Working Futures'. It revolved around new forms of shire administration and the designation of twenty Territory Growth Towns (TGT) that would become service hubs for the homelands. The NT government announced that no new housing would be constructed outside these towns, which were also seen as the sole sites for major health and schooling initiatives.

These facts underline that the NT Intervention and the remote communities debate are not simply the same thing. The Intervention was a major event *in the course of* the remote communities debate. The debate, however, long preceded the Intervention. Equally, the human rights violations that were part of the Intervention did not necessarily entail that all subsequent policy changes would be wrong. What is clear is that the pathologising of communities involved in the Intervention completed the work of some opinion writers. It created moral certainty in the public domain that some anti-separatists hoped would bring quite radical change. In this, the neoliberals at least would be disappointed. Moreover, the issues of inequality and cultural difference that shaped the debate before the Intervention continue to bear on the debate today.

Coercive Reconciliation (2007) reflected these cross-cutting issues. The collection was published as a critical response to the Intervention and edited by Melinda Hinkson and Jon Altman, both anthropologists and, at the time, members of CAEPR. The collection has two striking characteristics. All writers were critical of the suspension of the *Racial Discrimination Act 1975*. Yet, while contributors to the collection placed the greater emphasis on poverty and suffering, the editors placed it on cultural difference. Here are some representative comments from contributors to the volume:

On issues of inequality and distress:

> Research and reports into the high instance of violence and abuse in some Aboriginal communities consistently point to the fact that cyclical and chronic poverty, including poor health and poor living conditions, contribute to the breakdown of the social fabric in communities.
>
> Larissa Behrendt 2007:17. Professor of Law and Director of Research, Jumbunna Indigenous House of Learning, University of Technology, Sydney

There is little doubt that a set of major problems arose in Indigenous communities in the 1980s and 1990s ... factors [included] state under-investment and the difficulty of communities stuck between older cultural frameworks and new ones.

Guy Rundle 2007:40. Arena Publications editor

In the Northern Territory there has been a 125 per cent increase in [child protection] orders since 2001–2002 and the orders covering Aboriginal children in the Northern Territory since that time have increased 140 per cent ... The *Little Children are Sacred* report notes that:

> A lack of adequate family support infrastructure across most of the Territory to which FACS [Family and Community Support] could refer families identified as maltreating their child for assistance and support has meant that workers are left with little alternative in dealing with serious maltreatment cases but to place the child in out of home care.

It also found that Aboriginal children make up the majority of cases dealt with by FACS.

Mick Dodson 2007:93. Director of the ANU's National Centre for Indigenous Studies

The combined effects of poor health, alcohol and drug abuse, unemployment, gambling, pornography, poor education and housing, and a general loss of identity and control have contributed to violence and sexual abuse in many forms.

Existing government programs intended to help Aboriginal people break the cycle of poverty and violence need to work better ...

Alcohol remains the gravest and fastest growing threat to the safety of Aboriginal children ... Alcohol is destroying communities.

Rex Wild 2007:113, 115. Co-author of the *Little Children are Sacred* report

On issues of governance pertaining to distress in remote Aboriginal communities:

[A]part from numerous reports detailing the rising incidence of child abuse and neglect, the violence, suicides and suicide attempts, the juvenile offending and incarceration rates, the health statistics, the housing statistics, the unemployment rates, the lack of education achievement—all indicators of people in crisis—when I have spoken to ministers of the Crown, I have been brushed aside. From Robert Tickner (1990): 'I know the problems—you tell me the solutions', to Tony Abbott's office (2005): 'We know these problems—you don't have to keep describing them like this—can't your people just get over it?' I have to assume they knew all along.

> Judy Atkinson 2007: 152. Head of the College of Indigenous Australian Peoples, Southern Cross University

If the situation of young Aboriginal people and their families in Central Australia is to be described as a national emergency, it is one created in part by decades of inconsistent, incompetent and reactive government policy.

> Tristan Ray 2007:195. Coordinator of the Central Australian Youth Link-Up Service

And finally, on economics and governance:

There are numerous major barriers to commercial development [in Central Australia]. They include the remoteness of communities, which means high transport costs for getting goods from communities to markets. Communities' small populations also represent a limited market. All Aboriginal populations in Central Australia have populations of less than 1000. In thirty years there have only been two applications for leases for commercial operations within a community—both community stores. There are very few small business operations in remote communities, irrespective of the community's form of land tenure.

Another issue is the lack of a skilled, or even semi-skilled, labour force, due to low levels of literacy and numeracy. With such low levels of education, Aboriginal people are extremely limited in their ability to participate in the mainstream economy. Finally, remote areas lack the infrastructure needed to conduct business. Most communities have poor roads, and access to telecommunications is seriously limited. Both roads and effective communications are regarded as essential for most business. The CLC is concerned that the Australian Government is focusing on the permit system when the real barriers to Aboriginal engagement with the mainstream economy are ignored.

David Ross 2007:242. Director, Central Land Council,
Alice Springs, NT.

The introduction and the conclusion to the collection, written by Hinkson and Altman respectively, faulted the Intervention for its violations of human rights. The many humiliating restrictions that have come with income quarantining amply justify this stance (see Hinkson 2007:1–5). As retired HREOC commissioner Tom Calma remarked, it is an index of Indigenous standing in Australia that human rights were violated extensively as the proposed route to greater equality.[16] The push for government leasehold over Aboriginal land presented a like concern. Notwithstanding the need for flexibility if there is to be small business development and house ownership in towns on Aboriginal land, the tone of the initial discussions was confronting and sometimes bullying. Matters were exacerbated by the Coalition's record as a government keen to limit land rights and native title. Contributor to the collection David Dalrymple (2007) pointed out that the Land Rights Act in fact has its own section 19 that 'allows for long-term leasing'. Dillon and Westbury also have presented a detailed discussion of the land lease options for remote townships which allow a case-by-case approach (see Dillon and Westbury 2007:120–154, especially 149).

Yet Hinkson's introduction went beyond these issues to focus on difference. She remarked that 'this intervention is about much more than *fixing* existing conditions. At the heart of the government's coercive approach lies a clear intent: to bring to an end the recognition of, and support for, Aboriginal people living in remote communities pursuing culturally distinctive ways of life.' She elaborated: '[T]he NT intervention is aimed at nothing short of the production of a newly oriented, "normalised" Aboriginal population, one whose concerns with custom, kin and land will give way to the individualistic aspirations of private home ownership, career and self-improvement'; and concluded with a question: '[Will the Indigenous future] be one where "normalised" individuals pursue the questionable "equality" of neo-liberalism, or one in which cultural difference is genuinely valued and supported?' (Hinkson 2007:5–6, 11). With these remarks, Hinkson reduced the issue of disadvantage to a neoliberal agenda. Worse, some basic issues of equality were represented as quite incompatible with cultural difference. Does one need to eschew, for instance, the pursuit of English literacy, stable employment, and owning a house in order to remain culturally different in Australia? Clearly, many of Hinkson's contributors did not think so; nor would prominent Aboriginal leaders who reside in remote Australia.

Altman concluded the collection. His essay opened with a similar statement that the Intervention was driven by a 'radical plan ... to transform kin-based societies into market-based ones' (Altman 2007:307). Thereafter his remarks were more tempered. He proposed that the federal government, encouraged by Noel Pearson, Helen Hughes and others, had grasped at immediate and convenient explanations for community distress—welfare, grog and land rights—in order to avoid 'the true extent of the historical legacy and challenges of cultural difference' (Altman 2007:308). Pathology had triumphed over structural and cultural issues as the central ones in communities. He observed that, in the process, a 'conspicuous compassion' towards 'the child' had been matched with a 'conspicuous contempt for economic and cultural difference' (Altman 2007:312). Later, Altman elaborated. He proposed that economic 'sameness' and 'difference' are each acceptable conditions, provided that people choose them (Altman 2008a:279–280). He seemed to imply that Aboriginal people, in choosing 'economic difference', would choose a kin-based society over market entanglements. But would they also choose the adverse effects of enduring disadvantage in the larger society, among them lifestyle illness and substance abuse? Notwithstanding the heat of the moment, Altman's position was a simplification—a reduction of disadvantage simply to difference.

Defending the Indigenous sector against Noel Pearson

Rather than an overview for this chapter, I provide a coda. I have noted both here and in my introduction the respective failures of protagonists in the remote communities debate. While some anti-separatists rendered difference entirely in terms of pathology, some of those who defended the homelands were unwilling to acknowledge the distress in remote communities and the salience of poverty. Nothing underlines this situation more than the collection just discussed. In the writing of the anthropologists concerned, issues of rights—quite legitimate in themselves—entirely overshadowed issues of poverty and distress and the real policy dilemmas involved in addressing economic marginalisation. In *Coercive Reconciliation*, only non-anthropologists seemed to be clear that these latter factors were also an integral part of the circumstance that brought the NT Intervention.[17] Possibly it is unreasonable to ask that commissioned writing on policy issues should canvas social suffering. CAEPR was first and foremost a policy and consultancy group, not a department of social critics. Still, the fact of remote community distress was a background to CAEPR's work. It gave additional import to the view that major employment growth would be incompatible with the maintenance of cultural difference. One cannot but be uneasy about a tendency not to note the full cost of this policy position as well as its benefits. So far, this cost has included poverty and the experience of widespread, serious lifestyle disease.

Anger in response to this position may have led Noel Pearson into an alliance with those on the right who portrayed remote conditions in terms of the pathology of welfare dependency. As I have indicated in my discussion of Pearson's initial position, his focus was actually on marginalisation, ways to address it, and on the constraints involved in such a process. To restate those constraints: a range of cultural and other institutional factors make migration unattractive as a solution to marginalisation for remote Aboriginal Australians. At the same time, government-aided development in the homelands will always be less than required (it seems) to provide adequate employment, especially for the young. Pearson therefore argued for a community response with a social–moral component aimed at addressing how a condition akin to almost lifelong welfare might be reconstituted in ways that are more constructive for communities. Lacking recourse to a structural solution for a 'wicked problem', Pearson increasingly placed the emphasis on self-help as a response to a psychologised state of 'welfare dependency'.[18] When CAEPR's David Martin criticised Noel Pearson, the issue of community distress finally came to the fore in a publication by a CAEPR member. Like Peter Sutton, Martin placed the emphasis on cultural pathology as a counter to Pearson's ostensible focus on welfare dependency. One form of psychologised pathology was traded for another: the cultural as opposed to the so-called economic.

Three strands of Martin's critique are of particular interest (see Martin 2001). First, Martin contested Pearson's view that welfare dependency lies at the heart of the problems in remote Aboriginal communities. In an ironic twist, however, Martin did not criticise Pearson for reducing structural issues to mere psychologising, as one would normally expect in this type of critique (see Fraser 1999a). Rather, Martin described cultural factors that, in his view, made this dependency unremarkable within Aboriginal communities. Martin invoked a form of traditional Aboriginal relationship in which authority relations were rendered as nurturance. An older generation might 'look after' a younger one and in the process elicit services. Power and authority were camouflaged as 'help' that should be reciprocated by the young (see Myers 1986:210–218; Dussart 2000:85–97). In a resource-rich and socially dense environment this form of practice becomes demand sharing—the use of demands on one relative by another as a way of establishing the strength of their relatedness. In this case, the junior partner can demand of the senior one (see Peterson 1978, 1993, 1997).[19] Martin argued that, from the perspective of Aboriginal people, dependence on welfare may seem similar to making a demand of kin. On this view, government becomes the equivalent of a powerful relative. Moreover, such dependence can be read as a successful adaptation to encapsulation by the state. Individuals accept what's on offer and turn their attention to their own priorities—ceremony, perhaps, or camping on country. Although Martin does not cite A.P. Elkin, for this argument he might have (Elkin 1951).[20] Martin concluded that there is no crisis of dependency or of a specific *welfare* dependency in remote Aboriginal communities (Martin 2001:6–11). *Eo ipso,* community distress is not produced either by welfare dependency or its major causes.

A second strand of Martin's critique concerned issues of governance.[21] He questioned Pearson's notion of a regional 'interface' for community administration. Pearson had proposed that this structure should involve a statutory regional Indigenous authority as well as sub-regional, community, and family levels of governance. His intent was to bring the locus of policy formulation closer to the coalface of community life (Pearson 2000:67–82; CYI 2007:27–31). Martin's argument against this structure resembled that employed by anthropologist-critics of the Reeves Report: that regional authorities and their subgroups would be more prone to local family conflicts than an umbrella organisation—be it ATSIC or a large land council. In this argument, Martin privileged the established and expanding Indigenous sector as the agent of development (Martin 2001:5, 13–16). Moreover, like Rowse he suggested that CDEP was a matter of politics as much as economics; a vehicle for pursuing local autonomy and separate development. He chided Pearson for his focus on economics and lack of attention to an Indigenous politics (Martin 2001:19). Yet Martin failed to grasp another form of politics. Pearson had argued that in conjunction with the proliferation of service organisations, an artificial 'gammon' economy left remote Aboriginal people ostensibly receiving money for very little and being comprehensively directed by whites. His description and critique of a neo-colonial position—also disturbing for Nakata, writing of the Torres Strait—seemed to pass Martin by.[22]

Pearson's *Responsibility* statement was a general one, although its touchstone was Cape York communities in Queensland. Martin's doctoral research was in Aurukun on the Cape York Peninsula, where he had also worked in community administration. The third strand of his critique called on this experience. Martin proposed that Pearson's reliance on self-help or voluntarism as a response to community distress was unrealistic. In Martin's view, the communities in question were in fact too dysfunctional to 'take responsibility' for themselves. Martin wrote:

> [T]he difficulty in locating centres of moral authority within contemporary Aboriginal societies must not be underestimated. Attempts to institute the 'community', the 'family', or other such social units of Aboriginal society as sources of moral authority or suasion for the purposes of implementing welfare policy are likely to be ineffectual, or even actively resisted. There is a parallel difficulty in locating clear centres of political authority in these essentially acephalous societies. (Martin 2001:17)

Martin referred to the 'social devastation' in locales that Pearson and others were writing about. Old kinship structures had been severely weakened, along with traditional authority relations. New institutions either had a tenuous hold or often were ignored.[23] His counsel was that conditions in these communities required more and better governance: '[T]he fractured nature of the contemporary Indigenous polity [suggests] that government may need to be involved as "partners" at a far more intimate and hands-on level than Pearson envisages, including assisting with the development of new Indigenous governance institutions and facilitating capacity-building within those institutional arrangements' (Martin 2001:19).

Martin's critique of Pearson revolved around the view that, whatever the distress in communities, it should not be ascribed to welfare *per se* or to the forms of government support, such as CDEP, that the opinion writers likened to welfare. Dependency was not, in fact, an Aboriginal problem. Martin argued that the situation of community distress was intractable nonetheless. Violence, substance abuse and exploitation had become the norm in communities. Rather than marginalisation or conflicting forms of value, the cause that Martin underlined was traditional mores corrupted by current conditions. In his view, the sources of distress were as much traditional as modern and, to the degree that these traditional cultural factors specified an Aboriginal circumstance, they were in fact the crucial ones (see also Martin 2008). Aurukun was a research site for both Martin and Peter Sutton. In their writings they referenced each other and proposed that Pearson's lack of knowledge of tradition prevented an adequate analysis (see Sutton 2001:134–135, 2009:64–65 and Martin 2001:6–11, 2008). Both Martin and Sutton in turn were influenced by David McKnight's account of indigenous tradition collapsing under the burden of alcohol abuse on Mornington Island (McKnight 2002). Others have called this group 'the Queensland school'.[24] Characteristic of this school has been a stress on cultural pathology to counter explanations in terms of welfare dependency (see Austin-Broos 2010b). Where Sutton proposed that the issues were alcohol and collapse of old-style mission structures, Martin allowed the significance of economic marginalisation but nonetheless sought its remedy in the established Indigenous sector. Martin's solution was 'a far more intimate and hands-on' governance such as the Indigenous sector was already providing. Where Pearson saw this type of governance as part of the problem, Martin saw it as part of the solution. In their public statements Pearson, the opinion writers and the Queensland school too often reduced the issues in communities to psychologised pathologies.

In subsequent years, Pearson's Cape York Institute would come to rival CAEPR for influence and support in some government circles. David Martin left CAEPR in 2006. In 2009 he made this remark about remote community distress: 'I am convinced that our ... collective (anthropological) failure ... has played its part in creating ... sensationalized representation ... We KNEW what was happening ... but in our complicity with and subtle enforcement of the code of silence, we left the space of analysis of many of the realities of Aboriginal life vacated ... and it has been colonized by the likes of the journalists and conservative[s]' (cited in Austin-Broos 2010a:136). In Chapter 6 I draw the threads of this debate together, and then integrate the major themes of the book.

6

The politics of difference and equality

> We now know that narratives are made of silences, not all of which are deliberate or even perceptible as such within the time of their production.
>
> Michel-Rolph Trouillot, *Silencing the Past: Power and the production of history*

> [With regard to Aboriginal Australians]
> Cultural values and modes, whether originating before conquest or formed under conditions of ... exclusion cannot be cancelled by decree; moreover, the expropriation and marginalization, which are the common outcomes of colonization, have produced a [disturbing] level of poverty and deprivation.
>
> Jeremy Beckett, Aboriginality, Citizenship and Nation State

For almost two decades, the position of many anthropologists has been that determined reformers should look twice at traditional homeland communities: these remote Aboriginal Australians may sustain an order of value quite different from that of market society. Government policy and resources therefore should be used to safeguard these communities as such, rather than to make them into something else. This position raises the question: is the anthropologists' contention accurate? Is it an accurate description of all or even most remote Aboriginal communities or does it entail a reified account of culture shaped by classical ethnography? Evidence cited for the anthropologists' position includes Aboriginal people's reluctance to migrate from their homelands, and the flowering of fine Aboriginal art.[1] The latter confirms a sensibility that differs from that of other Australians. The former testifies to the importance that this sensibility accords to land rights and living remote. Moreover, remote elders often display knowledge, an aesthetic, and a delicacy of spirit that shouts an 'other' history of human experience. The evidence against the anthropologists' position is the suffering incurred by high mortality rates caused by lifestyle illness including diabetes, alcohol dependence, malnutrition, ischaemic heart disease, stroke and hypertension, respiratory infection, and kidney and liver disease.[2] This epidemiology, in conjunction with personal violence and abuse, speaks to conflicting values in communities rather than simply to an 'other' culture. Aboriginal people living on homelands are struggling with different ways of being that are in substantial conflict. Moreover, part of their distress is the product of poverty, experienced as such, and not simply the product of inferior services (see Austin-Broos 2010a).

I write this final chapter on the side of cultural difference but not the cultural difference evoked by a reified notion of tradition. Rather, the difference I have in mind is more like a conundrum: intimate conflicts within communities and individuals that reflect different histories and forms of tradition. What these communities have in common is the reproduction of cultural difference in the context of marked inequality. The interlinked histories of this form of cultural difference reveal the ways in which law and economy, the state and capitalism, have shaped and sometimes torn apart the attempt at continuity. The difference I am interested in is specified by the experience of remote encapsulated groups. That difference is not mere tradition. Neither is it pathology. Rather, it involves a range of highly specified cultures of marginalisation within a larger and more powerful society. Moreover, these are cultures that are seldom internally consistent. They harbour antagonistic institutional forms that are not aligned easily. This circumstance is reflected in conflicting orientations among individuals. The frustration that this conflict brings also contributes to violence and lifestyle disease. To respond effectively to the issues raised by these communities the nature of their making must be addressed along with their current complexity.

In the remote communities debate, a position that rendered cultural difference as bounded and reified—kin-based versus market-based society—also locked its adherents into a policy position that resisted labour market strategies, including mainstream education. Rather, the proposal was that community-based strategies alone could suffice for remote communities. Once committed to this position, as Martin has suggested, too many anthropologists overlooked the social suffering in communities; not only the violence and abuse but also the lifestyle disease that kills far too many Aboriginal people. Nonetheless, these communities *are* different by virtue of histories that stretch well beyond the advent of the Aboriginal Land Rights Act and beyond European invasion. The land rights legislation was significant because it provided homelands with legal standing within the state. Yet this standing is at odds with other institutions central to capitalism and its market society. The upshot has been that conflicts of value within communities and within the Aboriginal subject have also become a policy conundrum.[3] If anthropologists reified communities, anti-separatists sought to avoid this conundrum by a focus on welfare dependency and the pathologies of marginalisation. Their solution for remote communities has been a 'conformist' one that takes virtually no account of cultural difference.[4] In response to their position, some anthropologists have argued that the matter of pathology is not simply economic but cultural as well—wading further into the mire of one-sided recrimination. Each of these positions, for or against homelands life, has had its silences. Such is the challenge that the past has bequeathed to the present.

In this final chapter, I assess the remote communities debate. Then I return to the postcolonial critique and remark on the ways in which this critique bears on the more specific debate about remote communities. I note the implications of these two debates for anthropology and for the other humanistic social sciences. Opening the lens further still, I discuss the need to reconcile the politics of cultural difference and equality. To this end I focus on the issue of primary education in remote communities. Surprising as it may seem to some, I argue that this focus can and should constitute a radical politics both of difference and equality. Finally, I return to Mathew's story.

The failure of a debate

Unfortunately the remote communities debate was polarised very quickly. One form of polarisation came from the opinion writers and involved their pathologising of communities. Under the descriptions of communities that they gave, no member of the Australian public could do less than wish for rapid and wholesale change. Altman was quite right to propose that conspicuous compassion for the child was matched by a conspicuous contempt for cultural difference. As pathology became the new savagery, moral certainty was produced.

Yet recently Noel Pearson has shown the elusive nature of this certainty (see Pearson 2010b, 2010c). An opinion piece in *The Australian* underlined 'three key articles of liberal philosophy: self-interest, choice and private property'. Pearson wrote that 'The main actor in development is the individual. The main actor in the development story is not the government.' He argued that when governments did not understand this fact, they ended by 'thwarting and undermining the very development they claimed to be seeking'. In this reprint of an address to the CIS, Pearson attributed these ideas to Adam Smith. In his column for the following week, Pearson cited Johann Gottfried Herder and discussed his ideas on different forms of human cultivation (*Bildung*). Herder's formulations are direct antecedents of the modern, plural culture concept (see Darcy 1987:6–10). Taking up the matter of culture, Pearson remarked that although he did not resile from his CIS address and its universalism, there was something that 'Australian conservatives' did not understand—the culture involved in Aboriginal conservatism. He wrote:

> Aboriginal Australian traditional culture is evidence that when human behaviour is at an equilibrium, people build structures of tradition tied to language and land and pass these traditions on to the next generation . . . conservatism is the idea that distinct groups of people should continue to exist because deep difference . . . is an

> end in itself... The homogenisation inherent in liberalism and social democracy is risky because it robs us of many possible attempts to answer the unsolvable existential enigmas...
>
> Self-interest is the engine that drives the vehicle of social and economic progress. But tradition is the engine that drives the human will to exist. Conservatism makes the case for continued existence in a deep sense.

In the course of this second column Pearson was careful to underline that his defence of tradition, and especially Aboriginal languages, should not be taken as a defence of 'separate development' or 'multicultural diversity'. His concern was 'different worlds' and 'deep difference' that would nonetheless change with time.[5] Yet Pearson's pieces juxtapose the notions of a market individual and a traditional Aboriginal subject, ones that others also struggle to reconcile—including the residents of remote communities themselves. Indeed, the difficulty of this task goes to the heart of the remote communities debate.

The tensions involved in sustaining difference while pursuing economic equality explain why neoliberal policies actually failed to prevail following the NT Intervention (cf. Johns 2008). Helen Hughes proposed a developmental strategy popular in the Pacific region: free the land from traditional tenure, in this case via repeal of the Land Rights Act. From this reform would follow both an elaboration of private property, and competition between individuals and small businesses. Others demurred, even on the right. They argued that such a change would not have the desired effects in remote Australia, with its tiny populations and low income levels. Even small businesses would struggle to survive, and traditional owners would object in any case (see McDonnell 2005:32–33; see also Johns 2009:10). The repeal of land rights is no longer canvassed in most quarters. As Dillon and Westbury (2007:149) indicate, more targeted leaseholds have become the federal government policy preference.

More recently, Hughes has underlined education and promoted private rather than public initiatives in both primary and secondary schooling. Yet if the *major* engine of educational reform is to be philanthropy, Hughes fails to offer an appropriate strategy of private/

public sector initiatives that would work for the Territory. She offers no time frame for her policies and no suggestions for a scheme—other than welfare payments—that will bridge the period in which education is improved, lease negotiations are completed, and foreshadowed small business employment takes off. Moreover, Hughes has discarded or at least soft-pedalled her initial claim that major change could be wrought in communities without additional cost to governments—and yet she remains implacably opposed to increased public expenditure (Hughes and Warin 2005).[6] This denial of the state's real responsibilities ends in its own inconsistencies.

Gary Johns also lacks a time frame for his 'one big idea' of migration to core centres, now called Territory Growth Towns (TGT), and then to much larger centres of population in regional and urban Australia. Therefore he conveniently ignores the growth of an explosive situation in TGT as Aboriginal people are thrown more than usually together, on unemployment benefits, and with inadequate housing because, as Johns proposes, 'no job, no house'.[7] Better services in education and health can be and should be focused in these towns. However, this does not mean that outstations on homelands should be closed down (or given over to meagre Territory government support). For the foreseeable future, people need and want forms of retreat from the intensity of towns and the trouble and the stress it brings. This is a matter of addressing cultural difference in order to move towards equality of services. Such a move is no small matter and I shall return to it. Beyond these issues, how Johns would encourage the Aboriginal population of Central Australia, for instance, down to Port Augusta from Alice Springs remains unclear. There has been an intergenerational trickle in that direction for some time. How one would increase it, and to what specific end, are questions that require detailed answers. In the absence of such answers from the neoliberals Hughes and Johns, pathology filled the void. Worse, an Australian public was sufficiently indifferent not to notice that the issue of culture had been hijacked by pathology in league with idealised market solutions (see also Sanders 2008).

There was another source of polarisation—the reified idea of cultural difference that CAEPR writers and some other anthropologists have tended to sustain throughout the debate. In terms of policy debate, this reification was reflected in the strong preference for community-based employment programs as opposed to labour market ones, and the proposal (reinforced by other social scientists in the early 1990s) that issues of human capital did not bear significantly on communities where there were 'no labour markets'. Therefore the issue of English literacy and numeracy slipped off the agenda. This bifurcation of policy, made plausible by the proposal that all or most Aboriginal people *commonly* hunted and foraged, carried two implications. One was that many remote Aboriginal communities did retain a fairly traditional economic base into the last decade of the 20th century. The other implication was that the variation between remote communities in different regions of northern and Central Australia was fairly negligible on this count. Neither of these implications bears scrutiny.

This reification of tradition was accompanied by a proposal, supported strongly by Taylor, Altman and Rowse, that remote Aboriginal people could 'choose' their course—either along an indigenous route, or along one prescribed by market institutions. The hybrid economy model suggests a third alternative that involves both paths: an integration of customary ways, government support and market relations. This third way looks like plain commonsense. Nonetheless, the 'choice' suggested here deserves further scrutiny. A remark by CAEPR demographer John Taylor is a good place to start. In a discussion of the way in which conventional economics does not apply to remote communities, Taylor instanced the issue of locational disadvantage—the idea that rural residents in particular, in some parts of Australia, are disadvantaged by their limited access both to employment and services. Taylor cited the achievements of the land rights movement and its social corollary, which involved the construction of outstations on Aboriginal homelands. He remarked on the explosion of these tiny settlements in various regions of remote Aboriginal Australia:

> To the extent that such achievements are attainable only by virtue of remote residence on traditional lands . . . the ongoing dispersion

of population across these lands may be seen as . . . Aboriginal perceptions of *locational advantage*. As such this represents the spatial optimum in a locational trade-off . . . [The trade-off] involves reduced access to urban-based mainstream labour markets, opportunities for education, training and income generation as well as to better housing and other social facilities. Insofar as these are perceived as losses, they are set against the not insignificant social, cultural and economic gains acquired from residence on Aboriginal lands. (Taylor 1999:105–106, emphasis in original)

Taylor is right about the costs of being remote. But *did* remote Aboriginal people actually make the trade-off that Taylor describes, or, perhaps, did they assume that in the move to remote locales there would be gains without loss? This is why traditional owners among the Western Arrernte, for instance, described the homelands movement as 'decentralisation'. Their idea was that each family group would take the benefits of settlement back home to country. In the early 1990s, this included the idea that outstations might acquire their own shops and service stations, paradigms of 'whitefella business' at Ntaria. The question was, however, who would be the customers and clients? With the passing of an older generation, these ideas also passed but the puzzle of how to gain training and employment for youth residing on the homelands remained (see Austin-Broos 2009a:205–237). Similarly, an older Western Arrernte generation assumed that schooling would come to the outstations and that health services would come in the form of a mobile nursing unit. Both these assumptions glossed over highly politicised issues of governance and cost, and other issues as well.

It is not at all clear that traditional owners made the trade-off that Taylor describes. Nor is it entirely clear that Aboriginal elders in effect were prepared to choose poverty in Australian society by virtue of their residence on homelands. In this case, understandably, the 'choice' may not have been an informed one. Moreover, it has certainly been injudicious for defenders of the homelands to imply that this choice can ever be a simple or self-evident one for remote Aboriginal people. In fact, the choices are very hard; they are also choices that Aboriginal people must learn about, reflect on and revise in successive generations. I make these remarks mindful of Sahlin's observation that poverty is not just about goods but also an 'invention of civilisation'; an elaborated set of social relations that cannot be set aside by individual choice alone (Sahlins 1972:37). A recent exploration of this theme underlines that the 'scale of material difference' is what bears on individual wellbeing rather than 'material conditions' as such. For example, it is not modest housing *per se* but rather the web of conflicting forms of social relation, including forms of stratification, in which houses are ensconced that make their use a perennial source of stress and ill-health in remote communities (see Wilkinson and Pickett 2010:24–26). A final point concerning choice is that it varies between communities. Opportunities for traditional activities and major aspects of resource management vary between the tropical north-east and desert Central Australia. This variation between communities also extends to attitudes towards mainstream education, trade training and so-called urban employment in regional centres. With a long history of trade and craft development at Ntaria/Hermannsburg, consequent on marginal pastoralism, resulting land degradation and proximity to Alice Springs, the notion of community-based initiatives alone is hardly appropriate—although it may be more appropriate in some other regions.

Altman's hybrid economy model may seem to address these issues and move the debate along. As noted in the previous chapter, throughout the 2000s CAEPR views shifted towards a position that integrated some labour market thinking with a community-based approach to remote communities. Full-time employment became a more prominent concern. Notwithstanding, Altman's emphasis was still on 'self-sufficient' communities that made his proposals not simply community-based but also community-bounded. In the *Coercive Reconciliation* collection he wrote:

> [The hybrid economy] approach recognises that Aboriginal people engage with the market and the state and the customary (or non-market) sectors of their local economies. Such engagements can be highly productive, as well as minimising economic risk. For example, in the arts, customary activity and state patronage of

mediating community-controlled arts centres results in market sales. And in natural resource management, customary activity like fire management or hunting of feral species for food not only sustains culturally distinctive ways of life, but also generates benefits that can be sold as environment services ... Such diverse economic activity is buoyant in remote Aboriginal Australia ... The development challenge is how to foster all three sectors of this economy at variable rates, depending on local circumstances ... [and] promote self-sufficiency in remote Aboriginal communities. (Altman 2007a:316–317)

Altman's vision is an appealing one, especially for those interested both in environmental issues and Aboriginal affairs. In this and other descriptions of the hybrid economy, however, he claims that this economy is, or can be, self-sufficient. He also declines to mention other forms of employment (Altman 2005, 2006).

These include administrative jobs in the very resource centres that he advocates; jobs in local councils and in NT shire administration; jobs in TGT schools where education would be advanced by the recruitment of more trained local teachers. Altman makes no mention of local service industries including road-making and repair, building maintenance, power maintenance and the like.[8] Not only TGT but also smaller communities have stores and, occasionally, clinics where Aboriginal staff work. Service stations with workshops are also a perennial of the larger Aboriginal towns, sometimes with traditions of 'bush mechanics' that go back for generations. An Alice Springs organisation such as the Central Australian Aboriginal Media Association (CAAMA) employs regionally based Aboriginal people involved in making media products that have earned both national and international renown. Other Central Australians are involved in transport and communication between Aboriginal towns, and between these towns and regional hubs such as Katherine or Alice Springs. And is participation in mining and natural gas production anathema to all people who live remote? This expanded range of public and private sector forms of employment makes clear that the local economies of remote Aboriginal communities are not, have not been, and will not be 'self-sufficient' in any simple sense of the word.

The public sector will most likely be the major employer in many of them and, through welfare or targeted work schemes similar to CDEP, there will be significant federal government support. Furthermore, all these tasks today, including the resource management ones, require mainstream literate education in English and good numeracy skills that will not be easily acquired on small outstations or in the absence of stable schools and well-trained teachers.

Let me underline this point with a remark on hybrid economy mythology as I have encountered it in hallway conversation. Notoriously, mythology is not the product of an individual but rather of a more diffuse milieu and, in this case, of an anthropology that has grown uninterested in economics.[9] Advocacy for a hybrid economy in remote Aboriginal Australia generally focuses on industries connected with country rather than with urban or industrial settings, or even infrastructure maintenance. Art, craft, and land and sea management are the major ones. In discussions of labour market policy, mainstream education is described as 'assimilation' and therefore is often represented negatively as something external to Aboriginal life. Finally, options for orbiting, travel or migration are represented as 'mass migration' that totally destroys a community and culture. The idea of a bounded and self-sufficient local economy consistent with customary life is built on the back of this triad of 'the bad'. Yet, for all but a tiny minority of remote communities, this vision is misleading. Intentional or not, a focus on natural resource management and art, to the exclusion of most other types of employment, evokes ideas of activity based on traditional Aboriginal knowledge and its unproblematic reproduction. However, the conflict that Aboriginal people face is not between a self-sufficient life and a market-oriented capitalist one (cf. Sanders 2009). The very *mix* of activities current in communities is indicative of the fact that people are grappling with conflicting institutions *within their own domain*. For example, if land management is to be not only local but also a locally controlled concern, Aboriginal youth will need both secondary and tertiary education beyond their homelands. Or is the plan that local people will simply be the workers? The partner to silence on suffering and distress is the reification of cultural difference.

Things to learn from a failed debate

The remote communities debate involved three failures. One was a failure to acknowledge cultural difference and the complexities it brings to policy concerning marginalisation. Another was a failure to acknowledge disadvantage incurred by marginalisation and the suffering it brings to those who wish to live remote. In the remote communities debate, anti-separatists by and large suppressed the issue of cultural difference and anthropologists by and large suppressed the issue of distress. Finally, those anthropologists who did acknowledge social suffering did so by pathologising difference and entirely averting their gaze from the issue of an economic base for remote communities (see Sutton 2001, 2009; Martin 2001, 2008). These failures bring several insights.

The first one is that suffering and distress are salient in communities. This means that social inequality matters. Likewise, widespread and long-term welfare or welfare-like dependence matters because it is the link between inequality and suffering; the register of low status in a larger social order that brings demoralisation experienced as 'poverty'. Therefore communities require both federally funded programs of the CDEP type and effective strategies for mainstream schooling. In other words, community-based strategies and labour market/human capital ones should both be on the agenda. I return to education later in this chapter. CDEP or equivalent schemes deserve some additional comment here.

The debate about this scheme between anti-separatists and defenders of the homelands has centred on whether or not CDEP amounted merely to welfare payments. Technically, the CDEP scheme was not a welfare program. As Sanders and Morphy have pointed out, the scheme was a product of Aboriginal affairs administration and not social security as such (Sanders and Morphy 2001:1). Four factors have moved anti-separatists to designate the scheme as 'welfare'. In recent years, its apparent similarity to work-for-the-dole schemes elsewhere in Australia encouraged the 'welfare' designation. A more extreme version of this position was that any such community-wide government-supported scheme is in fact a welfare one. These are views that simply refuse Altman's policy realism regarding employment equity in remote communities. He argued that CDEP or a like approach is mandatory in communities that have so little alternative employment (see also Taylor and Hunter 2001).[10] Pearson acknowledged as much in his original *Responsibility* statement (Pearson 2000:55). In recent years, Gregory has also given Altman indirect support on this issue (Gregory 2006).

Another more situational factor has encouraged the 'welfare' designation: the difficulties involved in administering small projects on dispersed outstations. Generally, funding does not allow effective impersonal oversight of projects from a central resource hub (see Austin-Broos 2001). A scheme not intended as a welfare equivalent collapses into one because work requirements cannot be maintained. As senior Western Arrernte observed to me, 'Kids jus' run around'. A final factor, closely related to the previous one, is that more often than not the scheme has involved widespread, lifelong part-time employment in jobs that are not especially challenging or interesting. In addition, 'structured training and employment projects' intended to move participants into better and full-time employment have too often been travesties that do little more than undermine the notion of training. Window-dressing often prevailed in situations that were under-resourced and sliding into disorganisation (Austin-Broos 2009a:147–151, 205–237). Albeit unintentionally, then, a scheme that looked good in principle became the equivalent of almost lifelong unemployment or underemployment. As executed in the 1990s, many CDEP offered too little work of significance that was also poorly supervised. And this is why the 'welfare' designation cannot be just waved away. There are psychological impacts in a capitalist society from long-term unemployment that also undermine the ability to retain basic skills required for life in a modern state—such as literacy. Pearson's proposal to 'leech' the poison from welfare dependence should be seen in this light. Whether or not he intended it, his writing could be taken to pose the question: How is such a scheme sustained without extremely adverse effects? Understood this way, the focus is on the structural issue—the adverse effects of long-term underemployment at least—and not on a psychologised one: welfare dependency.

Welfare in remote Aboriginal communities is an issue only insofar that it reflects intractable forms of unemployment detrimental to health and happiness. In response to this issue, Pearson has proposed institution building, Martin more governance, and Sutton renovations of the self. Altman, the most constructive contributor, has sought to expand the range of regional industry that CDEP might draw on and contribute to (see also Altman 2008b). Yet the outlook is not bright.

Concern about CDEP led Gregory to discuss the distinction between 'supply' and 'demand' approaches to labour market issues (Gregory 2006). In effect, Gregory argued that policies geared to increase demand for workers within a community would always struggle to achieve enough. (A few years later, Boyd Hunter (2009a) of CAEPR agreed with him.[11]) Gregory was sceptical that small communities based on a mix of traditional and non-traditional activities, welfare and subsidised part-time work could produce a lifestyle, and especially levels of health, acceptable either to those involved or to governments. Importantly, he took poor health and other distress as evidence of the negative impact of underemployment and unemployment in remote communities. Therefore, he advocated forms of labour market policy concerned with human capital or the 'supply' side of labour markets. He favoured equipping the individual better to pursue employment when it is desired, and wherever it might be obtained. Migration for some individuals was an implication of his position. Nonetheless, Gregory remained flexible. He underlined that we don't really know with any precision, *for the range of communities involved*, why education outcomes are poor and why Aboriginal Australians turn away from labour migration (see Gregory 2006:136–137). Cultural difference, or past policies, or a combination of these factors might provide the explanation. And this may mean, Gregory concluded, that CDEP or like provisions should remain a mainstay of communities. Both approaches to employment are required.

The second insight to come from the remote communities debate concerns *not* suppressing cultural difference as a part of community life. I have argued against a CAEPR view that reifies this culture but there are other ways in which difference is crucial to communities and to policy-making for them. Peterson and others have proposed that remote Aboriginal unemployment has as much to do with cultural disengagement as it does with the disaffection of discouraged workers (Peterson 1985, 1998, 2005).[12] Some of these remarks concern cultural issues of intimate engagement among people who identify as kin. Others concern the fact that in remote communities being a relative and custodian of country remains as important, if not more important, than being an employed worker, even in a secure position. This is a cultural fact augmented by another fact—that much resourcing of the homelands has been channelled through land rights provisions and traditional owners. Both the poetics and the power of remote Aboriginal life are still embedded in kin and country. Consequences of this phenomenon are an absorbing politics of place and, within kin groups, demand sharing. Most parents at Ntaria that I know are adamant that youth should have jobs. At the same time, there is little doubt that, for many, land and resource politics linked with land are paramount. Mixed messages are sent to youth; for instance, that waged work on one's own country is beneath a custodian's dignity (Austin-Broos 2009a:131). With regard to demand sharing, this circulation of cash and commodities among kin means that consumer goods reflect and objectify the extent of a kinship network rather than an individual alone (see Peterson 1991, 1993). Possessive individualism, such as it is in communities, is channelled through this traditional system and, more often than not, does not result in personal accumulation. In the mundane everyday, this form of consumption, which circulates cash and goods rather than accumulating them, comprises the substance of the conflict between Aboriginal kinship and market institutions. Peterson remarks that consumption patterns will have to change before the call to work sounds clearly in the ears of youth. It may be also that these consumption patterns will change only with more and better mainstream education, individual orbiting and more sustained employment. This will come, however, only when the sole route to major resources is no longer traditional custodianship. From whichever way the matter is approached, there needs to be a better reconciliation of these conflicting institutional orders. For most communities, the cost of not pursuing this reconciliation seems too great in terms of health, personal safety, forms of esteem and the potentialities of youth. Nonetheless, different family groups within the one community and different communities across remote regions may pursue different types of reconciliation. If there is choice at all, this is where the choice lies.

A third insight from the debate, especially in the context of the NT Intervention, is that the rights–pathology axis (as I shall call it) should not provide the only terms in which remote Aboriginal communities are discussed among the humanistic social sciences. A focus on the highly paternalistic forms of welfare income management that came with the NT Intervention brought quite proper critique of the federal government's suspension of the *Racial Discrimination Act 1975*. In a considered sense, this action was a racist denial of human rights. It discriminated against one cultural group identified in law in racialised terms. Of late, this initiative has become more nearly simply paternalistic. Income management is being extended to relevant NT welfare recipients who are non-Indigenous. Yet, even if the paternalism ceased, unemployment would endure alongside land rights, and excessive lifestyle illness would endure within homeland communities. The fundamental point is that marginalisation is an issue of economy, society and culture and not merely a legal issue pertaining to the state.[13] Therefore, while it is important that the excesses of the state be critiqued, it is also important that critique be directed at policies fashioned to constrain consumption (of alcohol etc.) that go proxy for more ambitious initiatives concerning education and regional development. These should be initiatives that also seek to reconcile current cultural attachments in communities with employment and capacity growth. For this reason, Altman's tendency to reduce economy to culture and equality to difference is disappointing (see Altman 2007a, 2008a). Moreover, this position fails to address an important point: that these policies on the part of federal government are ad hoc, paternalistic and, in fact, wildly at variance with neoliberalism. Federal government policy is not neoliberal, but neither is it seriously geared to the inclusion of remote Aboriginal people in the Australian economy.

This latter fact is also obscured when both opinion writers and some anthropologists argue that the transgression of rights involved in income management is justified in order to control pathology including personal violence and child abuse. Just as controls on consumption modify but do not dispel impoverishment, trying to treat social pathology without addressing marginalisation fails to grasp the relevant issues. Repairing authority structures and building sets of integrated institutions along with a robust public opinion and confident local leaders are the types of measures that will have an enduring effect. These are interdependent projects that rely in turn on improving education and employment. Denying human rights to contain pathology is a stop-gap measure and socially corrosive in the longer term. In sum, it is important to note that neither side in the debate about pathology and rights entirely grasps the issues that produced the Intervention and its policy fallout.

Many writers have pondered the apparent slow pace of change in remote Aboriginal life. Many have invoked culture and some in a sense that is far more general than the ways discussed here. Peter Sutton and W.E.H. Stanner have both proposed that, due to past orientations, Aboriginal people are more tolerant of suffering than other Australians and less inclined to change. This is the 'assent to the tragic terms of life' that both write about (Stanner 1979 [1958]:62–63; Sutton 2001:148–149). I am more impressed by the enduring conflict between institutions in remote communities. I am also struck by how much needs to be grasped that lies beyond the immediate experience of remote Aboriginal people if they are to protect and nurture their communities themselves. Unfortunately, this process takes time, energy, and the work of Aboriginal leaders both local and national. I am sceptical regarding the 'assent to tragedy' argument and wonder whether or not the matter is actually one of institutional conflict produced by encapsulation and marginalisation, by inequality within the state. The deterioration in literacy over recent decades cannot but entrench this circumstance. In comparable conditions, any culture might find change hard.

The two debates

The debates discussed in this book can be thought of as two nested boxes. Some broader themes of the postcolonial critique are exemplified in a more concrete form in the remote communities debate. Postcolonial critics argued that classical ethnography concerned itself only with traditional culture. As a result, it did not notice or remark sufficiently on the passage of events that led to Indigenous encapsulation by the state and economic marginalisation. Much the same has been said by anti-separatists in the remote communities debate, albeit from the right and with regard to a specific time and place. A neoliberal critique proposed that anthropology had been too concerned with museum exotica to notice the suffering in communities. Ironically, perhaps, the charge of racism that postcolonial critics aimed at anthropology carried a comparable theme—that people were treated by the anthropologists only as interesting objects for research. Some postcolonial critics suggested that anthropology was thereby complicit in an Australian discourse that rendered Aboriginal inequality in terms of racial difference. From the right, some argued that anthropologists and others, as 'helping' professions, have maintained the welfare dependency of remote Aboriginal people in the name of cultural difference.

In these two critiques, racism and multiculturalism (with a welfare state component) in fact play comparable roles. Each proposes a self-interested pursuit on the part of anthropologists that has damaged Aboriginal people. Moreover, each critique promotes its own kind of moral certainty. Racism clearly should be swept aside, just as pathology should be. And this also goes for those in universities who perpetuate these conditions. With regard to classical ethnography, both charges are unjust. Although the focus of this book is cultural difference, historically interpreted, it does not reject or underestimate the role of classical ethnography in scholarship. Not only has that ethnography produced a significant record of human cultural difference as it pertains to Indigenous Australians, it also makes a continuing contribution to our understanding of the histories of Aboriginal life once encapsulated by the state and rendered marginal by capitalism.

Where classical ethnography is concerned, the outcome of critique should not be that task's demise but rather a broader agenda for anthropology overall. With regard to history, inequality and culture, clearly the two critiques rely on very different accounts of economy and law, capitalism and the state, within Australian society. My point is that, notwithstanding sometimes marked differences, there is a common theme in these critiques that demands attention.

Their common theme points to a particular lack in Australian anthropology. Anthropology has been poorly equipped to deal with the cultural difference and the inequality that actually exist in remote communities today. In part, this is due to the fact that the style of work by anthropologists who have moved away from classical ethnography so far has had limited impact on research in homeland communities. Neither the work of Beckett, Cowlishaw and their associates nor that of the anthropologists who have worked in NT towns has figured sufficiently in general understandings of remote Aboriginal Australia.[14] Interestingly this meant that, in the 1990s, anthropology by and large both rejected and did not reflect on the postcolonial critique launched by history and Indigenous studies. In turn, this is the reason why the call to culture war that the NT Intervention seemed to invite caused a breach in the ranks. Sutton, Clendinnen, Langton, Manne and latterly Martin treated social suffering as real whereas many anthropologists seemed committed to avoiding the issue.

In Chapter 1, I remarked that the failure to complete the postcolonial critique left a space that was filled by neoliberalism as the remote communities debate unfolded. The 'space' I refer to is a more contextualised understanding of what cultural difference is within remote communities today, and the manner in which it shapes the everyday priorities of remote Aboriginal people. As the debate unfolded, with its reports of violence, substance abuse and the like, the reified portrait of tradition produced in some ethnographic texts seemed no longer to apply. The gap between anthropology's portrayal and that in the daily press was too great and quickly undermined the discipline's plausibility; hence the slide in public discourse from the Dreaming to the nightmare of pathology. What was missing in the debate—at least in the public domain—was a more tangible grasp of today's lived experience in remote communities.[15] Integral to this situation is the fact that much anthropological research in remote Australia has been for consultancies that circumscribe the questions asked and the observations made. Classical ethnography in the present has not been old-style anthropology but rather a late-modern task defined by a form of politics—land rights politics—responsive to Aboriginal people but nonetheless controlled by the state. This work has crowded out a more critical and independent anthropology of the type that this book advocates.

Yet the problem has not been anthropology's alone. The postcolonial critique beyond anthropology also remains incomplete because its perpetrators seemed to accept an implicit division of labour: classical ethnography addressed the homelands while history and Indigenous studies addressed the NT past and coastal regions, past and present. The message seemed to be that classical ethnography addressed one form of Indigenous experience but this was not the only one. The problem with this position is that although it turned a critical lens on *fin de siècle* anthropology, it left classical anthropology in the present virtually untouched. In fact, by various subterfuges, some postcolonial critics managed to barely read anthropology's modern corpus.[16] This has meant that research concerning the homelands movement has often been removed from the perspectives of history and Indigenous studies as well. My proposal is that if anthropology is no longer simply classical ethnography, then its practice should be 'brought in' to a closer dialogue with these other disciplines and with colleagues who do not presently focus on remote communities. My suggestion is that the humanistic social sciences between them need now to take as their brief research and writing about *the full gamut* of Australian Indigenous experience from the homelands through rural and regional Australia to the costal cities. I have stated throughout this book that anthropology is something other than Indigenous studies. Understandings of cultural difference are important for Indigenous Australian peoples, and anthropology has honed tools for this type of work. In the remote communities debate, these tools have been in play too little, not too much. There is another reason to advocate greater engagement between the humanistic social sciences. In the past decade at least, the somewhat detached status of classical ethnography has left it wanting politically in the present—too small and isolated to counter the portraits of pathology that prevailed in the public domain prior to the NT Intervention. Moreover, those who continue to work in remote community consultancy and are not ethnographers require accounts of Aboriginal difference that are current and realistic.

These matters imply that in research on the full gamut of Indigenous experience, issues of both cultural difference and inequality should be in play. Issues of inequality do not supersede issues of difference and a focus on 'race' does not supersede attention to culture or local specifying practice. Correlatively, a politics of difference is not superior to equality politics. It is not more 'left'. Nor, in a global world, does identity or difference politics subsume the issues of a capitalist economy and the states that support it. It also would be helpful were there a turn away from simply a focus on the state and more attention paid to economy. It is difficult to grasp the enduring issues that bear on remote Aboriginal communities without addressing the pros and cons of employment policy and the forms of discourse that shape legislation via social policy. In fact, this book is a call to realign the relation between the politics of difference and equality.

Difference, equality and their politics

My call to rethink the politics of difference is not original. It has a history. In the course of the 1980s, the humanistic social sciences witnessed a significant change. A previously popular position proposed that political economy is the central politics of modern society. This view was maintained in the face of a growing focus on gender and a postcolonial politics of difference. The established position was that gender and race were 'soft' forms of politics that could be reduced to political economy. With the break-up of the Eastern bloc and the demise of the USSR, this genre of Marxism lost its force and critical writing turned more and more to gender and race and the phenomenon of *différence*. In the humanistic social sciences, and especially in anthropology, this difference politics was often proposed as superior to the older politics of socioeconomic equality. Some times equality politics was designated as 'sameness' politics in contrast to the 'difference' variety. The view was that a politics of difference pushed the question of inequality beyond the conventional limits of class to issues of multiculturalism and citizenship. In terms of political philosophy some of these ideas came with Will Kymlicka's (1995) views on group rights—a significant and often debated extension of liberalism's enlightenment agenda. Kymlicka's ideas conferred on minorities bearing cultural difference a uniform 'identity' that downplayed other aspects of the subject. The community or bounded whole was privileged as the political unit. Protect the group and its culture in order to protect the individual. In Australia, these ideas reinforced classical ethnography's propensity for reification. The politics of difference or identity were played out in terms of an Indigenous sector servicing a different, bounded culture (e.g. Peterson and Sanders 1998:27–28; Rowse 1998b:79).[17] In sum, the rights involved in a politics of difference were rights that individuals took from being members of the group. This was in part the issue in play when Altman, Rowse and Sanders proposed that 'statistical equality' and 'cultural difference' could be antagonistic. In their view, identifying cultural difference involved refusing the reduction of different types of right to (mere) equality. Yet this popular view has been questioned in recent years.

Walter Benn Michaels voiced his concerns in a book entitled *The Trouble with Diversity: How we learned to love identity and ignore inequality* (2006). Michaels was writing about the United States not as an economist or sociologist but rather as a professor of English literature. He brought a wealth of humorous comment and insight to his argument that a politics of representation and group rights cannot address the extraordinary marginalisation of some minority groups in today's global capitalism. In particular, it cannot address the disadvantaged lot of minorities that lack interest for a global market. Importantly, Michaels made the point that identity politics does not address poverty as such and that the poor, by and large, do not regard their condition as identity—something that they want to retain and to which rights attach. Rather, the poor aspire to be less poor; to move beyond poverty. When they demand rights, as in civil rights, these are rights relevant to this path out of poverty.

An earlier contribution had come from philosopher Nancy Fraser (1997b). In the 1990s she sought to formulate a 'post-socialist' politics that focused on two types of project that had become 'decoupled': the politics of recognition and the politics of redistribution. For the purposes of this book, I render her distinction as one between a politics of cultural difference and a politics of equality. Fraser made a crucial point about these politics: where one, the politics of cultural difference, leads a group to distinguish itself, to separate itself from the larger order so that it is 'recognised', a politics of equality is most successful when the group is more fully included in the larger order—with more opportunities and more options in the economy, for instance. First Nation peoples, in the main, are keen to retain their identities. On the other hand, the poor, by and large, would rather not be poor. Therefore these politics seem to pull in opposite directions. One draws away from the mainstream while the other draws towards it. Still, in Fraser's view, while these conditions may seem opposed, their politics intertwine. When it is racialised, cultural difference becomes a fault line along which inequality runs. Indigenous Australians know this well. Issues of difference—understood as savagery, pathology, deviance or intransigence—are used to explain why remote Aboriginal people are so often impoverished and have inferior services.

Fraser's comments accord with Michaels's but with one vital difference. Michaels tends to suggest that difference or identity politics has become a vacuous pursuit that masks inequality. Ruefully he remarks that we are all neoliberals now; right-wing or left-wing ones, but equally slow to acknowledge poverty as inequality. Fraser, on the other hand, gives each politics its own integrity, although, she allows, they are sometimes hard to reconcile. Nonetheless, we must try. We need to look for 'versions of the cultural politics of difference that can coherently combine with the social politics of equality'. Fraser suggests that we should pose the question repeatedly, 'For groups who are subject to injustices of both types, what combination of remedies work best to minimize [each]?' (1997b:12, 26). In the context of remote communities, her injunction suggests that we embrace both the politics of land rights with its cultural implications and that of greater economic equality.

A third writer complements Benn Michaels and Fraser: anthropologist Donald Robotham. He argues that anthropology, along with other humanistic social sciences, has become uninterested in economics to its detriment (Robotham 2005).[18] A part of his critique concerns the propensity to transform politics of equality into a politics of representation. Robotham instances Stuart Hall's acceptance of 'strategic essentialism' as a major concept and Paul Gilroy's optimistic views on cosmopolitanism and what it can bring to New World and Old World Africans in the trans-Atlantic (Gilroy 1993, 2000; Hall 1997). Robotham argues that, notwithstanding identity politics, the position of poor African peoples in the region has barely changed in the past twenty years. His views find a parallel in Beckett's when the latter writes that 'rehabilitating [a] minority's distinctive identity' can coincide with rendering 'poverty picturesque and social marginality an alternative lifestyle' (Beckett 1988:14). Not surprisingly, a part of Robotham's argument involves a critique of localism. He notes the common assumption that '"if globalization is de-localization", then the alternative must be "localization".' Yet, he observes, the notion of 'big versus small and bounded' fundamentally misconstrues the nature of economy today. In fact, maintaining small regional socialities requires quite elaborate and sophisticated forms of investment, and diverse chains of exchange of both goods and services. Neither identity nor bounded local groups ensure a small minority's wellbeing (see Robotham 2005:128, 135–141). This position suggests that with regard to employment policy for remote communities, both community-based and broader labour market measures need to be on the table.

These texts have influenced the arguments presented in this book. I conclude with a brief comment on politics and education before I return to Mathew's story.

Education for equality and difference

Within universities at least, political debate about remote Aboriginal communities has mainly focused on two issues. One is the maintenance of self-sufficient communities and the need for hybrid economies that include government-supported schemes to sustain them. The other is human rights and the urgent need for their restoration in the wake of the NT Intervention—rights removed from Aboriginal people in the name of containing pathologies that have violated other rights. In this chapter, I have not so much rejected these politics as discussed their limitations. My proposal has been that both forms of politics tend to deny the historical nature of difference today and the positioning of remote Aboriginal people in an economy as well as a state. Sometimes these issues have been conflated in a fashion that suggests that remote Aboriginal people have the right to live in self-sufficient communities separate from the rest of society. Whether or not Aboriginal people have this right, my argument has been that the state cannot alone provide it and, in any case, remote Aboriginal people have already changed in ways that mean it is a restrictive course for many. This book has argued throughout that separatism as the central focus of policy and politics does not serve remote communities well or acknowledge their nature today. For the anthropologists involved, separatism goes hand in hand with a reified notion of tradition produced by classical ethnography. It misconstrues the forms of difference that are now in play. For this reason, I propose to add a further dimension to a politics that does support land rights, human rights and appropriate development. I refer to widespread, forceful and persistent support for mainstream primary education in remote communities. This education lays the foundation for capacities that are relevant to economic participation and Indigenous citizenship. Moreover, such education is, or should be, a bridging practice between other institutions that are currently in conflict. Yet to advocate effectively for this education requires a politics that will prove quite radical because it seeks to address both inequality and cultural difference. In this concluding section of the chapter, I propose to explore some aspects of remote education and then return to this politics.

In anthropology at least, the education I am advocating has been seen as assimilationist. Its demands on time-space location and notions of authority and autonomy make mainstream education antagonistic to tradition in ways that extend well beyond the formal curriculum. Yet to leave the matter there overlooks the fact that remote Aboriginal people are Australian citizens; people who live within the state and are dependent on the state's mediation of a capitalist economy. Equal citizens require equal tools to engage the state directly as it affects them, and to address a range of labour markets if they so desire. In short, the view that excellent mainstream primary schooling is just assimilationist misidentifies who remote Aboriginal people are today and their options for a greater integration in Australian society. Let me take each issue in turn.

Aboriginal people in remote communities are not hunter-gatherers. More often they are employed part-time for a wage, and much of the discussion in this book has been devoted to this circumstance. Aboriginal people are also Australian citizens who vote and expect a range of competent service delivery from the state. They have an interest, often expressed, in pressing their claims for better services including those pertaining to health and education. The proper delivery of these services requires politically effective demands on government, and this politics in turn makes demands on communities. To be serviced properly, remote communities need to foster forms of public or shared opinion to support both the call for services and the productive use of them when and if those services arrive. In short, the growth of self-determination at the grassroots level requires the modification of family-based politics and the growth of a public opinion that can reside fairly comfortably alongside ongoing family interests. This task of building a public opinion will benefit from improvements in mainstream education at the community level. The task is crucial if self-determination, so-called, is to be a local phenomenon and not simply an attribute of peak national organisations—whether members of these organisations are elected or not. Finally, remote Aboriginal people are Indigenous citizens with an interest in the politics of difference or identity. Difference becomes identity when culture is objectified in public discourse as a contested phenomenon. Aboriginal people have the right to protect their identity and its continuity. They also need to be able to explain that continuity to others in and beyond Australia. Therefore it is crucial that as many men and women as possible have the range of relevant skills, indigenous and non-indigenous, required to accept senior positions in a land council. Identity politics also involves the proper conservation of song knowledge that remains on country. Recent ethnographic studies in this area testify to cultural continuity and also to related projects of local heritage conservation. These projects should involve Aboriginal people not simply as 'informants' but also as participants in the technologies and social organisation of conservation (see Marett 2005; Bradley et al. 2010). Mainstream education is required for this range of tasks that are cultural, political and economic. To deny the relevant capabilities to current and future generations who live remote is to undermine their right to cultural difference as citizens within the state and as members of a market society.

Iris Marion Young helps us to see that integration in Australian society is not simply assimilation. She has made a distinction between 'conformist' assimilation, 'transformational' assimilation and a 'radical democratic pluralism'. Her argument is that where the first form of assimilation simply requires conformity with a majority population, the second transformational type at least acknowledges that mainstream institutions represent interests of the majority and more powerful group, which should be required to make its own adjustments. In Young's view both these forms of assimilation cast aspersions, either explicitly or implicitly, on the minority group who must change more than the majority one. She argues that a radical democratic pluralism rejects this course (Young 1990:163–168). This third position acknowledges that a range of institutional relations *must* change in order that a cultural minority access the services in question. In short, my support for mainstream primary education in remote communities does not envisage one-sided conformity, but rather adjustments of some magnitude on both sides. I am advocating this latter course because remote Aboriginal cultural difference is an encapsulated difference which has now been shaped in the crucible of Australian economy and law for generations. The defence of cultural difference as it is today requires the tools of citizenship—not least the ability to advocate for oneself in the political arena.

At various points in this book I have referred to educationist Martin Nakata's writing on education in the Torres Strait Islands. I have connected his critique with Noel Pearson's call for a right to take responsibility in remote Aboriginal communities. I have pointed out that a psychologised position on welfare should not obscure the fact that Pearson's proposals are also postcolonial. He does not want the people he represents to be dependent on carers who are often strangers—culturally and historically ill-informed about remote communities. He argues strongly against the idea that Aboriginal people, even when remote, should remain as clients of the state. Therefore I submit that to advocate for mainstream primary education in communities is to support both equality and difference. Primary education is a fundamental right of citizenship. It is also a part of relevant labour market strategies. Finally, good primary education is the foundation for capabilities that those who live remote require to sustain their own self-determination and their identity politics. For all these reasons, education should be at the centre of politics about remote Aboriginal life.

It is well known that primary education outcomes are generally poor in NT remote communities (see Hughes and Hughes 2009). A marked gap exists between the performance of Aboriginal and non-Aboriginal students. In 2008, for instance, where 88 per cent of non-Aboriginal third graders reached a minimum reading standard, just over 30 per cent of Aboriginal third graders reached that standard. Matters did not improve very much in the ninth grade (see CRC 2009:103–106). As things stand, for the foreseeable future a majority of remote Aboriginal children will reach their teenage years with modest proficiency in English literacy. Given unemployment and discouragement, functional illiteracy is just around the corner. As illiteracy and disaffection from the workforce feed each other, more lives still will be destroyed by various forms of substance abuse.

Interestingly, some on both sides of the remote communities debate converge on the issue of education. In 2005, anthropologist Tess Lea, who with Bob Collins authored the NT report called *Learning Lessons* (1999), made this observation:

> The irony is that school improvement can be achieved. It requires technically competent and confident teaching, supported by effective school leadership, creating situations where poor performance is acted upon and peers drive excellence ... The bad news is that this is just about impossible to sustain within education environments where strong leaders have to be diplomats to survive, staff turnover remains high, teachers are diffident about their methods and approach, facilities are run down or non-existent, programs are not available and naming problems properly is considered disempowering, if not for the staff, then for 'the community'. Teachers will talk of the need for 'good professional development' and the creation of 'learning communities' in response to any suggestion that peer review of poor teaching practice is required ...
>
> The scenario worsens when the question of resources is looked squarely in the eye. (Lea 2005:158–159)

In 2005, Lea noted that forms of historical funding for education used by the Commonwealth Grants Commission advantaged states and territories already well-equipped to deliver schooling (2005: 159). In her view, resources to 'reduce the gap' were actually not available. Four years later, nothing much had changed, although the federal government was party to a pact to 'close the gap' nationwide between Indigenous and non-Indigenous education. A policy outcome of the NT Intervention, this commitment was part of the National Indigenous Reform Agreement (NIRA) between federal and state/territory governments. Helen Hughes reports that although some resources have been increased, the policy change required to promote better schools is still missing (Hughes and Hughes 2009:16).

Hughes describes parallel schooling for remote Aboriginal children. The 45 Homeland Learning Centres with modified curricula and the fifteen somewhat larger Community Education Centres far outnumber standard primary schools (Hughes and Hughes 2009:14). These centres have been the response to a plethora of issues including small and remote communities, poor school attendance, cultural unease, low salience of a school–work nexus, and rapid teacher turnover (on average teachers stay less than a year). Where nothing else is available, due to the cost and complexity of service delivery, some defence might be lodged of this system as an *interim* measure (see Schwab 1999, 2005; Schwab and Sutherland 2003). Yet the arrangement smacks of inequality hiding behind the guise of cultural difference. In fact, this education bears a marked resemblance to the NT's parallel system for the treatment of Aboriginal alcohol dependence. As Brady reports, these parallel arrangements too easily deprive Aboriginal people of mainstream innovations, informed advisors and good administration (Brady 2004:11).

Neither is the situation in primary schooling likely to improve soon without considerable political pressure. A recent discussion of services to rural Australia notes the brute fact of cost: 'For schools, spending per student is 12 per cent higher [than city costs] in moderately accessible regions, 34 per cent higher in remote areas and 60 per cent in very remote [areas]' (Gittins 2010). It is the latter category that includes most homeland communities. The COAG Reform Council (CRC) is monitoring performance outcomes for the NIRA. It is also overseeing national agreements for healthcare, education, skills and workforce development, disability, and affordable housing in the population generally. Given this nationwide competition for resources, and in the face of generally underfunded public education, better outcomes from remote schooling would be surprising (see also Caro and Bonner 2007). Aboriginal leaders Larissa Behrendt, Mick Dodson and Noel Pearson have remarked on this situation (see Pearson 2009a, 2010a; Behrendt 2010). All are of the view that *closing* the gap, rather than halving it, should be the aim for the current decade. CRC officers predict, albeit with regret, that the aim of halving the gap is unlikely to be reached.[19] In the face of this daunting situation, communities do struggle on. In Cape York, alcohol restrictions in towns and households have been followed by higher school attendance levels and longer school hours—but with adjusted curricula that address both mainstream skills and Aboriginal cultural tradition (see Koch 2010). In Ntaria/Hermannsburg, a 2010 report has enrolments increasing in the past three years and the rate of attendance at 80 per cent. Marked improvement is attributed to good teaching staff, much improved classrooms and equipment, and an extensive system of incentives supported especially by senior Western Arrernte women.[20]

Support for better primary education as part of a political agenda brings with it two confronting issues. Such support entails an acknowledgement that the matter concerns not just more 'standard' schooling but rather delivery of curricula in a fashion that can be received by remote Aboriginal children. My own experience at Ntaria has been that although parents may emphasise employment for youth, the relation between skills imparted by a primary curriculum and that employment are seldom discussed and, probably, not always clear. Consequently, the desire for employment is more fully developed than the desire for literate and numerate education. Put in other terms, cultural difference, unemployment and remoteness all mean that many parents in remote communities probably do not subscribe to a human capital view of literate and numerate education. Perception of links between education and employment that are taken for granted in rural and urban Australia may not be so evident in remote communities, and this circumstance among parents influences children. The work histories of parents and grandparents—not to mention many consociates previously employed in CDEP—do not provide the forms of experience that would ground a human capital view of remote education.[21] Therefore, why engage with it? The position that outsiders take on this issue will be influenced by whether it is seen as simply an outcome of cultural difference or as an outcome of difference in the context of economic marginalisation. Is the absence of a human capital approach to mainstream education a problem in communities, or not? My arguments throughout this book make clear that I think it is. However, I raise the issue to underline how difficult and complex delivering excellent primary education is in remote communities today. This issue bears on another.

My remarks indicate that supporting appropriate research and an evidence-based approach to primary teaching practice in remote communities would far exceed even the cost of remote education cited by Ross Gittins (see above). Mindful of this matter, perhaps, and of union constraints and the tangle of relations between relevant government departments, writers including Helen Hughes and Noel Pearson have turned to the private sector and philanthropy. These writers have promoted private sector scholarships and third sector funding of community initiatives. While innovations in specific communities should be encouraged, these initiatives cannot be decoupled from the fact that excellent primary education is a right of citizenship in the modern state, and a right that is accessible in rural and urban Australia. To advocate for greater economic inclusion and neglect this right is to take an inconsistent stance on employment in Australia's economy today. Equally, granting land rights and supporting homelands communities, centralised or not, entails that the state accept its responsibility to provide remote Aboriginal people with the basic tools of citizenship.

Generally, education in these terms is not seen as a radical politics. It becomes so in the context of contemporary ideas about efficient markets and the limited role of government in providing even basic services. These ideas have plagued discussions of remote communities along with the widespread view, promoted by the Intervention, that cultural difference as pathology is the cause of remote Aboriginal inequality. In short, an over-optimistic view of markets, a minimalist position on the state and a propensity to individualise and psychologise structural inequality while ignoring real differences have been hallmarks of the remote communities debate. To advocate for the development of excellent mainstream primary education that can be delivered in remote communities is to acknowledge this education as both a need in the integration process and a right of Aboriginal citizenship. My suggestion is that the state and society should bear the cost of this education, which will be great, and which will need for its success a supportive public opinion in communities. The radical part of this politics is contained in two propositions: first, that remote communities need to develop a relevant form of public opinion and, second, that the high cost of the education required is not thereby an 'unreasonable' demand on the state. These positions are counterintuitive in Australian politics today—a politics marked by romanticism of various types, conservatism and meek governance that comes with contemporary finance capitalism and its lack of interest in marginalised minorities, including those which are indigenous. I have limited the case to primary education because the routes to secondary and tertiary education relevant to different communities vary greatly and compound the issues involved. Therefore the course sketched here is a minimalist one, although it involves complex tasks and challenges that may seem overwhelming. Nonetheless, not to try such a course is unacceptable in a prosperous society that many like to think is fair and just.

•

Mathew proceeds today much as he has in recent decades, although he now spends more time at Ntaria. As he ages, he is also more involved in the lives of younger male relatives. He is not as thin as he used to be and has more periods without grog. Many things have happened in his family group. Mathew has a sister and two brothers-in-law serving on the MacDonnell Shire Council. One sister is a council office manager for a neighbouring community and another brother-in-law is a serving member of the Central Land Council. Others among his brothers-in-law are involved in vigorous native title arguments concerning the Western MacDonnell Ranges. Family members strategise endlessly. One brother and a son work in services at Ntaria and drive daily runs to Alice Springs for goods and mail. Another brother trained as a teacher's aide in Darwin but did not complete his course. He worked as a male assistant at Ntaria's health clinic and is now incapacitated due to illness. A sister works as a translator in the magistrate's court in Alice Springs, as does a distant cousin. One of Mathew's sons produced striking lithographs for a while, and one of Mathew's mother's cousins is an accomplished potter with an overseas market as well as a lively domestic one.

His family has suffered many tragedies, including the premature death of his father and four of his brothers. While his father died of a diabetes-related heart attack, all those brothers died of alcohol-related causes. There were many more such deaths among his brothers who were the sons of his father's brothers. Some of these deaths have been very traumatic. Mathew's mother died some years ago and, indeed, virtually all of that older generation has passed on.

One senior man in Mathew's family remains among the few Western Arrernte with an extensive knowledge of songs for his father's country and other sites. The responsibility weighs on him. Among Mathew's other women relatives, some have been subject to personal violence and at least two have lost their ability to bear children. Some have suffered disabling strokes. Notwithstanding, many family members live quite ordinary Ntaria lives of casual employment, regional travel, visits to the Big House outside Alice Springs, card playing, trips to the races and sometimes to the Alice Springs casino. They also support the Hermannsburg Bulldogs, Ntaria's football team. The code is AFL. Women and small children go to the Lutheran church quite often, and some men occasionally. When witchetty grubs (tyape) are in season, women and children hunt for them on Sunday afternoons.

Mathew's relatives still gather on country and talk of building more outstation houses. They believe that their old people have returned to the place and dwell among the other species there. Young people are sent to the outstation for a spell, and even take themselves there when there's fighting at Ntaria. In spring, the family musters brumbies and looks for one or two that might make a race horse. At a Tennant Creek meeting in mid-2010, the Central Land Council completed a lease agreement with Western Arrernte traditional owners. The Northern Territory government will build 26 new houses at Ntaria/Hermannsburg, but no new outstation houses. A Ntaria secondary school is due to be constructed, and the primary school now has an impressive computer room. Mathew's grandchildren will attend that school some day soon.

Notes

Foreword by Fred Myers

1 'Australianist anthropology', she writes,
> is much influenced by the ethnographies of an Aboriginal world governed by gerontocracy and supported by hunter-gatherer economies and ways of life. This world no longer exists in much of Australia, and where these institutions survive, they are compromised and altered by welfare dependency, modern consumerism and a range of conditions associated with the rapid transition to modernity. (Langton 2010: 92)

2 Indeed, she argues, 'the issues that concern remote communities would be fairly easy to address if they involved only cultural difference. It is because this is not the case that there is distress of the type now familiar in communities.'

Chapter 1: Two debates

1 To maintain confidentiality, the name and some personal details have been changed in this account, and in the one that concludes the book.
2 The relevant states are Queensland, South Australia and Western Australia.
3 *Samson and Delilah* was written and directed by Aboriginal filmmaker Warwick Thornton. It was released in 2009 to acclaim both in Australia and internationally. The film is distributed by Footprint Films.
4 Hunter (2010) also draws attention to this issue. On recent successes in the Ntaria School, see my comments in Chapter 6.
5 This is not to deny linguistics, which many would see as a social science as much as a humanities discipline. Generally, however, linguistics has not carried with it, at least in Australia, the brief to sustain social critique that is associated with the other three disciplines.
6 See my remarks on human capital and education in Chapter 6.
7 The particular texts that I have in mind are McGregor (1997), Cowlishaw (1987, 1999), Beckett (1987), Morris (1989), Wolfe (1999), Povinelli (2002), Nakata (2007) and Gray (2007). This is not to ignore the critical cast of the many regional histories of Indigenous

lives written in the past few decades. Some examples are Attwood (1989, 1994), Goodall (1996), Read (1981) and Curthoys (2002).

8   Examples include Shaw (1986), Beckett (1987), McGrath (1987) and Jebb (2001). Also see John Gray's critique of Ron and Catherine Berndt in this regard (Gray 2007:22–230).

9   For discussions of this important genre in Australian scholarship see Gibbons (2004), Attwood (2005) and Read, Peters-Little and Haebich (2008). Examples include Barker and Mathews (1977), Cohen (1987), Morgan (1987), Langford (1988), McGinness (1991), Lester (1993), Flick and Goodall (2004) and Kartinyeri and Anderson (2008).

10 'Homelands' is a term preferred by many academics and some community leaders for what are otherwise known as 'outstation communities'. The idea seems to be that where 'homelands' connotes an Aboriginal point of view, 'outstations' connotes one that is non-Aboriginal. In short, whence comes the identity of these communities? Within an Australian context, neither the terms 'homelands' nor 'separate development' seem to be connected with the terminology once used in South Africa. In the latter context, both terms would be taken to refer to policies that were part of an apartheid regime and therefore racist. As a matter of authenticity, so to speak, I will employ these terms in this book. They are significant to the extent that the terms tie outstation communities to the policy of land rights and to a politics of difference. Nonetheless, I do not endorse the terms.

Regarding mixed genres, some notable examples are Grimshaw and McGregor's (2006) collection on 'intercultural encounters', Beckett's (1987) history of Murray Islanders in the Torres Strait, Shaw's (1986) stories of Aboriginal stockmen, Rose's (1991) oral histories from Victoria River Downs, and a range of accounts of pastoral stations in the Kimberley and southern Arnhem Land (e.g. McGrath 1987; Cowlishaw 1999; Jebb 2001). See also Austin-Broos (2009a) for a different approach to history and culture not based on pastoralism.

11 The anthropologists who addressed these issues most directly were Peterson (1985) and Beckett (1988). Although Peterson (1998) has expressed some disagreement with Beckett, both present compelling analyses of the manner in which state policy entwined with economic change to constitute and sustain marginal communities (see also Austin-Broos 2009b). Peterson (1998) underlined that economic development brings with it a culture from which more traditional Aboriginal people are inclined to disengage even when this disengagement can prove destructive. Others have taken the view that unemployment has not been a salient experience for remote Aboriginal people (see Altman and Sanders 1991). I question this position in Chapters 5 and 6.

12 A major exception to the rule is Nicolas Peterson who, through four decades, has produced a string of critical articles on the circumstance of land rights while also playing a major role as a consultant anthropologist. I will cite his work extensively throughout this book.

13 The Bennelong Society aims to 'promote debate and analysis of Aboriginal policy in Australia' and to 'inquire into the causes of the present appalling plight of many contemporary Aboriginal people'. The society was preceded by an earlier one, the Galatians. The latter was formed in 1994 by a group of Uniting Church clergy following their church's annual national assembly, which had issued a covenanting statement on Aboriginal Australia. A Galatians pamphlet stated that the assembly's statement 'aroused concern because it included an apology for the work of Christian missionaries among Aboriginal people in previous generations'. This was seen as unsympathetic to those missionaries. In addition, the statement 'distinguished between members of the Uniting Church on the basis of race; and it committed the Uniting Church to Aboriginal "self-determination" and recognition of the need for dispossessed Aborigines to have "a secure land base"'. The Bennelong Society maintained these positions but as secular ones, and with more emphasis on economic development: see www.bennelong.com.au/aims.php and the Galatians Group (1994).

14 Initially, Sutton was trained as an anthropological linguist rather than a social and cultural anthropologist. He identifies as an anthropologist nonetheless.
15 In Chapter 5, I discuss all these writers in some detail, except for Nicolas Rothwell. All the others have been specifically opinion writers around an editorial theme whereas Rothwell as a feature writer has a more complex view, although he toes *The Australian*'s editorial line. He has celebrated fine Aboriginal art and its concomitant milieu while also dismissing academics who advocate for cultural difference (Rothwell 2008). More recently, he has written excellent critical essays on some new forms of government policy and on the troubled interface between federal and territory governance (Rothwell 2010a, 2010b). In his sometimes brilliant feature writing, Rothwell goes well beyond the fleeting regional engagement of other anti-separatists. At the same time, his thinking on policy issues is more variable and diffuse. Later in the book, I reference other of his writings which I think are important.
16 See below, Chapter 5.
17 For a genealogy of 'welfare dependency' within the US that shows many parallels with Australia's discourse, see Fraser (1997a).
18 The Gillard Labor federal government has appointed a minister for Indigenous Employment and Economic Development. He retains this portfolio along with others concerned with sport and homelessness. At time of writing, the minister, Senator Mark Arbib, had made no significant statement to parliament regarding his Indigenous portfolio.
19 For examples and summaries of the history culture wars, see Macintyre and Clark (2003), Manne (2003) and Attwood (2005).
20 I remark further on Sutton in Austin-Broos (2010a, 2010b).
21 Windschuttle's work on the first Tasmanians, which diminished Aboriginal culture and defended the settlers' culture, was a central part of the history wars: see Windschuttle (2002).
22 Altman (2007a, 2008a) tends to suggest that difference is the major issue: see Chapters 5 and 6 for my discussion of this position.
23 This term is Peter Sutton's and refers to the ethnography of traditional Aboriginal society as pursued in early anthropology and in the period of land claims.

Chapter 2: Culture and ethnography

1 Earlier work concerned forms of social structure, marriage, male rite and totemic or ancestral ceremonial. Concurrent with land claims, more was recorded of myth and song, especially in its public versions. Ideas about custodianship were debated and revised, and then tested at site hearings and in the courts. This was also a period in which the record of women's rite was amplified and women's roles in custodianship were better understood: see, for example, Bell (1983) and Dussart (2000).
2 Gruber's (1970) account of salvage anthropology focused on late 19th century ethnography that sought to record sociocultural life before 'the savage' died out. Some critics invoke the term today to describe any form of ethnography that addresses customary ways. If such a term is to be used at all, I would prefer 'retrieval' anthropology in the sense that a model of a whole life in the past is retrieved from present evidence in order to promote present understanding, or a claim to rights including compensatory claims.
3 The authors of these texts include A.P. Elkin (1979 [1938]), Catherine and Ronald Berndt (1988 [1964]), Kenneth Maddock (1982) and Ian Keen (2004). Lester Hiatt's work *Arguments about Aborigines* (1996) is an overview of scholarly debates, exemplary in its own right, rather than a textbook as such.
4 It is important to note, however, that both types of terminology class together kin that in other systems are separated. For example, English, a descriptive system, under the term 'cousin' lumps together relatives that other systems separate.

5 It is useful to note some genres, with some indicative publications. These include the growth in understanding of man–land relations brought by the writings of Strehlow (1970) on 'totemic geography' and the extension and refinement of some of his insights in the work of Munn (1964, 1973) and Morton (1987a, 1987b). Beginning with Kaberry (2004 [1939]) and moving through the work of C. Berndt (1950), Goodale (1971), Bell (1983), Hamilton (1987), Francesca Merlan (1991), Elizabeth Povinelli (1993) and others, women anthropologists have built understanding of the lives of Indigenous women in traditional society. Munn (1986), Morphy (1991) and Myers (2002) have given fascinating and far-reaching accounts of the traditional roots of Indigenous art and its modern context. Writings on ritual and cosmology are legion but include some notable interpretations by Berndt and Berndt (1951), R. Berndt (1962), Elkin (1977), Stanner (1966, 1979 [1953]), Tonkinson (1970), Hiatt (1971, 1975), Strehlow (1971, 1978), Morphy (1984) and Ian Keen (1994). Moreover, excluded from these citations are all the pre-1930s ethnographers who helped ground and shape many of these initiatives. Finally, Strehlow (1947, 1965), Warner (1958), Meggitt (1962), Lester Hiatt (1965), Peterson (1972, 1983, 1991), Myers (1986) and Keen (2004) have made seminal contributions to an appreciation of Indigenous sociality, from kinship practice and classification to the reproduction of identity and governance. In this they record both the filigreed specificity of everyday conventions, and the unique emotional register of traditional Aboriginal life. There are many other significant contributors.
6 Where this autonomy was once linked to the absence of centralised governance, it is strong today not least because bureaucratic governance has constructed Aboriginal 'families' in communities as end points of service and other resource deliveries.
7 A standard reference to the anti-*terra nullius* view is Connor (2005).
8 There has been some philosophical debate concerning this part of Locke's work. In James Tully's view (1994), Locke's portrayal of Native Americans provided a rationale for British settlers to usurp the lands of North America. The rationale lay in the fact that 'savages' residing in a 'state of nature' could not have governance or property and thereby could not have a system of property rights. Stephen Buckle (2001) has contested Tully's account and, by and large, argued against the view that John Locke was a colonial ideologue. In my discussion, I take Buckle as my guide just because his position is carefully argued and provides the more generous view of Locke. I do not wish to arbitrate these views but, rather, to show that on either reading Locke's positions miss the mark from an anthropological point of view.
9 If 'need' here is rendered in the phenomenological terms of Marx, as historically realised and historically produced, the questions become even more demanding: see Ollman (1971:73–78, 100).
10 Maddock worked on Beswick reserve, formerly Beswick station, and Cowlishaw at Mainora station and, later, at Bulman, where Rembarrnga people moved following sale of the station and the state development of their own cattle enterprise: see Maddock (1977); Cowlishaw (1999:202–220).
11 See Long (1992) for an illuminating account of the patrol officer's role.
12 The term 'governmentality' was made popular by Michel Foucault (2006) who emphasised that the exercise of power is not simply constraining but also constructive. It shapes its subjects in particular ways. Like many others, my difficulty with this perspective is that it can overestimate the state's impact and obliterate those areas of life in which people actually do assert some autonomy. This is not to deny the insight but rather to suggest that, from time to time, it needs to be reined in. Barry Morris (1989, 1997) has also pursued this type of analysis.
13 See also Andrew Lattas (1987, 1997) and Cowlishaw and Morris (1997). Patrick Wolfe (1999:197–198 fn 210) gives his own genealogy of *the* postcolonial critique both in Australia and elsewhere. I have not sought to do this but rather to focus on some particular writings of anthropologists, historians and practitioners of Australian

Indigenous studies. Hence I describe 'a postcolonial critique' and not the entire field which, as Wolfe indicates, is a complex one. I note, however, Marcia Langton's (1981) early contribution concerning the lack of interest in urban anthropology among ethnographers of Indigenous Australia. I also include one collection (Lea et al. 2006) appropriately entitled *Moving Anthropology*. Its contributions possibly were too disparate to achieve a proper task of critique.
14 For critiques of Povinelli see Merlan (2003) and Austin-Broos (2004). On Wolfe, see Merlan (1997).

Chapter 3: A postcolonial critique

1 See, for instance, the Galatians Group (1994).
2 Of those I discuss below, McGregor (1996, 1997) seems to have no particular interest in this task. Wolfe (1991, 1999) and Nakata (2007) play with it from time to time. Gray (2007) exemplifies a form of aggression that I find unfair to anthropology and unprofitable: see Austin-Broos (2009c) and Sutton (2009b).
3 Rivers led a Cambridge expedition to the Torres Strait Islands in 1898 and subsequently produced major anthropological work: see below my remarks on Martin Nakata's view of W.H.R. Rivers.
4 See 'Papers of John Carroll', State Library of NSW, item ID=421736.
5 I take this somewhat arcane expression from the title of Hiatt's book, published in 1996.
6 While Povinelli's accounts of state governmentality cover some ground that is similar to Wolfe's, her writings on incommensurability make clear that the ethnographic study of difference is a doable and worthwhile project (Povinelli 1995, 2002). Wolfe seems to doubt this. On 'governmentality', see Foucault (2006).
7 I have devoted some time to these issues in my own work: see Austin-Broos (1998, 2009a).
8 Although Nakata frequently cites Beckett's history with approval, nowhere in his major work of 2007 does Nakata acknowledge Beckett as an anthropologist.
9 Perhaps the only muted acknowledgement of the commonalities in these writers' works came in the fact that Merlan criticised them both: see Merlan (1997, 2003).

Chapter 4: Opposing separate development

1 On the Bennelong Society, see Chapter 1, note 13, above. The Centre for Independent Studies is a private think tank located in North Sydney. Its policy orientation is a strongly free-market one, and deeply opposed to government spending that interferes with the market. Its philosophy is neoliberal.
2 Although anti-separatist, Gregory has been a serious scholar of economics and social policy.
3 The scheme was suspended as part of the Intervention. Federal Labor has since revamped the scheme as it applies to remote Aboriginal communities. With a considerably reduced brief, the focus has switched from employment to training.
4 The hallmark of the scheme was that it came from the DAA and was intended as an employment strategy. The aim was for something better and beyond unemployment benefits from the Department of Social Security: see Sanders (1993).
5 By 'social suffering' I mean the sum total of harm or death due to personal assault, lifestyle disease and misadventure often exacerbated by high levels of substance abuse (see Farmer 1992; Kleinman 2001). By 'misadventure' I have in mind death from domestic and road accidents, for instance, and also suicide. The familiar category 'death from external causes' conflates these events with personal assault.
6 Of the twelve communities Tatz chose in the Northern Territory, eight were in Central or Western Desert regions and only four were in the north, which includes Arnhem

Land. The Aboriginal population of the north far exceeds that in the desert regions. Moreover, it is in the north and along its coast that one finds more propitious sites for some paid work that is integrated with a traditionally oriented community life. In short, Tatz's selection of communities provided him with a view that may have been more, rather than less, pessimistic.
7. The three states are WA, SA and Queensland.
8. The call came in the policy document *Aboriginal Employment Development Project* (AEDP 1986/87).
9. As Gregory (2005) remarks, this has been a worldwide phenomenon.
10. For more discussion of this position, see Chapter 5 below.
11. MRE are the income from mining royalties on Aboriginal land paid into federal government consolidated revenue and then returned to the Aboriginal Benefits Reserve (formerly the Aboriginal Benefits Trust Account).
12. Among others who assisted Reeves were anthropologist John Avery and retired professor of economics Richard Blandy. It is clear that much of the comment on economics and remote Aboriginal life comes from Blandy.
13. Nicolas Rothwell reports on recent developments among the Yolngu on northern Arnhem Land for the use of mining royalties to improve educational facilities: see Rothwell (2010c).
14. Cowlishaw has argued that Sutton has pathologised Aboriginal people. In my view she has a point, given that Sutton ultimately refused all relevant contextualisation of a socioeconomic and historical kind, and seemed unwilling to endorse Noel Pearson's vote of confidence in his own people: see Cowlishaw (2003); Sutton (2005).
15. Since the publication of this statement, Pearson has been a prolific writer on Aboriginal issues, as a columnist in *The Australian* and as a policy advisor (see Pearson 2007, 2009a, 2009b). I focus on this early publication as a succinct statement of his position.
16. In Chapter 5, I will note the similarities and differences between Pearson's initial plan, and CAEPR director Jon Altman's 'hybrid economy' (2005, 2006).
17. See Langton (2008) for a more recent statement on the Intervention and conditions in remote communities.
18. Langton (2010) provides an update for her position that focuses on poverty. The collection of which her article is a part was published after this book went to press: see Altman and Hinkson (2010).
19. Boyd Hunter (2008) provides an analysis of this rhetoric.
20. For the Bennelong Society, see Chapter1, note 13, above. The Menzies Research Centre is an organ of the Liberal Party, Australia and 'works to promote the principles of individual liberty, free speech, competitive enterprise, limited government and democracy: see www.mrcltd.org.au. More recently, Gary Johns has been a member of the Public Policy Institute at the Australian Catholic University.
21. Where Hayek is concerned, his ideas about freedom through individual competition have been influential with neoliberals: see Hayek (1944: espec. 27–31). Milton Friedman and members of the Chicago school of economics, at the University of Chicago, were widely influential in academic and policy circles from the beginning of the 1980s. This school endorsed monetarism, free markets as efficient markets, rational expectations and real business cycle theory. Members of the school were very critical of government intervention in the economy and of more than minimal government expenditure. Since the Global Financial Crisis in 2008, this position has received greater scrutiny: see, for instance, Akerlof and Shiller (2009), Fox (2009) and Quiggin (2010).

Chapter 5: Defending the homelands

1. Altman retired from his position in 2010 to become a senior professorial fellow at the ANU.

2   Readers will note that I have not made H.C. Coombs and his support for NT outstation life the touchstone of my discussion about politics and policy (see Coombs et al. 1983). Rather, I take my departure from the Hawke Labor government's proposal for 'employment equity' in remote Aboriginal communities and the policy responses to this proposal. One reason for not making Coombs the touchstone is that his position is linked with longstanding debates about assimilation and separation (see Partington 1996). I do not wish to rehearse these particular arguments. Their terms are simplistic and have only a limited relevance for the debates of the 21st century.

3   Ironically, Altman and Pearson actually agree on this, at least so far as Pearson's early writing is concerned (Pearson 2000).

4   This collection comprises mainly papers delivered to a panel of the 2009 annual conference of the Australian Anthropological Society at Macquarie University in Sydney. Like the collection on the Intervention, this one had an independent publisher, while the first two were published by CAEPR. All the collections have been edited by teams closely associated with CAEPR.

5   In the most recent collection, Hinkson underlines that not all anthropologists agree (Hinkson 2010:2). I have been a contributor myself to two of the collections (Austin-Broos 2001, 2010a).

6   I spell out these issues in the background briefing below.

7   The latter term is employed in the cover notes of the fourth collection, *Culture Crisis* (Altman and Hinkson 2010).

8   See Hughes (2007:18) for a different reading of this distribution, sourced from Taylor (2006). Hughes proposes that only 27 per cent of Indigenous Australians live in remote or very remote areas. The regional category is 30 per cent, and major cities, 40 per cent. One would tend to assume that, in Hughes's terms, only Aboriginal people who live remote or very remote lack access to the labour market.

9   Interestingly, these discussions did not include a comparison between mainland Aboriginal people and Torres Strait Islanders. The latter have a longer history of better education and extensive experience with labour migration for work. They are also a different—gardening—culture which allows some further insight into the position of remote Aboriginal Australians.

10   CDEP are described in more detail in Chapter 4, above.

11   Altman (2007b) put the overall shortfall in government service funding at $4 billion, and itemised its major components. His estimate included a full-time job for every participant in CDEP at the time, and a housing projection that rested on government as the sole source of housing for the remote Aboriginal population. These would be unusual conditions for government to fulfil in any circumstances—Indigenous or non-Indigenous, anywhere in Australia. Notwithstanding, Taylor and Altman's general point, of large shortfalls, was well taken.

12   Interestingly, the CAEPR perspective is supported by Dillon and Westbury's critical review of bureaucratic 'architecture' as it pertains to servicing NT Indigenous communities. Although he does not cite them, Sutton's (2009a) argument that problems in communities are not simply problems of servicing can be usefully juxtaposed with their work.

13   Sutton had borrowed this term from Nicolas Peterson.

14   In 1995 Altman did acknowledge that 'the payments of royalties to incorporated bodies in areas affected by mining can result in excessive regional politicking for these moneys with a concomitant lack of attention to longer-term economic opportunities' (Altman 1995:298). He did not reiterate this view in his response to the Reeves Report. Neither was the issue canvassed that some monies dispensed by organisations in Central Australia, for instance, have been spent on consumer goods; for example, white goods including washing machines. Another option might have been enhancing school equipment as a parents and teachers association might do in other parts of Australia. Private expenditure can be relevant to public goods.

15 These matters were crystallised in an ASSA workshop chaired by myself and Gaynor Macdonald in 2004. I sought to bring together anthropologists and economists. My introduction to the subsequent publication describes this workshop: see Austin-Broos and Macdonald (2005).
16 HREOC stands for Human Rights and Equal Opportunities Commission. Tom Calma was being interviewed by *The 7.30 Report*, ABC1, 26 January 2010.
17 My position on the matter of rights differs from Francesca Merlan's as she argued it in 2009. She seems to suggest that the (cultural) salience of 'rights' as an issue in communities should bear on how seriously other Australians treat the issue. Given that both non-Aboriginal and Aboriginal Australians are citizens of the state, this seems to me an untenable position. Issues of rights must be taken seriously. Nonetheless, as Merlan argues and as my discussion shows, rights were not the only issue in the NT Intervention or in the circumstances of remote communities: see Francesca Merlan, http://inside.org.au/more-than-rights/.
18 This term actually comes from Boyd Hunter of CAEPR (see Hunter 2007, 2009a, 2009b). He describes it as a term used in the planning literature to characterise a multi-dimensional problem.
19 Merlan (1991) and Austin-Broos (2009a:142–151) have written of the manner in which these relations can become corrupted, especially in the context of gender relations.
20 See my discussion in Chapter 3 above.
21 Martin is extensively published in this area and influenced by the work of Merlan (2005): see, for example, Martin (2003, 2005).
22 See Nakata (2007) and Chapter 3, above.
23 It is a common observation that administrative ideas of family, as an income-earning isolate, and of community, as a structure of settlements, are not in fact Indigenous institutions.
24 Barry Morris and Andrew Lattas, www.arena.org.au/2010/09/embedded-anthropology-and-the-intervention/.

Chapter 6: The politics of difference and equality

1 Myers (2002) provides an excellent account of the development of Indigenous work among the Pintupi both as art and as industry.
2 Respiratory infection is often linked with human T-cell lymphotropic virus type 1 (HTLV-1), a rare condition worldwide but also found in other impoverished locales including rural Nigeria. The virus renders subjects vulnerable to lethal bloodstream infections. Integral to the development of these conditions is constant re-infection by parasites via scabies and other skin lesions associated with crowded and insanitary housing. A form of immune deficiency, HTLV-1 is associated with the high incidence of serious pneumonias. For a thorough and sobering discussion of the situation among Aboriginal people in Central Australia, see Einsiedel and Woodman (2010).
3 It is not my contention that these are new conundrums. They have existed in less remarked-on forms throughout the history of debates in Aboriginal policy about 'separation' and 'assimilation'. Since the Land Rights Act, however, these debates have been more explicit in both political and policy milieus.
4 I take the notion of 'conformist assimilation' from Iris Young (1990): see my discussion in the final section of this chapter.
5 Pearson indicates no wariness concerning the way in which German romantic ideas regarding language and attachment to land can lead to nationalism in the first instance and, ultimately, to racism: see Williams (1989) and Dumont (1994).
6 Given that government is the problem and not the solution for Hughes, it is not surprising that she spends little time on federal/Territory funding and administrative relations. On the other hand, Dillon and Westbury (2007), for whom government is the

answer, discuss issues of governance thoroughly but spend very little time on economy and culture.
7 Notwithstanding Johns's recommendations, at time of writing, the federal Labor government has embarked on a Strategic Indigenous Housing and Infrastructure Program (SIHIP). Nicolas Rothwell has reported on the major implementation issues involved in the project, which is a joint federal and Territory one: see Rothwell (2009).
8 See Williams (2010) for a recent non-government organisation initiative in this area of service employment.
9 This charge cannot be levelled at Jon Altman, who has Aboriginal regional economies as a focus of his research. It is applicable, however, to Australian anthropology generally: see Austin-Broos (2009b).
10 As Hunter suggests, CDEP is a 'second best' solution for a 'wicked problem'. Finding a 'best' solution is hard: see Hunter (2007, 2009a, 2009b). He writes, 'A "wicked problem" is a term used in the planning literature to characterise a complex multi-dimensional problem.'
11 While Hunter underlined the positive outcomes of CDEP, he also remarked that 'it is important not to lose sight of the fact that economic development and mainstream employment opportunities are, in the long run, even more important factors [than CDEP] for ensuring there is a constructive social environment in Indigenous communities' (Hunter 2009a:45). On these matters, Hunter and Gregory are in accord.
12 Both Austin-Broos (2006) and Tonkinson (2007) have also discussed issues concerning the meaning of work in remote Aboriginal communities.
13 My view might be compared with that of Barry Morris and Andrew Lattas, www.arena.org.au/2010/09/embedded-anthropology-and-the-intervention/.
14 Beckett's and Cowlishaw and Morris's works are cited in Chapter 1. The urban studies I have in mind are Sansom (1980), Collmann (1988) and Merlan (1998). Writing by Kowal (2006) and Lea (2008) on health delivery in remote communities represents a focus on white administrators rather than remote Aboriginal people. The call to study 'whites' not 'blacks' seems to me a limited revision of the ethnographic project. Many of the relations in the state and society that bear most on the wellbeing of Aboriginal people are not ones actually present at the interface.
15 Examples of the works that can build this new portrait include Merlan (1991), Brady (2004), Musharbash (2008) and Austin-Broos (2009a).
16 The critic who came closest was certainly Patrick Wolfe (1999). Nonetheless, his globalising view that swept from the 19th century right through the land rights period entirely failed to grasp the complex politics of land rights in the context of Aboriginal politics nationwide. Nor was he able to grant any value to classical ethnography.
17 For the way in which Australian issues were inserted into a comparative discussion of Indigenous rights, see Ivison, Patton and Sanders (2000).
18 For my own account of the manner in which anthropology has 'disappeared' economy, see Austin-Broos (2009b).
19 Personal communication, Paul McClintock, COAG Reform Council Chairman, November 2009.
20 These matters were reported nationwide on ABC television's *7.30 Report* for 14 September 2010: see www.abc.net.au/7030/content/2010/s3011783.htm.
21 By 'a human capital view of education' I mean here a view that even general education provides capacities relevant to labour market success. Becker (1993) first introduced this concept to contemporary sociological analysis. Both Bourdieu (1986) and Putnam (2000) have remarked on the relevance of social capital or social positioning to the acquisition of human capital. For example, schooling is an easier enterprise in an urban environment where the nexus between types of education and work is readily apparent. The matter is not so easy in remote communities today, where many of these relations are not directly experienced.

References

Akerlof, George and Robert Shiller. 2009. *Animal Spirits: How human psychology drives the economy, and why it matters for global capitalism.* Princeton: Princeton University Press.

Altman, Jon. 1983. *Aborigines and Mining Royalties in the Northern Territory.* Canberra: Australian Institute of Aboriginal Studies.

——1991. Conclusion. In J. Altman (ed.), *Aboriginal Employment Equity by the Year 2000*, pp. 155–174. Monograph No. 2. Canberra: Academy of Social Sciences in Australia and Centre for Aboriginal Economic Policy Research, ANU.

——1995. Land Rights and Aboriginal Economic Development: Lessons from the Northern Territory. *Agenda.* 2(3):291–299.

——1999. The Proposed Restructure of the Financial Framework of the Land Rights Act: A critique of Reeves. In J. Altman, F. Morphy and T. Rowse (eds), *Land Rights at Risk?*, pp. 109–122. Research Monograph No. 14. Canberra: Centre for Aboriginal Economic Policy Research, ANU.

——2001. 'Mutual Obligation', the CDEP Scheme, and Development: Prospects in remote Australia. In F. Morphy and W. Sanders (eds), *The Indigenous Welfare Economy and the CDEP Scheme,* pp. 125–134. Research Monograph No. 20. Canberra: Centre for Aboriginal Economic Policy Research, ANU.

——2005. Economic Futures on Aboriginal Land in Remote and Very Remote Australia: Hybrid economies and joint ventures. In D.J. Austin-Broos and G. Macdonald (eds), *Culture, Economy and Governance in Aboriginal Australia,* pp. 121–134. Sydney: Sydney University Press.

——2006. The Indigenous Hybrid Economy: A realistic sustainable option for remote communities? Topical Issue No. 2. Canberra: Centre for Aboriginal Economic Policy Research, ANU.

——2007a. In the Name of the Market? In J. Altman and M. Hinkson (eds), *Coercive Reconciliation,* pp. 307–324. North Carlton: Arena Publications.

——2007b. Stabilise, Normalise and Exit = $4 billion. Topical Issue No. 8. Canberra: Centre for Aboriginal Economic Policy Research, ANU.

——2008a. From 'After the Dreaming' to 'After Land Rights': W.E.H. Stanner's legacy as Indigenous policy intellectual. In M. Hinkson and J. Beckett (eds), *An Appreciation of*

Difference: W.E.H. Stanner and Aboriginal Australia, pp. 271–282. Canberra: Aboriginal Studies Press.

——2008b. Submission to the Australian Government's *Increasing Indigenous Employment Opportunity* Discussion Paper. Topical Issue No. 16. Canberra: Centre for Aboriginal Economic Policy Research, ANU.

Altman, Jon and Kirrily Jordan. 2009. The Untimely Abolition of the Community Development Employment Program. CAEPR Topical Issue No. 5/2009. Canberra: ANU College of Arts and Social Sciences.

Altman, Jon and Tim Rowse. 2005. Indigenous Affairs. In Peter Saunders and James Walter (eds), *Ideas and Influence: Social science and public policy in Australia*, pp. 159–177. Sydney: UNSW Press.

Altman, Jon and Will Sanders. 1991. Government Initiatives for Aboriginal Employment: Equity, equality and policy realism. In J. Altman (ed.), *Aboriginal Employment Equity by the Year 2000*, pp. 1–18. Monograph No. 2. Canberra: Academy of Social Sciences in Australia and Centre for Aboriginal Economic Policy Research, ANU.

Altman, Jon (ed.). 1991. *Aboriginal Employment Equity by the Year 2000*. pp. 155–174. Monograph No. 2. Canberra: The Academy of Social Sciences in Australia and Centre for Aboriginal Economic Policy Research, ANU.

Altman, Jon and Melinda Hinkson (eds). 2007. *Coercive Reconciliation: Stabilise, normalise, exit Aboriginal Australia*. Melbourne: Arena Publications.

——(eds.). 2010. *Culture Crisis: Anthropology and politics in Aboriginal Australia*. Sydney: UNSW Press.

Altman, Jon, Frances Morphy and Tim Rowse (eds). 1999. *Land Rights at Risk? Evaluations of the Reeves Report*. Research Monograph No. 14. Canberra: Centre for Aboriginal Economic Policy Research, ANU.

Anderson, Warwick. 2003. *The Cultivation of Whiteness: Science, health, and racial destiny in Australia*. New York: Basic Books.

Asad, Talal. 1973. Two European Images of Non-European Rule. In T. Asad (ed.), *Anthropology and the Colonial Encounter*, pp. 103–118. London: Ithaca Press.

Atkinson, Judy. 1990. Violence in Aboriginal Australia: Colonisation and gender. *The Aboriginal and Islander Health Worker*. 14(2):5–21, 14(3):4–27.

——2007. Indigenous Approaches to Child Abuse. In J. Altman and M. Hinkson (eds), *Coercive Reconciliation*, pp. 151–162. Melbourne: Arena Publications.

Attwood, Bain. 1989. *The Making of the Aborigines*. Sydney: Allen & Unwin.

——1994. *A Life Together, a Life Apart: A history of relations between Europeans and Aborigines*. Melbourne: Melbourne University Press.

——2005. *Telling the Truth about Aboriginal History*. Sydney: Allen & Unwin.

Austin-Broos, Diane. 1998. Falling through the 'Savage Slot': Post-colonial critique and the ethnographic task. *Australian Journal of Anthropology*. 9:295–319

——2001. Outstations and CDEP: The Western Arrernte in Central Australia. In F. Morphy and W. Sanders (eds), *The Indigenous Welfare Economy and the CDEP Scheme*, pp. 167–176. Research Monograph No. 20. Canberra: Centre for Aboriginal Economic Policy Research, ANU.

——2003. Places, Practices and Things: The articulation of Arrernte kinship with welfare and work. *American Ethnologist*. 30:118–135

——2004. Book review essay—Anthropology and Indigenous Alterity. *Australian Journal of Anthropology*. 15:213–216.

——2005. Introduction. In D. Austin-Broos and G. Macdonald (eds), *Culture, Economy and Governance in Aboriginal Australia*, pp. 1–5. Sydney: Sydney University Press.

——2006. 'Working for' and 'Working' among Western Arrernte in Central Australia. *Oceania*. 76:1–15.

——2009a. *Arrernte Present, Arrernte Past: Invasion, violence and imagination in Indigenous Central Australia*. Chicago: University of Chicago Press.

———2009b. Capitalism, as Culture and Economy. *The Australian Journal of Anthropology.* 20:301–317.

———2009c. Review—*A Cautious Silence: The politics of Australian anthropology* by Geoffrey Gray. *American Anthropologist.* 35:4077–4081.

———2010a. Quarantining Violence: How anthropology does it. In J. Altman and M. Hinkson (eds), *Culture Crisis: Anthropology and politics in Aboriginal Australia,* pp. 136–149. Sydney: UNSW Press.

———2010b. Review article—Making a Difference: The politics of writing about suffering. *Oceania.* 80:102–112.

Austin-Broos, Diane and Gaynor Macdonald (eds). 2005. *Culture, Economy and Governance in Aboriginal Australia.* Sydney: Sydney University Press.

Australia. 1987a. *Aboriginal Employment Development Policy Statement: Policy Paper No. 1.* Canberra: Australian Government Publishing Service.

———1987b. *Aboriginal Employment Development Policy Statement: Policy Paper No. 2.* Private and Public Employment Strategies. Canberra: Australian Government Publishing Service.

———1987c. *Aboriginal Employment Development Policy Statement: Policy Paper No. 3.* Community-based Employment, Enterprise and Development Strategies. Canberra: Australian Government Publishing Service.

Barker, Jimmie and Janet Mathews. 1977. *The Two Worlds of Jimmie Barker.* Canberra: Aboriginal Studies Press.

Baum, Bruce. 2008. *The Rise and Fall of the Caucasian Race: A political history of a racial identity.* New York: New York University Press.

Becker, Gary. 1993 (3rd ed.). *Human Capital: A theoretical and empirical analysis with special reference to education.* Chicago: University of Chicago Press.

Beckett, Jeremy. 1978. George Dutton's Country. *Aboriginal History.* 2:2–31.

———1987. *Torres Strait Islanders: Custom and colonialism.* New York: Cambridge University Press.

———1988. Aboriginality, Citizenship and Nation State. In *Aborigines and the State in Australia,* pp. 3–18. *Social Analysis,* Special Issue No. 24, December.

———1993. Walter Newton's History of the World—or Australia. *American Ethnologist.* 20:675–695.

Behrendt, Larissa. 2007. The Emergency We Had to Have. In J. Altman and M. Hinkson (eds), *Coercive Reconciliation: Exit Aboriginal Australia,* pp. 15–20. North Carlton: Arena Publications.

———2010. Back to the Future for Indigenous Australia. In Nick Dyrenfurth and Tim Soutphommasane (eds), *All That's Left: What Labor should stand for,* pp. 113–134. Sydney: New South.

Bell, Diane. 1983. *Daughters of the Dreaming.* Sydney: Allen & Unwin.

Benny and the Dreamers. 1993. Motion picture. Alice Springs: CAAMA Productions.

Berndt, Catherine. 1950. Women's Changing Ceremonies in Northern Australia. *L'Homme.* 1:1–87.

Berndt, Ronald. 1962. *An Adjustment Movement in Arnhem Land.* Cahiers de l'Homme. Paris and The Hague: Mouton.

Berndt, Ronald (ed.). 1982. *Aboriginal Sites, Rights and Resource Development.* Canberra: Academy of the Social Sciences in Australia.

Berndt, Ronald and Catherine Berndt (eds). 1951. *Sexual Behaviour in Western Arnhem Land,* Viking Fund Publications in Anthropology, No. 16. New York: Viking.

———(eds). 1965. *Aboriginal Man in Australia.* Sydney: Angus and Robertson.

———(eds). 1988 [1964]. *The World of the First Australians.* Canberra: Aboriginal Studies Press.

Blainey, Geoffrey. 1997 (3rd ed.). *Triumph of the Nomads.* Sydney: Macmillan.

Boas, Franz. 1940. *Race, Language and Culture.* New York: The Free Press.

Bourdieu, Pierre. 1986. The Forms of Capital. In J. Richardson (ed.), *Handbook of Theory of Research for the Sociology of Education,* pp. 241–258. New York: Greenwood Press.

Bradley, John with Yanyuwa families. 2010. *Singing Saltwater Country: Journey to the songlines of Carpentaria*. Sydney: Allen & Unwin.
Brady, Maggie. 2004. *Indigenous Australia and Alcohol Policy: Meeting difference with indifference*. Sydney: UNSW Press.
Brennan, Frank. 1995. *One Land, One Nation: Mabo—towards 2001*. St Lucia: University of Queensland Press.
Buckle, Stephen. 2001. Tully, Locke and America. *British Journal for the History of Philosophy.* 9:245–281
Camfoo, Nellie and Gillian Cowlishaw. 1995. *Nellie Camfoo: Her story*. Katherine, NT: Barunga Press.
Caro, Jane and Chris Bonner. 2007. *The Stupid Country: How Australia is dismantling public education*. Sydney: UNSW Press.
Chapman, Bruce. 1991. Aboriginal Employment, Income and Human Capital: Towards a conceptual framework. In J. Altman (ed.), *Aboriginal Employment Equity by the Year 2000*, pp. 133–140. Monograph No. 2. Canberra: Academy of Social Sciences in Australia and Centre for Aboriginal Economic Policy Research, ANU.
Clendinnen, Inga. 2009. Truth-tellers Take Charge. *The Australian*. July. Australian Literary Review 12–13.
Cohen, Bill. 1987. *To My Delight: The autobiography of Bill Cohen, a grandson of the Gumbangarri*. Canberra: Aboriginal Studies Press.
Collins, Bob and Tess Lea. 1999. *Learning Lessons: An independent inquiry into Aboriginal education in the Northern Territory*. Darwin: Northern Territory Department of Education.
Collmann, Jeffrey. 1988. *Fringe-dwellers and Welfare: The Aboriginal response to bureaucracy*. St Lucia: University of Queensland Press.
Connor, Michael. 2005. *The Invention of Terra Nullius*. Sydney: Macleay Press.
Coombs, H.C., M. Brandl and W. Snowdon. 1983. *A Certain Heritage: Programs for and by Aboriginal families in Australia*. Canberra: Centre for Resource and Environmental Studies, ANU.
Cowlishaw, Gillian. 1987. Colour, Culture and the Aborigines, *Man*. 22:221–37.
——1988. *Black, White or Brindle: Race in rural Australia*. Cambridge: Cambridge University Press.
——1999. *Rednecks, Eggheads and Blackfellas*. Sydney: Allen & Unwin.
——2003. Euphemism, Banality, and Propaganda: Anthropology, public debate and Indigenous communities. *Australian Aboriginal Studies*. 1:2–18.
——2009. *The City's Outback*. Sydney: UNSW Press.
Cowlishaw, Gillian and Barry Morris (eds) 1997. *Race Matters: Indigenous Australians and 'our' society*. Canberra: Aboriginal Studies Press.
CRC (COAG (Council of Australian Governments) Reform Council). 2009. *National Education Agreement: Baseline performance report for 2008*. Canberra: Commonwealth of Australia.
Curthoys, Ann. 2002. *Freedom Ride: A freedom rider remembers*. Sydney: Allen & Unwin.
CYI (Cape York Institute). 2007. *From Hand Out to Hand Up*. Cape York Welfare Reform Project. Design Recommendations. 3 Vols. Cairns: Cape York Institution for Policy and Leadership.
Dalrymple, David. 2007. Abnormalisation of Land Tenure. In J. Altman and M. Hinkson (eds), *Coercive Reconciliation*, pp. 213–222. Melbourne: Arena Publications.
Darcy, Anthony. 1987. Franz Boas and the Concept of Culture: A genealogy. In D. Austin-Broos (ed.), *Creating Culture: Profiles in the study of culture*, pp. 3–17. Sydney: Allen & Unwin.
Darwin, Charles. 2008 [1871]. *Descent of Man*. In *Evolutionary Writings*, pp. 231–333. Edited by J.A. Secord. Oxford: Oxford University Press.
DATSIPD (Department of Aboriginal and Torres Strait Islander Policy and Development). 2000. *The Aboriginal and Torres Strait Islander Women's Task Force on Violence Report*. Brisbane: Queensland Government.

Dillon, Michael and Neil Westbury. 2007. *Beyond Humbug: Transforming government engagement with Indigenous Australia.* West Lakes: Seaview Press.
Dodson, Mick. 2007. Bully in the Playground: A new stolen generation? In J. Altman and M. Hinkson (eds), *Coercive Reconciliation,* pp. 85–96. Melbourne: Arena Publications.
Dousset, Laurent. 2005. *Assimilating Identities: Social networks and the diffusion of sections.* Oceania Monograph No. 57. Sydney: University of Sydney.
Dumont, Louis. 1994. *The German Ideology: From France to Germany and back.* Chicago: University of Chicago Press.
Duncan, Ron. 2003. Agricultural and Resource Economics and Economic Development in Aboriginal Communities. *Australian Journal of Agricultural and Resource Economics.* 47(3):307–324.
Dussart, Françoise. 2000. *The Politics of Ritual in an Aboriginal Settlement: Kinship, gender and the currency of knowledge.* Washington: Smithsonian Institution Press.
Einsiedel, Lloyd and Richard Woodman. 2010. Two Nations: Racial disparities in bloodstream infections recorded at Alice Springs Hospital, Central Australia, 2001–2005. *Medical Journal of Australia.* 192:567–571.
Elkin, Adolphe P. 1951. Reaction and Interaction: A food gathering people and European settlement in Australia. *American Anthropologist.* 53:164–186.
——1977. *Aboriginal Men of High Degree.* St Lucia: University of Queensland Press.
——1979 [1938]. *The Australian Aborigines.* Sydney: Angus and Robertson.
Farmer, Paul. 1992. *AIDS and Accusation: Haiti and the geography of blame.* Berkeley: University of California Press.
——2002. On Suffering and Structural Violence: A view from below. In Joan Vincent (ed.), *The Anthropology of Politics: A reader in ethnography, theory and critique,* pp. 424–437. Oxford: Blackwell.
Fforde, Cressida. 2004. Collection, Repatriation and Identity. In C. Fforde, J. Huber and P. Turnbull (eds), *The Dead and their Possessions: Repatriation in principle, policy and practice,* pp. 25–46. One World Archaeology 43. New York: Routledge.
Fison, Lorimer and A.W. Howitt. 1991 [1880]. *Kamilaroi and Kurnai.* Canberra: Aboriginal Studies Press.
Flick, Isabel and Heather Goodall. 2004. *Isabel Flick: The life story of a remarkable Aboriginal leader.* Sydney: Allen & Unwin
Fordham, Adrian and R.G. (Jerry) Schwab. 2007. *Education Training and Indigenous Futures: CAEPR policy research, 1990–2007.* Canberra: Centre for Aboriginal Economic Policy Research, ANU.
Fortes, Meyer. 1969. *Kinship and the Social Order: The legacy of Lewis Henry Morgan.* London: Routledge & Kegan Paul.
Foucault, Michel. 2006. Governmentality. In A. Sharma and A. Gupta (eds), *The Anthropology of the State: A reader,* pp. 131–143. Oxford: Blackwell.
Fox, Justin. 2009. *The Myth of the Rational Market: A history of risk, reward, and delusion on Wall Street.* New York: HarperCollins Publishers.
Fraser, Nancy. 1997a. A Genealogy of 'Dependency': The tracing of a keyword of the US welfare state. *Justice Interruptus: Critical reflections on the 'post socialist' condition,* pp. 121–150. New York: Routledge.
——1997b. From Redistribution to Recognition? Dilemmas of justice in a 'post-socialist' age. *Justice Interruptus,* pp. 11–40. Reprinted in S. Seidman and J. Alexander (eds), *The New Social Theory Reader,* pp. 285–293. London: Routledge.
Galatians Group. 1994. *The Churches: Native to Australia or alien intruders?* Armadale: Galatians Group.
Gibbons, Sacha. 2004. Aboriginal Testimonial Life-writing and Contemporary Cultural Theory. PhD Thesis. School of English, Media Studies and Art History, University of Queensland.
Gilroy, Paul. 1993. *The Black Atlantic: Modernity and Double Consciousness.* Cambridge, MA: Harvard University Press.

———2000. *Against Race: Imagining political culture beyond the color line.* Cambridge, MA: Harvard University Press.
Gittins, Ross. 2010. Our Highly Taxed and Deprived Country Folk, and Other Myths. *Sydney Morning Herald.* 15 September. Opinion 13.
Glaskin, Katie, Myrna Tonkinson, Yasmine Musharbash and Victoria Burbank (eds). 2008. *Mortality, Mourning and Mortuary Practices in Indigenous Australia.* Farnham: Ashgate.
Goodale, Jane. 1971. *Tiwi Wives: A study of women of Melville Island, Northern Australia.* Seattle: University of Washington Press.
Goodall, Heather. 1996. *Invasion to Embassy: Land in Aboriginal politics in New South Wales, 1770–1972.* Sydney: Allen & Unwin.
Goot, Murray and Tim Rowse. 2007. *Divided Nation? Indigenous affairs and the imagined public.* Melbourne: Melbourne University Press.
Gray, Geoffrey. 2007. *A Cautious Silence: The politics of Australian anthropology.* Canberra: Aboriginal Studies Press.
Green, Jennifer. 2007. The Alchera Story—Spencer and Gillen's unforeseen legacy. Unpublished typescript.
Gregory, Bob. 1991. 'The American Dilemma' Down Under. In J. Altman (ed.), *Aboriginal Employment Equity by the Year 2000,* pp. 141–154. Monograph No. 2. Canberra: Academy of Social Sciences in Australia and Centre for Aboriginal Economic Policy Research, ANU.
———2005. Between a Rock and a Hard Place: Economic policy and the employment outlook for Indigenous Australians. In D. Austin-Broos and G. Macdonald (eds), *Culture, Economy and Governance in Aboriginal Australia,* pp. 135–150. Sydney: Sydney University Press.
———2006. Asking the Right Questions? In B. Hunter (ed.), *Assessing the Evidence on Indigenous Socioeconomic Outcomes: A focus on the 2002 NATSISS,* pp. 127–137. Research Monograph No. 26. Canberra: Centre for Aboriginal Economic Policy Research, ANU.
Gregory, Bob and Anne Daly. 1997. Welfare and Economic Progress of Indigenous Men of Australia and the US, 1980–1990. *The Economic Record.* 73, No. 221 (June):101–119.
Grimshaw, Patricia and Russell McGregor (eds). 2006. *Collisions of Cultures and Identities: Settlers and Indigenous peoples.* Melbourne: Department of History, University of Melbourne.
Gruber, Jacob. 1970. Ethnographic Salvage and the Shaping of Anthropology. *American Anthropologist.* 72:1289–1299.
Hall, Stuart. 1997. What is this 'Black' in Black Popular Culture? In D. Morley and K-H. Chen (eds), *Stuart Hall: Critical dialogues in cultural studies,* pp. 465–475. New York: Routledge.
Hamilton, Annette. 1987 [1980]. Dual Social System. In W.H. Edwards (ed.), *Traditional Aboriginal Society,* pp 34–52. South Melbourne: Macmillan.
———1998 [1982]. Descended from Father, Belonging to Country. In W.H. Edwards (ed.), *Traditional Aboriginal Society* (2nd ed.), pp. 90–108. South Yarra: Macmillan.
Harris, John F. 2005. *The Survivor: Bill Clinton in the White House.* New York: Random House.
Harris, Patricia. 2000. Participation and the New Welfare. *Australian Journal of Social Issues.* 35:279–300
Hayek, Friedrich A. 1944. *The Road to Serfdom.* London: Routledge and Kegan Paul.
Hiatt, Lester. 1965. *Kinship and Conflict: A study of an Aboriginal community in northern Arnhem Land.* Canberra: Australian National University.
———1971. Secret Pseudo-procreation Rites among the Australian Aborigines. In L. Hiatt and C. Jayawardena (eds), *Anthropology in Oceania,* pp. 77–88. Sydney: Angus and Robertson.
———1975. Swallowing and Regurgitation in Australian Myth and Rite. In L. Hiatt (ed.), *Australian Aboriginal Mythology. Essays in honour of W.E.H. Stanner,* pp. 143–162. Canberra: Australian Institute of Aboriginal Studies.
———1996. *Arguments about Aborigines: Australia and the evolution of social anthropology.* Cambridge: Cambridge University Press.
Hinkson, Melinda. 2007. Introduction—In the Name of the Child. In J. Altman and M. Hinkson (eds), *Coercive Reconciliation,* pp. 1–14. Melbourne: Arena Publications.

―――2010. Introduction—Anthropology and the Culture Wars. In J. Altman and M. Hinkson (eds), *Culture Crisis: Anthropology and politics in Aboriginal Australia*, pp. 1–13. Sydney: UNSW Press.
Hinkson, Melinda and Jeremy Beckett (eds). 2008. *An Appreciation of Difference: W.E.H. Stanner and Aboriginal Australia*. Canberra: Aboriginal Studies Press.
Howitt, A.W. 1996 [1904]. *The Native Tribes of Southeast Australia*. Canberra: Aboriginal Studies Press.
Howson, Peter. 2000. Reality and Fantasy: The abject failure of Aboriginal policy. *Quadrant*. April:20–24.
Hughes, Helen. 2005. The Economics of Indigenous Deprivation and Proposals for Reform. *Issue Analysis*. No. 64. Sydney: Centre for Independent Studies.
―――2007. *Lands of Shame: Aboriginal and Torres Strait Islander 'homelands' in transition*. Sydney: Centre for Independent Studies.
Hughes, Helen and Mark Hughes. 2009. *Revisiting Indigenous Education*. CIS Policy Monograph No. 94. Sydney: Centre for Independent Studies.
Hughes, Helen and Jenniss Warin. 2005. A New Deal for Aborigines and Torres Strait Islanders in Remote Communities. *Issue Analysis*. No. 54. Sydney: Centre for Independent Studies.
Hunter, Boyd. 2007. Conspicuous Compassion and Wicked Problems: The Howard Government's national emergency in Indigenous affairs. *Agenda*. 14:35–51.
―――2008. Revisiting the Role of Rhetoric in Economics. A review of Helen Hughes's *Lands of Shame: Aboriginal and Torres Strait Islander 'homelands' in transition*, Centre for Independent Studies, 2007. *The Economic Record*. 84:279–281
―――2009a. A Half-hearted Defence of the CDEP Scheme. *Family Matters*. 81:43–54.
―――2009b. Prospects for Closing the Gap in a Recession: Revisiting the role of macroeconomic factors in Indigenous employment. Topical Issue No. 1. Canberra: Centre for Aboriginal Economic Policy Research, ANU.
―――2010. Pathways for Indigenous School Leavers to Undertake Training or Gain Employment. *Closing the Gap Clearinghouse*. Resource Sheet No. 2. Melbourne: Australian Government, Australian Institute of Health and Welfare, Australian Institute of Family Studies.
Ingold, Tim. 1986. *The Appropriation of Nature: Essays on human ecology and social relations*. Manchester: Manchester University Press.
Ivison, Duncan, Paul Patton and Will Sanders (eds). 2000. *Political Theory and the Rights of Indigenous Peoples*. Cambridge: Cambridge University Press.
Japanangka, Dick Leichleitner and Pam Nathan. 1983. *Settle Down Country*. Malmsbury: Kibble Books.
Jebb, Mary Anne. 2002. *Blood, Sweat and Welfare: A history of white bosses and Aboriginal pastoral workers*. Crawley, WA: University of Western Australia Press.
Johns, Gary. 2006a. *Aboriginal Education: Remote schools and the real economy*. Barton, ACT: Menzies Research Centre Ltd.
―――2006b. What Is to Become of Aborigines Forced to Move. *The Australian*. 11 October. Opinion 16.
―――2008. After the Intervention: Some serious questions about remote economies. The Bennelong Society. The NT Emergency: Appraisal and future. Conference 2008. See www.bennelong.com.au/conferences.
―――2009. *No Job No House: An economically strategic approach to remote Aboriginal housing*. Barton, ACT: Menzies Research Centre Ltd.
Johns, Gary (ed.). 2001. *Waking up to Dreamtime: The illusion of Aboriginal self-determination*. Singapore: Media Masters.
Jones, Frank 1991. Economic Status of Aboriginal and Other Australians: A comparison. In J. Altman (ed.), *Aboriginal Employment Equity by the Year 2000*, pp. 27–46. Monograph No. 2. Canberra: Academy of Social Sciences in Australia and Centre for Aboriginal Economic Policy Research, ANU.
Kaberry, Phyllis. 2004 [1939]. *Aboriginal Women: Sacred and profane*. London: Routledge.

Kartinyeri, Doreen and Sue Anderson. 2008. *Doreen Kartinyeri: My Ngarrindjeri calling.* Canberra: Aboriginal Studies Press.

Keen, Ian. 1994. *Knowledge and Secrecy in an Aboriginal Religion.* Oxford: Oxford University Press.

——2004. *Aboriginal Economy and Society: Australia at the threshold of colonisation.* Oxford: Oxford University Press.

Keesing, Roger. 1975. *Kin Groups and Social Structure.* New York: Holt, Rinehart and Winston.

Kenny, Anna. 2008. From Missionary to Frontier Scholar: An introduction to Carl Strehlow's masterpiece, *Die Aranda- und Loritja-Stämme in Zentral-Australien.* PhD Thesis, University of Sydney.

Kimber, Richard and M.A. Smith. 1987. An Aranda Ceremony. In J. Mulvaney and P. White (eds), *Australians to 1788,* pp. 220–236. Sydney: Fairfax, Syme and Weldon.

Kleinman, Arthur. 2000. The Violences of the Everyday. In V. Das, A. Kleinman and P. Reynolds (eds), *Violence and Subjectivity,* pp. 226–241. Berkeley: University of California Press.

Koch, Tony. 2010. Indigenous Communities Are Thriving in the New 'Dry.' *The Australian.* 2 September: 1–2.

Köpping, Klaus-Peter. 1983. *Adolf Bastian and the Psychic Unity of Mankind.* St Lucia: University of Queensland Press.

Kowal, Emma. 2006. Moving towards the Mean: Dilemmas of assimilation and improvement. In T. Lea, E. Kowal and G. Cowlishaw (eds), *Moving Anthropology: Critical Indigenous studies,* pp. 65–78. Darwin: Northern Territory University Press.

Kymlicka, Will. 1995. *Multicultural Citizenship.* Oxford: Oxford University Press.

Lalor, Myles and Jeremy Beckett. 2000. *Wherever I Go: Myles Lalor's 'oral history.'* Melbourne: Melbourne University Press.

Langford, Ruby. 1988. *Don't Take Your Love to Town.* Ringwood: Penguin.

Langham, Ian. 1981. *The Building of British Social Anthropology: W.H.R. Rivers and his Cambridge disciples in the development of kinship studies, 1893–1931.* Boston: D. Reidel.

Langness, L.L. 1975. *The Study of Culture.* San Francisco: Chandler & Sharp Publishers, Inc.

Langton, Marcia. 1981. Urbanizing Aborigines: The social scientists' great deception. *Social Alternatives.* 2(2):16–22.

——2002. A New Deal? Indigenous development and the politics of recovery. Dr. Charles Perkins AO. Memorial Oration. The University of Sydney, 4 October.

——2008. Trapped in the Aboriginal Reality Show. *Griffith Review.* Autumn:145–162.

——2008–2009. The End of 'Big Men' Politics. *Griffith Review.* Summer:11–38.

——2009. Foreword. In P. Sutton, *The Politics of Suffering: Indigenous Australia and the end of the liberal consensus,* pp. ii–vi. Melbourne: Melbourne University Press.

——2010. The Shock of the New: A postcolonial dilemma for Australianist anthropology. In J. Altman and M. Hinkson (eds), *Culture Crisis: Anthropology and politics in Aboriginal Australia,* pp. 91–115. Sydney: UNSW Press.

Lattas, Andrew. 1987. Savagery and Civilisation: Towards a genealogy of racism in Australia. *Social Analysis.* 21:39–58.

——1997. Aborigines and Contemporary Australian Nationalism: Primordiality and the cultural politics of otherness. In G. Cowlishaw and B. Morris (eds), *Race Matters: Indigenous Australians and 'our' society,* pp. 223–258. Canberra: Aboriginal Studies Press.

Lattas, Andrew and Barry Morris. 2010. The Politics of Suffering and the Politics of Anthropology. In J. Altman and M. Hinkson (eds), *Culture Crisis: Anthropology and politics in Aboriginal Australia,* pp. 61–87. Sydney: UNSW Press.

Lea, Tess. 2005. 'Learning Lessons': A retrospective. In D. Austin-Broos and G. Macdonald (eds), *Culture, Economy and Governance in Aboriginal Australia,* pp. 151–164. Sydney: Sydney University Press.

——2008. *Bureaucrats and Bleeding Hearts: Indigenous health in Northern Australia.* Sydney: UNSW Press.

Lea, Tess, Emma Kowal and Gillian Cowlishaw (eds). 2006. *Moving Anthropology: Critical Indigenous studies.* Darwin: Northern Territory University Press.

Lester, Yami. 1993. *Yami: The autobiography of Yami Lester.* Alice Springs: Institute for Aboriginal Development.

Lévi-Strauss, Claude. 1973. *Totemism.* Harmondsworth: Penguin.

Levitus, Robert. 1999. Local Organisations and the Purpose of Money. In J. Altman, F. Morphy and T. Rowse (eds), *Land Rights at Risk?*, pp. 123–130. Canberra: Centre for Aboriginal Economic Policy Research.

Long, Jeremy. 1992. *The Go-betweens: The origins of the patrol officer service in the Northern Territory.* Occasional Papers No. 31. Darwin: State Library of the Northern Territory.

Lowie, Robert. 1937. *History of Ethnological Theory.* New York: Holt, Rinehhart and Winston.

McClure, Patrick. 2000. *Participation Support for a More Equitable Society: Final report of the Reference Group on Welfare Reform.* Canberra: Commonwealth of Australia.

McConvell, Patrick. 1985a. The Origin of Subsections in Northern Australia. *Oceania.* 56:1–33.

——1985b. Time Perspective in Aboriginal Australian Culture: Two approaches to the origin of subsections. *Aboriginal History.* 9(1):53–80.

McDonnell, John. 2005. Land Rights and Aboriginal Development. *Quadrant.* June. XLIX No. 6:30–33.

McGinness, Joe. 1991. *Son of Alyandabu: My fight for Aboriginal rights.* St Lucia. Queensland University Press.

McGrath, Ann. 1987. *Born in the Cattle.* Sydney: Allen & Unwin.

McGregor, Russell. 1996. Intelligent Parasitism: A.P. Elkin and the rhetoric of assimilation. *Journal of Australian Studies.* No. 50/51:118–130

——1997. *Imagined Destinies: Aboriginal Australians and the doomed race theory, 1880–1939.* Melbourne: Melbourne University Press.

Macintyre, Stuart and Anna Clark. 2003. *The History Wars.* Melbourne: Melbourne University Press.

McKnight, David. 2002. *From Hunting to Drinking: The devastating effects of alcohol on an Australian Aboriginal community.* London: Routledge.

Macpherson, Crawford. 1962. *The Political Theory of Possessive Individualism: Hobbes to Locke.* Oxford: Clarendon Press.

Maddock, Kenneth. 1977. Two Laws in One Community. In R. Berndt (ed.), *Aborigines and Change in the 1970s,* pp. 13–32. Canberra: Australian Institute of Aboriginal Studies.

——1982. *The Australian Aborigines: A portrait of their society.* Harmondsworth: Penguin.

Manne, Robert. 1998. The Stolen Generations. *Quadrant.* XLII:53–63.

——(ed.). 2003. *Whitewash: On Keith Windschuttle's fabrication of Aboriginal history.* Agenda. Melbourne: Black Inc.

——2007. Pearson's Gamble, Stanner's Dream. *The Monthly: Australian politics, society and culture.* August: 30–40.

Marcus, Julie. 2001. *The Indomitable Miss Pink: A life in anthropology.* Sydney: UNSW Press.

Marett, Allan. 2005. *Songs, Dreamings, and Ghosts: The Wangga of north Australia.* Middletown, CN: Wesleyan University Press.

Martin, David. 2001. Is Welfare Dependency 'Welfare Poison'? An assessment of Noel Pearson's proposals for Aboriginal welfare reform. Discussion Paper No. 213. Canberra: Centre for Aboriginal Economic Policy Research, ANU.

——2003. Rethinking the Design of Indigenous Organisations: The need for strategic engagement. Discussion Paper No. 248. Canberra: Centre for Aboriginal Economic Policy Research, ANU.

——2005. Governance, Cultural Appropriateness and Accountability within the Context of Indigenous Self-determination. In D. Austin-Broos and G. Macdonald (eds), *Culture, Economy and Governance in Aboriginal Australia,* pp. 187–202. Sydney: University of Sydney Press.

——2008. Domesticating Violence: Homicide among remote-dwelling Australian Aboriginal people. In Domestic-related Homicide: Keynote papers from the 2008 International

Conference on Homicide, pp. 49–61. AIC Report No. 104. Research and Public Policy Series. Canberra: Australian Institute of Criminology.

Mathew, John. 1899. *Eaglehawk and Crow: A study of the Australian Aborigines, including an inquiry into their origin and a survey of Australian languages.* London: David Nutt.

Meggitt, Mervyn. 1962. *Desert People: A study of the Walbiri Aborigines of Central Australia.* Sydney: Angus and Robertson.

Memmott, Paul and Rachel Stacy. 1999. *Indigenous Family Violence: Summary research report to accompany the round table on family violence findings.* Brisbane: Paul Memmott and Associates and AERC, University of Queensland.

Merlan, Francesca. 1991. Women, Productive Roles, and Monetisation of the 'Service Mode' in Aboriginal Australia: Perspectives from Katherine, Northern Territory. *Australian Journal of Anthropology.* 2:259–291.

——1997. Reply to Patrick Wolfe. *Social Analysis.* 40:10–19.

——1998. *Caging the Rainbow: Places, politics and Aborigines in a north Australian town.* Honolulu: University of Hawaii Press.

——2003. Review—Elizabeth Povinelli's *The Cunning of Recognition. Journal of Anthropological Research.* 59:385–387.

——2005. Explorations towards Inter-cultural Accounts of Socio-cultural Reproduction and Change. *Oceania.* 75:176–182.

Michaels, Walter Benn. 2006. *The Trouble with Diversity: How we learned to love identity and ignore inequality.* New York: Metropolitan Books/Henry Holt and Company.

Morgan, Lewis H. 1877. *Ancient Society.* London: Macmillan.

Morgan, Sally. 1987. *My Place.* Fremantle: Fremantle Arts Centre Press.

Morony, Ron. 1991. The Community Development Employment Projects (CDEP) Scheme. In J. Altman (ed.), *Aboriginal Employment Equity by the Year 2000,* pp. 101–106. Monograph No. 2. Canberra: Academy of Social Sciences in Australia and Centre for Aboriginal Economic Policy Research, ANU.

Morphy, Frances and Will Sanders (eds). 2001. *The Indigenous Welfare Economy and the CDEP Scheme.* Research Monograph No. 20. Canberra: Centre for Aboriginal Economic Policy Research, ANU.

Morphy, Howard. 1984. *Journey to the Crocodile's Nest.* Canberra: Australian Institute of Aboriginal Studies.

——1991. *Ancestral Connections: Art and an Aboriginal system of knowledge.* Chicago: Chicago University Press.

——1996. Empiricism to Metaphysics: In defence of the concept of the Dreamtime. In Tim Bonyhady and Tom Griffiths (eds), *Prehistory to Politics: John Mulvaney, the humanities and the public intellectual,* pp. 163–189. Melbourne: Melbourne University Press.

——1997. Gillen—Man of Science. In J. Mulvaney, H. Morphy and A. Petch (eds), *My Dear Spencer: The letters of F.J. Gillen to Baldwin Spencer,* pp. 23–50. Melbourne: Hyland House Publishing.

——1999. The Reeves Report and the Idea of the 'Region'. In J. Altman, F. Morphy and T. Rowse (eds), *Land Rights at Risk?*, pp. 33–38. Canberra: Centre for Aboriginal Economic Policy Research, ANU.

——2005. Indigenous Art as Economy. In D.J. Austin-Broos and G. Macdonald (eds), *Culture, Economy and Governance in Aboriginal Australia,* pp. 19–28. Sydney: Sydney University Press.

Morris, Barry. 1989. *Domesticating Resistance: The Dhan-Ghadi Aborigines and the Australian state.* Oxford: Berg.

——1997. Racism, Egalitarianism and Aborigines. In G. Cowlishaw and B. Morris (eds), *Race Matters: Indigenous Australians and 'our' society,* pp. 161–176. Canberra: Aboriginal Studies Press.

Morton, John. 1987a. Sing Subjects and Sacred Objects: More on Munn's 'transformation of subjects into objects' in Central Australian myth. *Oceania.* 58(2):100–118.

―― 1987b. The Effectiveness of Totemism: 'Increase ritual' and resource control in Central Australia. *Man.* 22:453–474.
―― 1998. Essentially Black, Essentially Australian, Essentially Opposed: Australian anthropology and its uses of Aboriginal identity. In Jürg Wassmann (ed.), *Pacific Answers to Western Hegemony: Cultural practices of identity construction,* pp. 355–385. London: Berg.
Mulvaney, John. 1975. *The Prehistory of Australia.* Harmondsworth: Penguin.
Mulvaney, John and J.H. Calaby. 1985. *'So Much that is New': Baldwin Spencer 1860–1929.* Melbourne: Melbourne University Press.
Munn, Nancy. 1964. Totemic Design and Group Continuity in Walbiri Cosmology. In M. Reay (ed.), *Aborigines Now,* pp. 83–100. Sydney: Angus and Robertson.
―― 1973. The Transformation of Subjects into Objects in Walbiri and Pitjantjatjara Myth. In R. Berndt (ed.), *Australian Aboriginal Anthropology,* pp. 141–173. Nedlands: University of Western Australia Press.
―― 1986. *Walbiri Iconography: Graphic representation and cultural symbolism in a Central Australian society.* Chicago: University of Chicago Press.
Musharbash, Yasmine. 2008. *Yuendumu Everyday: Contemporary life in remote Aboriginal Australia.* Canberra: Aboriginal Studies Press.
Myers, Fred. 1980. A Broken Code: Pintupi political theory and contemporary social life. *Mankind.* 12:311–326.
―― 1986. *Pintupi Country, Pintupi Self: Sentiment, place and politics among Western Desert Aborigines.* Canberra: Australian Institute of Aboriginal Studies.
―― 2002. *Painting Culture: The making of an Aboriginal high art.* Durham, Duke University Press.
Nakata, Martin. 2007. *Disciplining the Savages and Savaging the Disciplines.* Canberra: Aboriginal Studies Press.
Neill, Rosemary. 2002. *White Out: How politics is killing black Australia.* Sydney: Allen & Unwin.
Ollman, Bertell. 1971. *Alienation: Marx's conception of man in capitalist society.* Cambridge: Cambridge University Press.
Paine, Robert (ed.). 1977. The White Arctic: Anthropological essays on tutelage and ethnicity. *Newfoundland Social and Economic Papers,* No. 7. Toronto: Institute of Social and Economic Research, Memorial University of Newfoundland.
Partington, Geoffrey. 1996. *Hasluck versus Coombs: White politics and Australia's Aborigines.* Sydney: Quaker Hill Press.
Pearson, Christopher. 2005. Slum Total of a Failed Vision. *The Australian.* 5–6 March. Inquirer 18.
Pearson, Noel. 2000. *Our Right to Take Responsibility.* Cairns: Noel Pearson and Associates.
―― 2009a. Radical Hope: Education and equality in Australia. *Quarterly Essay.* 35:1–105.
―― 2009b. *Up from the Mission: Selected writings.* Agenda. Melbourne: Black Inc.
―― 2010a. Some Magic Bullets for Education. *The Australian.* 27–28 March. Commentary 14.
―― 2010b. Closing the Gap with Adam Smith. *The Australian.* 24–25 July. Commentary 14.
―― 2010c Conservatism, Too, Is Relevant to Our Culture. *The Australian.* 31 July. Focus 12.
Peterson, Nicolas. 1972. Totemism Yesterday: Sentiment and local organisation among the Australian Aborigines. *Man.* 7:12–32.
―― 1976. The Natural and Cultural Areas of Aboriginal Australia: A preliminary analysis of population groupings with adaptive significance. In N. Peterson (ed.), *Tribes and Boundaries in Australia,* pp. 50–71. Canberra: Australian Institute of Aboriginal Studies.
―― 1983. Rights, Residence and Process in Australian Territorial Organisation. In N. Peterson and M. Langton (eds), *Aborigines, Land and Land Rights,* pp. 134–148. Canberra: Australian Institute of Aboriginal Studies.
―― 1985. Capitalism, Culture and Land Rights: Aborigines and the state in the Northern Territory. *Social Analysis.* 18:85–101.
―― 1991. Cash, Commoditisation and Authenticity: When do Aboriginal people stop being hunter-gatherers? *Senri Ethnological Studies.* 30:67–90.
―― 1993. Demand Sharing: Reciprocity and the pressure for generosity among foragers. *American Anthropologist.* 95:860–74.

———1998. Welfare Colonialism and Citizenship: Politics, economics and agency. In N. Peterson and W. Sanders (eds), *Citizenship and Indigenous Australians: Changing conceptions and possibilities,* pp. 101–117. Cambridge: Cambridge University Press.

———1999. Reeves in the Context of the History of Land Rights Legislation: Anthropological perspectives. In J. Altman, F. Morphy and T. Rowse (eds), *Land Rights at Risk?,* pp. 25–32. Canberra: Centre for Aboriginal Policy Research.

———2005. What Can Pre-colonial and Frontier Economics Tell Us about Engagement with the Real Economy? Indigenous life projects and the conditions of development. In D. Austin-Broos and G. Macdonald (eds), *Culture, Economy and Governance in Aboriginal Australia,* pp. 7–18. Sydney: Sydney University Press.

Peterson, Nicolas and Will Sanders. 1998. Introduction. In N. Peterson and W. Sanders (eds), *Citizenship and Indigenous Australians: Changing conceptions and possibilities,* pp. 1–32. Cambridge: Cambridge University Press.

Polanyi, Karl. 1944. *The Great Transformation.* New York: Farrar and Rinehart.

Povinelli, Elizabeth. 1993. *Labor's Lot: The power, history and culture of Aboriginal action.* Chicago: University of Chicago Press.

———1995. Do Rocks Listen? The cultural politics of apprehending Australian Aboriginal labor. *American Anthropologist.* 97:505–518.

———2002. *The Cunning of Recognition: Indigenous alterities and the making of Australian multiculturalism.* Durham: Duke University Press.

Putnam, Robert. 2000. *Bowling Alone: The collapse and revival of American community.* New York: Simon and Schuster.

Quiggan, John. 2010. *Zombie Economics: How dead ideas still walk among us.* Princeton: Princeton University Press.

Ray, Tristan. 2007. Youth Well-being in Central Australia. In J. Altman and M. Hinkson (eds), *Coercive Reconciliation,* pp. 195–204. North Carlton: Arena Publications.

Read, Peter. 1981. *The Stolen Generations: The removal of Aboriginal people in New South Wales 1883 to 1969.* Occasional Paper No. 1. Sydney: NSW Ministry of Aboriginal Affairs.

Read, Peter, Frances Peters-Little and Anna Haebich (eds). 2008. *Indigenous Biography and Autobiography.* Canberra: ANU E Press

Reeves, John, QC. 1998. *Building on Land Rights for the Next Generation.* The Review of the Aboriginal Land Rights (Northern Territory) Act 1976. Report. 2 Vols. Canberra: ATSIC.

Reynolds, Henry. 1982. *The Other Side of the Frontier: Aboriginal resistance to the European invasion of Australia.* Ringwood: Penguin.

———2003. Terra Nullius Reborn. In Robert Manne (ed.), *Whitewash: On Keith Windschuttle's fabrication of Aboriginal history,* pp. 109–138. Agenda. Melbourne: Black Inc.

Robotham, Donald. 2005. *Culture, Society and Economy: Bringing production back in.* London: Sage.

Rose, Deborah. 1991. *Hidden Histories: Black stories from Victoria River Downs, Humbert River and Wave Hill stations.* Canberra: Aboriginal Studies Press.

Ross, David. 2007. Permits Protect. In J. Altman and M. Hinkson (eds), *Coercive Reconciliation,* pp. 239–248. Melbourne: Arena Publications.

Rothwell, Nicolas. 2008. Indigenous Insiders Chart an End to Victimhood. *The Australian.* 3 September. Australian Literary Review 14.

———2009. Houses Must Be Safe Homes. *The Australian.* 10–11 October. Inquirer 4

———2010a. Landscape of Despondency as Bureaucrats Rebuild the Bush. *The Australian.* 30–31 January. Inquirer 4.

———2010b. Failure of Leadership in Remote Education. *The Australian.* 20–21 March. Inquirer 6.

———2010c. Garma Consensus for Local Solutions. *The Australian.* 21–22 August. Inquirer 6.

Rowley, C.D. 1972. *The Destruction of Aboriginal Society.* Ringwood: Penguin Books Australia.

Rowse, Tim. 1998a. *White Flour, White Power.* Melbourne: Cambridge University Press.

―――1998b. Indigenous Citizenship and Self-determination: The problem of shared responsibilities. In N. Peterson and W. Sanders (eds), *Citizenship and Indigenous Australians: Changing conceptions and possibilities*, pp. 179–100. Melbourne: Cambridge University Press.
―――2000. *Obliged to Be Difficult*. Cambridge: Cambridge University Press.
―――2001. The Political Dimensions of Community Development. In F. Morphy and W. Sanders (eds), *The Indigenous Welfare Economy and the CDEP Scheme*, pp. 39–46. Research Monograph No. 20. Canberra: Centre for Aboriginal Economic Policy Research, ANU.
―――2002. *Indigenous Futures: Choice and development for Aboriginal and Islander Australians*. Sydney: UNSW Press.
―――2005. The Indigenous Sector. In D. Austin-Broos and G. Macdonald (eds), *Culture, Economy and Governance in Aboriginal Australia*, pp. 207–224. Sydney: Sydney University Press.
Rundle, Guy. 2007. Military Humanitarianism in Australia's North. In J. Altman and M. Hinkson (eds), *Coercive Reconciliation*, pp. 37–46. North Carlton: Arena Publications.
Sahlins, Marshall. 1972. The Original Affluent Society. In *Stone Age Economics*, pp. 1–39. Chicago: Aldine.
―――2000. *Culture in Practice*. New York: Zone Books.
Sandall, Roger. 2001. *The Culture Cult: Designer tribalism and other essays*. Boulder: Westview Press.
Sanders, Will. 1985. The Politics of Unemployment Benefits for Aborigines: Some consequences of marginalisation. In D. Wade-Marshall and P. Loveday (eds), *Employment and Unemployment*, pp. 137–162. Darwin: North Australian Research Unit, ANU.
―――1993. The Rise and Rise of the CDEP Scheme: An Aboriginal 'workfare' program in times of persistent unemployment. Discussion Paper No. 54. Canberra: Centre for Aboriginal Economic Policy Research, ANU.
―――2001. Adjusting Balances: Reshaping the CDEP scheme after 20 good years. In F. Morphy and W. Sanders (eds), *The Indigenous Welfare Economy and the CDEP Scheme*, pp. 47–50. Research Monograph No. 20. Canberra: Centre for Aboriginal Economic Policy Research, ANU.
―――2008. In the Name of Failure: A generational revolution in Indigenous affairs. In C. Aulich and R. Wettenhall (eds), *Howard's Fourth Government: Australian Commonwealth administration*, pp. 185–205. Sydney: UNSW Press.
―――2009. Ideology, Evidence and Competing Principles in Australian Indigenous Affairs: From Brough to Rudd via Pearson and the NTER. Discussion Paper No. 289. Canberra: Centre for Aboriginal Economic Policy Research, ANU.
Sanders, Will and Frances Morphy. 2001. Introduction. In F. Morphy and W. Sanders (eds), *The Indigenous Welfare Economy and the CDEP Scheme*, pp. 1–10. Research Monograph No. 20. Canberra: Centre for Aboriginal Economic Policy Research, ANU.
Sansom, Basil. 1980. *The Camp at Wallaby Cross: Aboriginal fringe dwellers in Darwin*. Canberra: Australian Institute of Aboriginal Studies.
―――1982. The Aboriginal Commonality. In R. Berndt (ed.), *Aboriginal Sites, Rights and Resource Development*, pp. 117–138. Nedlands: University of Western Australia Press.
Schild, Basil. 2008. God like whitefella more better, I reckon. Paper presented at Lutheran World Federation Conference, 'Theology of the South'. Hong Kong, January 2008.
SCRGSP (Steering Committee for the Review of Government Service Provision). 2009. *Overcoming Indigenous Disadvantage: Key indicators 2009*. Canberra: Productivity Commission.
Schwab, R.G. (Jerry). 1999. *Why Only One in Three? The complex reasons for low Indigenous school retention*. Research Monograph No. 16. Canberra: Centre for Aboriginal Economic Policy Research, ANU.
―――2005. Education and Community. In D. Austin-Broos and G. Macdonald (eds), *Culture, Economy and Governance in Aboriginal Australia*, pp. 165–173. Sydney: Sydney University Press.

Schwab, R.G. (Jerry) and Dale Sutherland. 2003. Indigenous Learning Communities: A vehicle for community empowerment and capacity development. *Learning Communities: International journal of learning in social context*. 1:53–70.

Sen, Amartya. 1993. Capability and Well-being. In Martha C. Nussbaum and A. Sen (eds), *The Quality of Life*, pp. 30–53. Oxford: Clarendon Press.

Shaw, Bruce. 1986. *Countrymen: The life histories of four Aboriginal men*. Canberra: Australian Institute of Aboriginal Studies.

Shergold, Peter. 2001. The Indigenous Employment Policy: A preliminary evaluation. In F. Morphy and W. Sanders (eds), *The Indigenous Welfare Economy and the CDEP Scheme*, pp. 67–74. Research Monograph No. 20. Canberra: Centre for Aboriginal Economic Policy Research, ANU.

Spencer, Baldwin and Frank Gillen. 1899. *The Native Tribes of Central Australia*, London: Macmillan.

——1927. *The Arunta*. London: Macmillan.

Stanner, William (W.E.H.). 1965. Aboriginal Territorial Organisation: Estate, range, domain and regime. *Oceania*. 36:1–26.

——1966. *On Aboriginal Religion*. Oceania Monographs No. 11. Sydney: University of Sydney.

——1968. *After the Dreaming: Black and white Australians—an anthropologist's view*. Sydney: Australian Broadcasting Commission.

——1979 [1953]. The Dreaming. In *White Man Got No Dreaming: Essays 1938–1973*, pp. 23–40. Canberra: Australian National University Press.

——1979 [1958]. Continuity and Change among the Aborigines. In *White Man Got No Dreaming: Essays 1938–1973*, pp. 41–66. Canberra: Australian National University Press.

——1979 [1963]. The History of Indifference Thus Begins. In *White Man Got No Dreaming: Essays 1938–1973*, pp. 165–191. Canberra: Australian National University Press.

Stocking, George. 1982. *Race, Culture and Evolution: Essays in the history of anthropology*. Chicago: Chicago University Press.

——1992. The Ethnographer's Magic: Fieldwork in British anthropology from Tylor to Malinowski. In *The Ethnographer's Magic and other Essays*, pp. 12–59. Madison: University of Wisconsin Press.

Strehlow, Theodore (T.G.H.). 1947. *Aranda Traditions*. Melbourne: Melbourne University Press.

——1965. Culture, Social Structure and Environment. In R. M. Berndt and C. Berndt (eds), *Aboriginal Man in Australia*, pp. 122–145. Sydney: Angus and Robertson.

——1970. Geography and the Totemic Landscape in Central Australia: A functional study. In R. Berndt (ed.), *Australian Aboriginal Anthropology* pp. 92–140. Nedlands: University of Western Australia Press.

——1971. *Songs of Central Australia*. Sydney: Angus and Robertson.

——1978. *Central Australian Religion: Personal monototemism in a polytotemic community*. Special Studies in Religion 2. Bedford Park: Australian Association of the Study of Religion.

Sutton, Peter. 1999. The Reeves Report and the Idea of the 'Community'. In J. Altman, F. Morphy and T. Rowse (eds), *Land Rights at Risk?*, pp. 39–52. Canberra: Centre for Aboriginal Economic Policy Research, ANU.

——2001. The Politics of Suffering: Indigenous policy in Australia since the 1970s. *Anthropological Forum*. 11:125–173.

——2005. Rage, Reason and the Honourable Cause: A reply to Cowlishaw. *Australian Aboriginal Studies*. 2:35–43.

——2009a. *The Politics of Suffering: Indigenous Australia and the end of the liberal consensus*. Melbourne: Melbourne University Press

——2009b. Review article—Australian Anthropologists and Political Action, 1925–1960. *Oceania*. 79(2):202–219.

Tatz, Colin. 1990. Aboriginal Violence: A return to pessimism. *Journal of Social Issues*. 25(4):245–260.

Taylor, John. 1991. Aboriginal Labour Migration for Employment: The evidence. In J. Altman (ed.), *Aboriginal Employment Equity by the Year 2000*, pp. 65–78. Research Monograph No. 2. Canberra: Academy of Social Sciences in Australia and Centre for Aboriginal Economic Policy Research, ANU.

——1999. The Social, Cultural and Economic Costs and Benefits of Land Rights: An assessment of the Reeves analysis. In J. Altman, F. Morphy and T. Rowse (eds), *Land Rights at Risk?*, pp. 99–108. Canberra: Centre for Aboriginal Economic Policy Research, ANU.

——2006. Population and Diversity: Policy implications of emerging Indigenous demographic trends. Discussion Paper No. 286. Canberra: Centre for Aboriginal Economic Policy Research, ANU.

——2007. Demography is Destiny, Except in the Northern Territory. In J. Altman and M. Hinkson (eds), *Coercive Reconciliation*, pp. 173–184. Melbourne: Arena Publications.

Taylor, John and Boyd Hunter. 2001. Demographic Challengers to the future of CDEP. In F. Morphy and W. Sanders (eds), *The Indigenous Welfare Economy and the CDEP Scheme*, pp. 95–108. Research Monograph No. 20. Canberra: Centre for Aboriginal Economic Policy Research, ANU.

Taylor, John and Linda Roach. 1998. The Relative Economic Status of Indigenous People in the Northern Territory, 1991–1996. Discussion Paper No. 156. Canberra: Centre for Aboriginal Economic Policy Research, ANU.

Tesfaghiorghis, Habtemariam and Alan Gray. 1991. The Demographic Structure and Location of the Aboriginal Population: Employment implications. In J. Altman (ed.), *Aboriginal Employment Equity by the Year 2000*, pp. 47–64. Monograph No. 2. Canberra: Academy of Social Sciences in Australia and Centre for Aboriginal Economic Policy Research, ANU.

Thomas, Martin. 2007. *Culture in Translation: The anthropological legacy of R.H. Mathews*. Canberra: ANU E Press and Aboriginal History.

Thomson, Donald. 2003. *Donald Thomson in Arnhem Land*, compiled and introduced by N. Peterson. Carlton: Miegunyah Press.

Thorley, Peter. 2001. Uncertain Supplies: Water availability and regional archaeological structure in the Palmer River catchment, Central Australia. *Oceania Archaeology*. 36:1–14.

Tonkinson, Robert. 1970. Aboriginal Dream-spirit Beliefs in a Contact Situation: Jigalong, Western Australia. In R. Berndt (ed.), *Australian Aboriginal Anthropology*, pp. 277–291. Perth: University of Western Australian Press.

——2007. Aboriginal 'Difference' and 'Autonomy' Then and Now: Four decades of change in a Western Desert society. *Anthropological Forum*. 17:41–60.

Toohey, Justice John. 1998. Extract from Warlmanpa, Warlpiri, Mudburra and Warumungu land claim, Aboriginal Land Commissioner's Report No. 11, 1982. In A. Wright (ed.), *Take Power Like This Old Man Here: An anthology of writings celebrating twenty years of land rights in Central Australia, 1977–1997*, p. 217. Alice Springs: Central Australian Land Council.

Trouillot, Michel-Rolph. 1991. Anthropology and the Savage Slot: The poetics and politics of otherness. In R. Fox (ed.), *Recapturing Anthropology: Working in the present*, pp. 17–44. Santa Fe, New Mexico: School of American Research Press.

——1995. *Silencing the Past: Power and the production of history*. Boston: Beacon Press.

Trovato, Frank. 2001. Aboriginal Mortality in Canada, the United States and New Zealand. *Journal of Biosocial Science*. 33:1, 67–86.

Tully, James. 1994. Rediscovering America: The *Two Treatises* and Aboriginal rights. In G. Rogers (ed.), *Locke's Philosophy: Content and context*, pp. 165–196 Oxford: Clarendon Press.

Tylor, Edward B. 1903 (4th ed.). *Primitive Culture: Researches into the development of mythology, philosophy, religion, language, art and custom*. London: John Murray.

Viner, Ian. 1999. Whither Land Rights in the Northern Territory? Whither Aboriginal self-determination? A review of the Reeves Report. *Australian Indigenous Law Reporter*. 4(1):1–18.

Walsh, Michael. 1993. Languages and their Status in Aboriginal Australia. In M. Walsh and C. Yallop (eds), *Language and Culture in Aboriginal Australia,* pp. 1–14. Canberra: Aboriginal Studies Press.

Ward, Russell. 1958. *The Australian Legend.* Melbourne: Oxford University Press.

Warner, W. Lloyd. 1958. *A Black Civilization.* Chicago: Harper and Row.

Weber, Max. 1949. *The Methodology of the Social Sciences.* E. Shils and H. Finch (trans.). New York: The Free Press.

Wild, Rex. 2007. Unforeseen Circumstances. In J. Altman and M. Hinkson (eds), *Coercive Reconciliation,* pp. 111–120. Melbourne: Arena Publications.

Wild, Rex and Pat Anderson. 2007. *Ampe Akelyernemane Meke Mekarle 'Little Children are Sacred'.* Report of the Northern Territory Board of Inquiry into the Protection of Aboriginal Children from Sexual Abuse. 2 Vols. Darwin: Northern Territory Government.

Wilkinson, Richard and Kate Pickett. 2010. *Spirit Level: Why equality is better for everyone.* London: Penguin Books

Williams, Brackette. 1989. A Class Act: Anthropology and the race to nation across an ethnic terrain. *Annual Review of Anthropology.* 18:401–444

Williams, Nancy. 1999. The nature of 'permission'. In J. Altman, F. Morphy and T. Rowse (eds), *Land Rights at Risk?,* pp. 53–64. Canberra: Centre for Aboriginal Economic Policy Research, ANU.

Williams, Sue. 2010. Plumbing the Depths of Simple Home Repair. *The Australian.* 28–29 August. Inquirer 5.

Windschuttle, Keith. 2002. *The Fabrication of Aboriginal History. Volume I, Van Diemen's Land, 1803–1847.* Sydney: Macleay Press.

Wolfe, Patrick. 1991. On Being Woken Up: The Dreamtime in anthropology and in Australian settler culture. *Comparative Studies in Society and History.* 31(2):197–224.

——1994. Nation and Miscegenation: Discursive continuity in the post-Mabo era. *Social Analysis.* 36:93–152.

——1999. *Settler Colonialism and the Transformation of Anthropology: The politics and poetics of an ethnographic event.* London and New York: Cassell.

Yallop, Colin. 1993. The Structure of Australian Aboriginal Languages. In M. Walsh and C. Yallop (eds), *Language and Culture in Aboriginal Australia,* pp. 15–32. Canberra: Aboriginal Studies Press.

Young, Iris Marion. 1990. *Justice and the Politics of Difference.* Princeton: Princeton University Press.

Index

1967 referendum, 7–8

AA (Alcoholics Anonymous), 6
Abbott, Tony, 127
Aboriginal Benefits Reserve, 87, 116
Aboriginal Benefits Trust Account, 116
'Aboriginal dependency', 62, 64, 66, 91, 93
Aboriginal Development Commission, 83
Aboriginal Employment Development Project, 107, 109
'Aboriginal industry', 18, 83, 92
Aboriginal Land Rights (Northern Territory) Act 1976, 82–83, 86–89 *see also* land rights
Aboriginal protector, 43–44
Aboriginal traditional culture
  British culture and, 47–48
  conservatism of, 138–139
  custodianship, 39–42
  governance in, 36–37
  ideology and ritual, 29–33
  inequality in, 10
  kinship and classification, 33–36
  languages, 28
  law, 29, 30, 32, 36–37
  migration, 27
  negotiations with the state, 43
  tradition as pathology, 19, 91, 133
abuse *see* alcohol abuse; child sexual abuse
Academy of the Social Sciences in Australia, 85, 107, 109
African Americans, 101
African ethnography, 70
alcohol abuse, 3, 6, 94, 120, 134
alcohol restriction, 164
Alice Springs jail, 3–4, 7
Altman, Jon, 121, 156
  ASSA, 85–86
  CAEPR, 80, 106–111
  CDEP, 120, 147, 148, 150
  hybrid economy, 122–123, 141, 143–145
  MRE, 117–118
  NT Intervention, 125–129, 138
ancestral figures, 30, 31, 35, 67

animism, 67
anthropology, 149 *see also* postcolonial critique; remote communities debate
  engagement with other social sciences, 23, 154–155
  failure in critical thought by, 8–9
  tools of, 22–23, 154
Arnhem Land, 43–44, 63, 64–65, 107, 110
Arrernte, 57, 66, 69 *see also* Western Arrernte
Asiatics, 60
assimilation, 61, 63, 64–65, 145, 161
Atkinson, Judy, 90, 127
ATSIC (Aboriginal and Torres Strait Islander Commission), 5, 83, 107, 121, 122
Aurukun, 93, 132, 133
Australasian Association for the Advancement of Science, 59
Australian Anthropological Society, 113
Australian National University, 106
Australian, The, 15–16, 80, 90, 91
avoidance behaviour, 34

Bastian, Adolf, 67
Baudrillard, Jean, 98
Beckett, Jeremy, 27, 45–47, 75, 77, 135, 153
Behrendt, Larissa, 125, 164
Bennelong Society, 15, 80, 90, 99, 119
biogeneticism, 56
Boas, Franz, 53, 57–58, 59
bush mechanics, 144

CAEPR *see* Centre for Aboriginal Economic Policy Research
Calma, Tom, 128
Cambridge Anthropological Expedition (1898), 72
Camfoo, Ted, 44
Cape York Institute, 20, 134
Cape York Peninsula, 132, 164
capitalism, 49–50
  the Dreaming and, 66

Index

effect on traditional society, 10, 11, 13, 38
finance, 167
global, 96, 156–157
imperialism and, 71
land rights and, 137
marginalisation, 13–14, 76, 136, 152
transition through parasitism to, 63–64, 65
Carroll, Dr Alan, 59
CDEP (Community Development Employment Projects)
  all in/all out provision, 121
  CAEPR, 16, 101, 102–103, 107, 108, 110, 118–123
  demise of ATSIC, 122
  dismantling of, 17, 124
  establishment and role, 83–84, 86, 89, 132
  neoliberal agenda, 97–98
  oversight of projects, 147
  as welfare, 96, 146–148
Central Australian Aboriginal Media Association, 144
Central Land Council, 83, 87, 114, 117, 127–128, 168
Centre for Aboriginal Economic Policy Research
  CDEP, 16, 101, 102–103, 107, 108, 118–123
  Coercive Reconciliation (2007), 125, 130
  CYI, 134
  establishment and role, 106–109
  MRE, 116–119
  Reeves Report, 89, 113–118
  support for homelands movement, 80
Centre for Independent Studies (CIS), 80, 98
Chicago school of economics, 103
child protection orders, 126
child removal, 44, 61
child sexual abuse, 16, 51, 90
Chinese, 60
citizenship, 47, 79, 160, 166
classical ethnography
  doomed race theory, 53–60
  ethnographries of continuity, 25–27, 37–38, 49–50
  for homelands movement, 77–78
  integration of historical and ethnographic method, 72–78
  intelligent parasite theory, 60–66
  postcolonial critique, 47–48, 152–155
  timeless dreamer theory, 66–72
Cleland, J.B., 61

Cleland, Dr W.L., 59, 60
Clendinnen, Inga, 20, 153
Clinton administration, 119
COAG Reform Council (CRC), 164
Coercive Reconciliation (2007), 125–129, 130, 143
Collins, Bob, 163
colonisation, 36, 66, 72, 74, 75, 94
  colonists' rights, 39, 41
  decolonisation, 74
  welfare colonialism, 46–47
colonists' rights, 39–41
Commonwealth Grants Commission, 163
Community Development Employment Projects *see* CDEP
Community Education Centres, 163–164
conflicting institutions, 145, 149, 151
consumption patterns, 149
Coombs, H.C., 65, 96, 107
corporations, Indigenous, 83
cosmopolitanism, 158
Cowlishaw, Gillian, 27, 43–45, 69, 71, 77, 153
cultural continuity, 25–27, 37–38, 49–50
cultural difference
  anti-separatists and, 105
  as crucial to communities and policy-making, 148–150
  cultural interface research, 75
  cultural values in interpretation of, 71–72, 76
  definition of, 9–10
  education for equality and difference, 159–167
  equality of services and, 140
  as focus of anthropology, 52
  identity in regional and urban Australia, 48–49
  inequality and, 6–7, 136
  inequality *versus*, 12, 112
  market institution weakness and, 123
  as pathology, 90–93
  pathology *versus*, 129
  politics of difference, 155–158
  politics of equality in research, 76–77
  process of change, 49–50
  statistical equality *versus*, 156
  traditional and new practices, 9–10
cultural models, 42–43
cultural pathology
  cultural difference as, 90–93
  cultural difference *versus*, 18–19, 129
  discourse of, 76

cultural pathology (*continued*)
   housing, 97, 142
   Martin, 131–132
   neoliberal agenda, 103–104
   rights–pathology axis, 150–151
   Sutton, 104
   as target of NT Intervention, 51–52
   of tradition, 19, 91, 133
cultural reification, 18, 81–82, 140–141
cultural values, 71–72, 76
culture wars, 19–20, 108, 153
Cunning of Recognition, The (Povinelli), 47
custodianship *versus* property, 39–42

DAA (Department of Aboriginal Affairs), 5, 83
Dalrymple, David, 128
Daly, Anne, 100
Darwin, Charles, 52, 53–54, 57
deaths, avoidable, 85
demand sharing, 119, 131, 149
demography, 121
disadvantage (socioeconomic), 6, 17–18, 21, 37, 74, 76, 86, 89, 94, 104, 112, 116, 118, 120, 124, 129, 141, 146, 156, xii
discouraged worker syndrome, 7, 149
Dodson, Mick, 126, 164
doomed race theory, 53–60
Dreaming, the, 58, 66–71
dreams, 67, 69
Duncan, Roy, 99
Dutton, George, 45–46

economy, Aboriginal *see also* hunter-gatherer economy
   barriers to economic development, 127–128
   current forms of employment, 144–145
   'gammon economy', 132
   traditional, 28, 70
   welfare economy, 95
economy and law, state *see also* market economics
   creation of inequality, 10–11, 49–50
   English law, 39
   separation of powers, 40
education
   as assimilation, 145
   bilingual programs, 98
   costs, 164, 165–166
   for equality *and* difference, 150, 159–167
   funding, 163
   for labour market, 109, 112
   link with employment, 165
   neoliberal agenda, 98–100, 139–140, 166
   outcomes, 148, 162
   parallel schooling, 163–164
   Pearson, 95, 166
   Reeves Report, 89
   Torres Straits Islanders, 74–75, 76
Elkin, A.P., 61–63, 64, 66, 131
employment *see* unemployment/employment
encapsulation (and the state), 10–12, 18, 38, 43, 49–50, 94, 111
environmental services, 144
epidemiology, 85, 136
equality, politics of, 155–158
eugenics, 54, 59–60
Europe, 40, 57
European settlement, 9, 38, 41
evolutionism, 53–58, 59, 67–68, 72

FACS (Family and Community Support), 126
family-based politics, 160
Fforde, Cressida, 60
fine Aboriginal art, 9, 81, 110–111, 122, 136, 143–144, 145
fire, 28
Fison, Lorimer, 55, 58
Fortes, Meyer, 74
Frank, Andre Gunter, 96
Fraser, Nancy, 157–158
Frazer, James, 56
From Handout to Hand Up (CYI), 20

gender, 6, 30–31, 32, 37
German ethnology, 57–58
ghetto–jail complex, 7
Gillen, Frank, 56, 57, 58, 66, 67
Gilroy, Paul, 158
global capitalism, 96, 156–157
governance, 36–37, 126–128, 132
government policies and practices *see also* Northern Territory government
   assimilation, 61, 63, 64–65
   closing the gap, 124, 163, 164
   education, 109, 112
   marginalisation, 7
   neoliberalism and, 150
   rations, 44
   segregation, 60–61
   self-determination, 82–83, 160
   subsidies, 38–39

government transfers (or support), 16, 19, 47
governmentality, 45, 95, 174n12
Gregory, Bob, 79, 82, 100–103, 105, 109, 147, 148
group rights, 156

Hall, Stuart, 158
Hasluck, Paul, 65
Hawke Labor government, 85–86, 107, 109
Hayek, Friedrich, 103
Herder, Johann Gottfried, 138
Hermannsburg *see* Ntaria/Hermannsburg
Hinkson, Melinda, 125–129
history (discipline) *see* humanistic social sciences
Hobbes, Thomas, 91
Homeland Learning Centres, 163–164
homelands movement
  critics of, 80, 96–97
  as decentralisation, 142
  land rights legislation, 82–83, 137
  legal status, 137
  outstations, 2, 141–142, 168
  research in, 14–16, 44–45, 47, 77–78
  resourcing of, 149–150
Horn Expedition to Central Australia, 57
House of Representatives Standing Committee on Aboriginal and Torres Strait Islander Affairs, 88
housing, 97, 100, 140, 143
Howard Coalition government, 86, 124, 128
Howitt, A.W., 55, 56, 58, 59
Howson, Peter, 15–16, 82, 90–92, 103
Hughes, Helen, 15–16, 82, 96–99, 100, 103, 104, 129, 139–140, 163, 166
human capital, 11, 102, 109–110, 112, 141, 148, 165, 181n21
human rights recognition, 79, 159
human rights violations, 124, 125, 128, 150–151
humanistic social sciences, 8–9, 14, 15, 154–155 *see also* postcolonial critique; remote communities debate
Hunter, 121, 123
hunter-gatherer economy, 9, 10, 13, 38, 53, 68, 86, 91, 160
  resource regions, 28–29
  transition to capitalism, 62–64
Huxley, T.H., 55
hybrid economy, 122–123, 141, 143–145

identity politics, 156–157
ideology, traditional, 29–33
income management, 6, 150, 151 *see also* quarantining of welfare incomes
increase rites, 32
Indigenous sector, 82–84, 101, 107, 113, 115, 117, 129–134
Indigenous studies *see* humanistic social sciences
inequality (socioeconomic), 11
  Coercive Reconciliation (2007), 125–126
  cultural difference and, 6–7, 136
  cultural difference *versus*, 12, 112
  imperialism as structure, 71
  neoliberal agenda, 128–129
  reality of, 42–50
  in traditional culture, 10
initiation, 2, 32, 34, 36–37
intelligent parasites, 62–63

Jalpalpa (Glen Helen), 31
Johns, Gary, 15–16, 82, 99–100, 103, 140

Kariera, 34
King, Martin Luther, 2
kinship and classification, 6, 25, 33–36
knowledge, traditional, 29–31, 40, 41
Kymlicka, Will, 156

labour in traditional culture, 28
labour market policies
  employment equity, 85–86, 109
  Locke's view of property, 39–40
  pastoral labour, 43–46, 69
  two-tier wages system, 96
Lalor, Myles, 45
land rights *see also* homelands movement
  Aboriginal support for, 49, 71
  CAEPR response to Reeves Report, 113–118
  claim hearings, 40, 48, 49–50, 67, 68
  claim process, 71, 77
  communal property in, 77
  consultancies, 92, 154
  High Court ruling on discrimination, 38–39
  land trusts, 87
  legislation, 26, 42, 47–49, 80, 82–83, 137
  MRE formula, 116–117
  Reeves Report, 86–89
  repeal failure, 139
  role of land rights institutions, 115–116
  as separatism, 65

land rights (*continued*)
   sunset clause on claims, 87
   as welfare, 76
Langton, Marcia, 20, 82, 95–96, 104, 153
languages, 25, 28, 37, 69, 74–75
Lea, Tess, 163
leasehold land, 128, 139, 168
legal system *see* economy and law, state
Levitus, Robert, 117–118
liberalism, 39, 92, 138, 156 *see also* neoliberalism
Liebermann, Lou, 88
life histories, 45–46
life spans, 94
Little Children are Sacred report (2007), 16, 19, 80, 103, 124, 126
localism, 96, 141–142, 158
Locke, John, 27, 39–42
Lowie, Robert, 74
Luritja, 4

Mabo judgment, 39, 84
MacDonnell Ranges, 31, 167
Maddock, Kenneth, 68–69
Manne, Robert, 20, 153
marginalisation, 7, 13–14, 46–47, 64, 76, 130, 150–151, 152
market economics, 96–105
market economy disengagement, 38–39, 46–47, 81, 149
market institution weakness, 123
marriage, 34, 35, 44
Martin, David, 93, 108–109, 131–134, 137, 148, 153
Marxism, 155
Mathew, John, 55
Mathews, R.H., 58
Mathew's story, 1–4, 5–7, 21, 167–168
McClure Report, 118–119, 121
McGregor, Russell, 52, 59–60, 76
McKnight, David, 134
Menzies Research Centre, 99
Michaels, Walter Benn, 156–157
migration, 27, 55 *see also* outmigration
mining, 14, 38
Mining Royalty Equivalents, 87, 89, 113–114, 116–119
mission stations, 38, 51
Morgan, Lewis Henry, 56–57, 73–74
Mornington Island, 134
Morony, Ron, 110
Morphy, Howard, 70, 114–115, 118
mortuary ceremonies, 32–33

multiculturalism, 152, 156
Murdoch, Rupert, 80

Nakata, Martin, 72–76, 162
National Aboriginal Conference, 83
National Aboriginal Consultative Council, 83
National Indigenous Reform Agreement, 163
National Museum of Victoria, 56
national security, 122–123
Native Affairs Branch (NT), 43–44
Native Americans, 39–41, 101
native title, 84, 167
natural resource management, 122, 144, 145
need, 41
Neil, Rosemary, 90
neoliberal agenda, 82, 103–104, 119, 128–129, 139–140, 150, 153, 158
neoliberalism, 39
Neville, A.O., 61
New South Wales, 39, 41, 43–45
News Limited, 80
Newton, Walter, 45
Northern Land Council, 83, 87, 114, 117
Northern Territory government
   inalienable land transfer, 82–83
   leasehold land, 128, 139, 168
   self-government, 87
   servicing remote communities, 112–113
   Territory Growth Towns, 99, 124–125, 140
   'Working Futures' program, 17, 124
Northern Territory Intervention, 17, 124–129
   CAEPR, 108
   cultural pathology target, 51–52
   permits, 88
   remote communities debate, 12, 20–21, 79–80, 124
   supporters of, 20
Northern Territory National Emergency Response Bill (2007), 124
Northern Territory Pastoral Lessees' Association, 44
Ntaria/Hermannsburg, 1, 5–6, 7, 142, 164–165, 168

oral histories, 45–46
outmigration, 102, 109–110, 112, 130, 136, 148
   mass migration, 145
outstations *see* homelands movement

Pacific region, 139
pastoralism, 43–46, 69
paternalism, 150
payback, 3–4, 37
Pearson, Christopher, 91–92, 103
Pearson, Noel, 148
   Aboriginal conservatism, 138–139
   anthropology, 8
   anti-separatistism, 82
   CDEP, 16, 120, 121
   citizenship, 79
   community mobilisation, 93
   defending Indigenous sector against, 129–134
   education, 76, 113, 162, 164, 166
   marginalisation, 130
   Martin's critique of, 108–109
   NT Intervention, 20, 129
   Our Right to Take Responsibility, 15, 93–95, 118–119, 132–133, 147
   regional interface, 132
   welfare dependency, 62, 94, 104, 119, 131
Peterson, Nicolas, 77, 81, 114–118, 120, 149
philanthropy, 139–140, 166
Pink, Olive, 64, 65
Pintupi, 37
political economy, 155–156
politics of difference, 155–158
politics of equality, 155–158
Polyani, Karl, 111
polygyny, 34
population, 5, 29, 38, 109
Port Augusta (SA), 140
post-socialist politics, 157–158
postcolonial critique, 13–15, 52–53, 59, 76–78, 104, 152–155
poverty, 65, 103–104, 125, 136, 142, 143, 146, 156–157
Povinelli, Elizabeth, 27, 47–49, 66, 71, 77
private property, 26, 39–40, 42, 81, 99, 103, 123, 124, 138, 139
private sector funding, 139–140, 166
Productivity Commission, 85
property *versus* custodianship, 39–42
public indifference, 140
public opinion building, 160, 165

Quadrant, 15, 80, 90, 91, 100
quarantining of welfare incomes, 17, 124, 128
Queensland, 90
Queensland school, 134

race/racism, 53–54, 94–95, 111–112, 150, 152
Racial Discrimination Act 1975, 17, 20, 124, 125, 150
Radcliffe-Brown, 74
Ramsey Smith, Dr William, 59–60
Ray, Tristan, 127
reconciliation debate, 51
Reeves QC, John, 82, 86, 91
Reeves Report, 86–89, 104–105, 108, 113–118, 132
regional associations, 29, 31–32
regional development, 28, 132, 150
remote communities
   Aboriginal requests for CDEP, 119
   choice (to live remote), 86, 111, 141–143, 150
   continuities in Aboriginal life, 25–26
   education cost, 164, 165–166
   effect of postwar changes, 14
   homeland communities, 14
   population, 5, 29, 38, 109
   postwar changes in conditions, 14
   rights to education, 166
remote communities debate, 17–21, 79–82, 124, 125, 135–137
   failure of, 138–145, 146–151
   postcolonial critique, 152–155
reserves, 64–65
Reynolds, Henry, 20
rights, 20–21
rights–pathology axis, 150–151
ritual, 29–33, 40, 64
Rivers, W.H.R., 58, 72–74
Robertson, Boni, 90
Robotham, Donald, 158
Roman Catholicism, 92
Roman principle, 40
Ross, David, 128
Rothwell, Nicolas, 15–16
Rowse, Tim, 107, 111–112, 141, 156
Royal Anthropological Society of Australasia, 59
Rundle, Guy, 126
rural Australia, 94, 120, 166

Sahlins, Marshall, 8, 143
Samson and Delilah (film), 6
Sandall, Roger, 91–92, 103
Sanders, Will, 120–121, 123, 156
savagery, 48, 51–52, 54–56, 103, 138, 157
segregation, 64–65

self-determination, 82–83, 160
sexuality, 48
Smith, Adam, 138
social engineering, 118
social services, 10–11, 38, 95, 112–113, 118, 140, 142, 160
social suffering, 18, 84–85, 108–109, 125–126, 130, 153
socioeconomic standing *see* disadvantage (socioeconomic)
sociology, 74
song knowledge, 31, 32, 161, 168
'sorry', 4
Spencer, Baldwin
   as anthropologist, 55–59, 67, 69
   as protector of Aborigines, 60–61, 64
Spicer Report (1997), 120–121
Stanner, W.E.H., 64–66, 69, 70, 96, 151
state, the, 11
status, 33, 41, 58–59
Stolen Generations, 13
strategic essentialism, 158
Strehlow, Carl, 57–58
Strehlow, T.G.H., 31
superorganic Aboriginality, 68–69, 70, 80
supply and demand, 148
survival of the fittest, 53–54
Sutton, Peter, 148
   anti-separatism, 82, 103, 104
   Martin, 133–134
   Reeves Report, 114, 118
   'The Politics of Suffering', 15, 18, 19–20, 92–93, 151
   welfare dependency, 62

Tasmania, 55, 92
Tatz, Colin, 84–85, 90
Taylor, John, 109–110, 116, 118, 121, 123, 141
technology, Aboriginal, 28
terra nullius, 39
Thomson, Donald, 64–65
Tickner, Robert, 127
Tindale, Norman, 64
Torres Straits Islanders, 72–76
traditional ownership, 14, 48, 83, 87, 108, 113–114, 116–118, 139, 142, 149, 168
training allowances, 96
Trans-Continental Railway, 62
Tylor, E.B., 67

unemployment/employment, 7–8, 14, 16, 101
   advent of benefits, 119
   background briefing on, 109–113
   CDEP *versus* benefits, 121
   current forms of employment, 144–145
   employment equity, 85–86
   links between education and employment, 165
   long-term unemployment, 147–148
   statistical equality in, 156
United States, 119, 156–157

Viner, Ian, 88
violence, 12, 15–16, 18, 19, 22, 36–37, 38, 84–85, 90–93, 98, 103, 108, 120, 125–126, 133, 136–137, 151, 153, 168

Walkabout, 68
walkabout, 68, 70
War Porn, 98
Warin, Jenness, 97
Warlpiri, 65
Weber, Max, 71–72, 76
Welfare Branch (NT), 43–44
welfare colonialism, 46–47
welfare dependency *see also* 'Aboriginal dependency'
   Elkin, 62
   land rights as welfare, 76
   Martin, 131–133
   neoliberal agenda, 16
   Pearson, 62, 94, 104, 119, 131
welfare economy, 94, 95
welfare pedestal, 120
welfare state, 14, 47, 152
Western Arrernte, 1, 5, 34, 35, 57, 65, 147, 168 *see also* Arrernte
Western MacDonnell Ranges, 31, 167
Whitlam Labor government, 83
Wilcannia (NSW), 45
Wild, Dr John, 59
Wild, Rex, 126
wildlife harvesting, 122
Windschuttle, Keith, 20, 92
Wolfe, Patrick, 48–49, 52, 66–71, 76, 77, 80
Woodward, Justice, 116
work-for-the-dole, 146
World War II, 14–15, 63, 74

Young, Iris Marion, 161
youth, 10–11, 119–120, 142, 149, 165